COERCION AND CONSENT

COERCION AND CONSENT:
Studies on the modern state

JOHN A. HALL

Polity Press

First published in 1994 by Polity Press
in association with Blackwell Publishers.

Editorial office:
Polity Press
65 Bridge Street
Cambridge CB2 1UR, UK

Marketing and production:
Blackwell Publishers
108 Cowley Road
Oxford OX4 1JF, UK

238 Main Street
Cambridge, MA 02142, USA

ISBN 0 7456 1194 X
ISBN 0 7456 1195 8 (pbk)

A CIP catalogue record for this book is available from the British Library and the Library of Congress.

Typeset in 10 on 12 pt Sabon by TecSet Ltd, Wallington, Surrey
Printed in Great Britain by T.J. Press, Padstow, Cornwall

This book is printed on acid-free paper

To Patricia Crone
with
admiration and affection

CONTENTS

ACKNOWLEDGEMENTS

Earlier versions of five of these essays have been published previously. 'Capstones and Organisms' appeared in *Sociology*, vol. 19, 1985. A shortened version of 'State Power and Patterns of Late Development' appeared in vol. 28 of *Sociology* in 1994. 'Consolidations of Democracy' first appeared in David Held's *Prospects for Democracy*, published by Polity in 1992. 'Nationalism, classified and explained', reprinted by permission of *Daedalus*, Journal of the American Academy of Arts and Sciences, is from the issue entitled 'Reconstructing Nations and States', summer 1993, vol. 122, no. 3. Please note that the comments made about post-communist societies in the last two essays mentioned have been revised, in line with the argument made in the third essay in this volume. 'Will the United States decline as did Britain?' first appeared in Michael Mann's *The Rise and Decline of the Nation State*, published by Blackwell in 1990. Further, the conclusion draws on some arguments made in 'Peace, Peace at Last?', which appeared in a *Festschrift* for Ernest Gellner, *Transition to Modernity*, edited by J. A. Hall and I. C. Jarvie and published by Cambridge University Press in 1992. I am grateful to all the various journals and publishers – and to Ding-xin Zhao, the co-author of the fourth essay – for permission to make use of this material.

I also wish to thank my colleagues, especially Michael Smith, at McGill for welcoming me so warmly to such an excellent department. Happily, I remain indebted to Michael Mann, Ernest Gellner, Anatoly Khazanov and Nicos Mouzelis. Most importantly, I could not have finished this volume without the love of Linda Blair.

JOHN A. HALL

INTRODUCTION

Claude Lévi-Strauss may have been wrong to insist that human thought depends upon the capacity to make binary oppositions.[1] But social scientists do tend to think in either/or terms. Unfortunately, this style of reasoning brings error more often than enlightenment. Nowhere is this more true than in modern political sociology, and in particular in studies of the modern state. Background intellectual assumptions have led us to equate coercion with the strength of a state. Brutality is seen as power, and held to equal effectiveness. In similar vein, the necessity to seek consent is equated with the weakness of a state. To engage in the politics of give and take, to be checked and balanced, means, according to this view, a diminution of force and direction. These presumptions may well have their origins in the inter-war period; at the least, the experiences of those years added to a bias whose roots may be deeper still. Both fascism and communism had the capacity to decide where dull democracy dithered, supine in the face of challenges to its very existence.

This book has a central argument, variously addressed by essays dealing with a set of interrelated topics. If the matter is put negatively, the argument amounts to questioning the assumptions identified and the binary logic upon which they rest. In positive terms, the book insists that societies based on consent can generate great energies, including energies that allow them to coerce with mighty effectiveness. Just as importantly, coercion can weaken, by putting people's backs up and so leading them to resist or retreat in the face of initiatives from above. It

[1] C. Lévi-Strauss, *The Savage Mind*, University of Chicago Press, Chicago, 1966.

would be idle to deny that this view is based on a particular notion of power. If one definition of power stresses its zero-sum aspect, that is the ability to make somebody do what you wish, an equally important if neglected definition stresses that power is not a fixed sum – and that agreement can increase its very quantity. Underneath this latter view is a general metaphysic, clearly prescriptive but distinctively descriptive as well, that is highlighted in Oscar Wilde's observation that 'selfishness is not living as one wishes to live, it is asking others to live as one wishes to live'.[2] Differently put, societal energy is likely to be enhanced when social institutions are designed so that the contributions made by many can be synthesized and utilized.

A particularly striking attempt within social science to move beyond the binary division between coercion and consent was made in Michael Mann's important essay on the nature of state power.[3] Mann initially follows the traditional either/or view of state power in drawing a contrast between states that are more or less arbitrary – that is a distinction between despotic and more constitutional regimes. But his training as a historical sociologist naturally made him aware that there is a second dimension to state power, seen most clearly in the capacity to get things done. This sort of infrastructural power was very limited in classic agrarian circumstances but became much enhanced with the creation of modern systems of communication. A particular benefit of this appreciation of the logistics of power is that it clearly highlights the fact that classic agrarian empires were but puny leviathans, sitting on top of societies they could scarcely see, let alone penetrate and organize. The power of the state depends at all times upon its ability to raise taxes, and this was necessarily limited before the state could directly reach into one's pay packet.

But Mann's scheme is curiously static. Above all, what can be said about the comparative strength of constitutional and authoritarian regimes? The first chapter of this book suggests that even in pre-industrial circumstances constitutionalism – whose provenance is explained – enhanced state strength; a more particular point made against Mann is that the main change in human powers pioneered in European history, that is the triumph of capitalism, depended upon (and did at least something to enhance) constitutionalism. With the advantage of hindsight, it is all too easy to see that Mann overdid his insistence on the stability of

[2]   Oscar Wilde, *The Soul of Man Under Socialism*, in Oscar Wilde, *De Profundis and Other Writings*, Penguin, London, 1973, p. 49.
[3]   M. Mann, 'The Autonomous Power of the State: Its Origins, Mechanisms and Results', *European Journal of Sociology*, vol. 25, 1984.

authoritarian regimes in industrial circumstances. Germany would not have lost its pre-eminence for so long, chapter 7 annd 8 point out, had a more constitutional regime checked the foreign policy fantasies of its leaders; more striking still, the self-destruction of the Soviet Union, analysed in the chapter 3, demonstrates that vast edifices can be built on quicksand even in the industrial era.[4] A consideration of Tocqueville, whose insights form a leitmotiv of this book, encourages important generalizations at this point.

Tocqueville insisted that the strength of a state depended upon its legitimacy. One of the main discoveries of the *Old Regime and the French Revolution* was that French absolutism had begun the increase in state infrastructural reach through the creation of an official bureaucracy, manned by the *intendants*, that is by establishing a centrally directed official authority system, in charge of law and taxation, designed to reach into every corner of society. But Tocqueville's analytic point was that the French state remained very weak. He made this particularly clear in the important appendix dealing with Languedoc. In that region, the aristocracy had retained local liberties – which was to say that they had refused the offer, accepted by their peers, of tax exemption in return for the destruction of representative assemblies. Tocqueville found government in Languedoc to be efficient. The meeting of estates provided knowledge and pride, whilst the aristocracy was prepared to pay taxes to a government that it felt to be its own. And what was true of a province was true of modern societies as a whole. Tocqueville was well aware that the English state was more powerful than that of France. In this he was correct: the English won the War of the Atlantic because consent allowed military might to flourish on sound finances.[5]

It would be naive in the extreme to deny the contention, familiar to us from the Greeks, that constitutional regimes can become corrupt. No-holds-barred demands by everybody for immediate and total gratification must mean an absence of cohesion and an inability to act. Maximal

---

[4]   This emphasis on the viability of authoritarianism is especially present in M. Mann, 'Ruling Class Strategies and Citizenship', *Sociology*, vol. 21, 1987.

[5]   For modern demonstrations of England's greater fiscal strength, see, *inter alia*: P. O'Brien, 'The Political Economy of British Taxation, 1688–1815', *Economic History Review*, vol. 41, 1988; J. C. Riley, 'French Finances, 1727–1768', *Journal of Modern History*, vol. 59, 1987; J. F. Bosher, *French Finances, 1770–1795*, Cambridge University Press, Cambridge, 1970; P. Mathias and P. O'Brien, 'Taxation in England and France', *Journal of European Economic History*, vol. 5, 1976; J. Goldstone, *Revolution and Rebellion in the Early Modern World*, University of California Press, Berkeley, 1991; J. Brewer, *The Sinews of Power*, Alfred Knopf, New York, 1989.

societal energy results not just from the recognition of functional specificity *per se;* as important is the ability of different power groups to work
together in some sort of 'politics of reciprocal consent'.[6] It is at this point
that Tocqueville makes his greatest contribution to the social sciences.

To say that he knew about the corruption of democracy would be to
understate his concern severely. From his earliest days, he was obsessed
with the problem of liberty in the modern era. His early work is based on
assumptions that he shared with others of his generation. Roughly speaking, he felt that modern individualism would encourage social isolation
and a destruction of public virtue. So he was surprised to discover that
Americans could combine liberty with equality. He confided to his travel
journal his contempt for the middle classes, noting, almost reluctantly,
that 'in spite of their petty passions, their incomplete education and their
vulgar manners, they clearly can provide practical intelligence'.[7] It is
extremely important to realise that Tocqueville came to change these
initial and basic presuppositions.[8] He moved away from a view based
on modern social conditions to one that was far more state-centred:
'Almost all the vices, miscalculations and disastrous prejudices I have
been describing owed their origin, their continuance, and their proliferation to a line of conduct practised by so many of our Kings, that of
dividing men so as the better to rule them'.[9] The vices, miscalculations
and prejudices to which Tocqueville is here referring boil down in essence
to one: people so distrust each other that they cannot cooperate in
liberty – yet the blame for this sorry condition is not their own but
that of their rulers. Put differently, social atomization is less an emergent
property of a new social order than the result of a particular style of
domination.

The tremendous insight at work here is that the character of social
action is determined massively by interaction with the state: in the
second and sixth chapters this principle helps us make sense of
working-class and nationalist movements. The principle can be looked
at in a different way. Tocqueville is in effect arguing that it is normal *in*

---

[6] This happy expression is used by R. J. Samuels in *The Business of the
Japanese State*, Cornell University Press, Ithaca, 1987 to describe the way in
which state elites and business elites bargain with each other to a common end.
[7] A. de Tocqueville, *Journey to America*, ed. J. P. Mayer, trans. G. Lawrence,
Doubleday, New York, 1971, p. 259, cited by R. Boesche, *The Strange Liberalism
of Alexis de Tocqueville*, Cornell University Press, Ithaca, 1987, p. 89.
[8] I make this argument at length in 'Trust in Tocqueville', *Policy Organisation
and Society*, vol. 5, 1992.
[9] A. de Tocqueville, *The Old Regime and the French Revolution*, trans. S.
Gilbert, Anchor Books, New York, 1955, p. 136.

conditions of political liberty for groups to work together and for cross-class coalitions to be formed. Political participation is held to take human beings out of themselves and thereby to increase their understanding: 'Feelings and ideas are renewed, the heart enlarged, and the understanding developed only by the reciprocal action of men one upon another.'[10] This insight lies at the back of the contention of chapter 2, namely that liberal regimes gain stability by diffusing conflict throughout society. As this might seem excessively optimistic, it makes sense to highlight the fact that Tocqueville's thought about the possibility of liberal regimes as a whole is deeply pessimistic. In a sense, he has no sociology of *transition*: France lost its liberty in the old regime and is held unlikely thereafter to regain it, whilst England's culture of liberty could be maintained within the era of equal social conditions.

This sense of historical constraint, indeed of historical determinism, is a salutary corrective to naive views, currently popular, suggesting that democracy is bound to spread throughout the globe, and it accordingly lies at the back of the treatment of democratization in chapter 5. It is as well to note, immediately, that this treatment goes some way past Tocqueville, most notably by demonstrating that trust has on particular occasions been created and by considering those features of social organization in addition to political culture that matter for the consolidation of democracy. All the same, I have great sympathy for the one activist principle that can be found in Tocqueville: the only long-term cure for political distrust and social conflict is the exercise of liberty. The people can be trusted to learn to cooperate – so that, in Sting's rather different formulation, 'if you love someone, set them free'. If that formulation is too grand for some, the same analytic point can be couched in more Machiavellian guise: the offer of participation coopts, thereby taming radicalism.

Further discussion of all these points can safely be left to the chapters themselves. But a final introductory remark about the nature of modernity can usefully underscore the nature of the argument as a whole. That discussions of modernity have tended to be exceedingly abstract is perhaps a pity, yet it is scarcely disastrous in itself. But the combination of abstraction with culturalism, that is the view – so massively present in the influential work of Talcott Parsons – that meaning makes the world go round, did lead to intellectual catastrophe. This perspective on modernity failed to give proper account to base forces of production and coercion, and understood ideology itself in an unhelpfully traditional manner. Such

---

[10]   A. de Tocqueville, *Democracy in America*, trans. G. Lawrence, Anchor Books, New York, 1969, p. 515.

views did reflect and make some sense of the historical experience of the modern United States, but they were little use in understanding the twentieth century as a whole – for the brute reason that they failed to place the world wars at the centre of their attention.

The underlying assumption of the book is that modernity has structures. The most obvious of these for present purposes is that of the state. There is nothing complex about the definition of the state at work: the state has personnel who gain ascendancy by functional means – above all by seeking to monopolize violence, to encourage economic development and, in modern circumstances, to ensure normative integration. One point that is implicit in this definition can usefully be brought into the open: the state's emphasis on territorializing social relations means that it faces outwards as much as inwards. The most obvious consequence of this is that states are in opposition to each other, seeking security because they are fearful for their survival. But as important as existence within the larger society of state competition has become the ever more pressing need to swim inside capitalist society. There are complex relations between these two larger societies. If the first emergence of capitalism was allowed by European multipolarity, the dynamism of capitalism then had a major impact on the state: an increase in absolute wealth together with the ease of taxing moveable goods made it possible for states to penetrate their civil societies ever more effectively, and in consequence to wage more absolute war. By the end of the eighteenth century, this led to the politics of nationalism and of representation. Differently put, the 'modernization' of the state, as forgotten theorists understood,[11] has a neglected political dimension. This is not to discount the economic aspect, merely to note that it has been better appreciated by social science. This is scarcely surprising. After a single country had mysteriously, even accidentally pioneered new means of production, other states necessarily made it their business to force development.[12] The fourth chapter, which proposes a theory of the type of state most likely to achieve late development, makes it clear that this generalization holds as true today as it did in the recent past. Once competing states had their own industrial machines, wars between them became utterly ruinous, raising the

---

[11] H. Sidgwick, *The Development of the European Polity*, Macmillan, London, 1903; R. MacIver, *The Modern State*, Oxford University Press, Oxford, 1926.
[12] The classic statement remains A. Gershenkron, 'Economic Backwardness in Historical Perspective', in B. Hoselitz, ed., *The Progress of Underdeveloped Areas*, Chicago University Press, Chicago, 1952. Cf. G. Sen, *The Military Origins of Industrialisation and International Trade Rivalry*, Frances Pinter, London, 1984.

question, discussed in some detail in chapters 7 and 8, as to whether the successful workings of capitalist society depend upon the leadership of a single great and liberal power.

But perhaps all these concerns are outdated. Currently influential postmodernist social theory, not just abstract and culturalist but scandalously relativist as well, makes much of the more general claim that nation states are withering away. Obsolescence has been caused, it is claimed, by a globalization of production that has at once made traditional geopolitical gain meaningless and effectively removed any hope of the national management of an economy. The conclusion considers this view, suggesting that it makes no sense of much of the contemporary world and but little of its advanced component.

1

CAPSTONES AND ORGANISMS

The state is once again at the forefront of our attention. Although this development is, given the importance of political coercion and military activity in history, much to be welcomed, it must be admitted that there are few solid results to show for considerable labours.[1] Two particular problems, especially manifest in Marxist attempts to come to terms with the state, spring to mind. Firstly discussions of the state have tended to be formal and abstract, as the merest glance at the writings of, say, Nicos Poulantzas on the capitalist state demonstrates. Underlying this is, one suspects, an attitude quite familiar from traditional political science which habitually considers that the state can be treated timelessly on the grounds that the problems and tasks of government must be met in any historical circumstance. Secondly, it is not clear whether marxists really do allow for the independent impact of politics, as talk about 'relative autonomies' of one sort or another indicates. It is worth while distinguishing three positions in this connection. Naive marxism denies the importance of the state altogether, whilst more sophisticated marxists take coercion seriously yet remain true to the commanding heights of

[1] This statement, written in 1984, needs immediate qualification. Happily, the formalism of much of the initial attention given to the state, most particularly by marxists, did not last long; it is now possible to point to considerable substantive achievements, many of which are noted and discussed in this book. None the less, I have not revised this chapter so as to remove references to marxism: the chapter was occasioned by and gains its force from debate about whether state forms had an autonomous impact on the rise of capitalism.

their ideology by insisting that the state's autonomy is only relative: that is that the laws of historical motion remain dependent upon class.

A third position, stating that marxism can remain marxism whilst admitting that political power, and not just economic exploitation by class, is an autonomous source of evil in human affairs, has never yet been spelt out. Frankly, I believe that this last position can *never* be created without the destruction of the conceptual apparatus and the promise of salvation inherent in marxism.[2]

It would be possible to present an account of recent attempts to grapple with the state at a conceptual level, but an entirely different tack is adopted here. An account of the relation between political forms and the triumph of capitalism, concentrating on a comparison between the West and China, is offered in order that some advance may be made beyond the impasses noted. For the sake of clarity, it is as well to spell out my attitude towards the problems that have been highlighted. Firstly, formalistic concern with the state seems to me misguided as different types of state are present in the historical record. Secondly, I shall argue that political forms matter. A strong line is thus being taken against existing marxist accounts, although something will be said in favour of the more sophisticated versions of that approach.

One final preliminary is in order. Discussion centres on two classic theories of the relation between state forms and economic development, both neglected recently to our loss. The first of these is that of Max Weber, who insisted that bureaucratic states in the pre-industrial epoch killed off capitalist development.[3] The second is Adam Smith's contention that, in the West, there was, to use the Weberian term, an 'elective affinity' between commerce and liberty.[4] These are interesting and powerful claims which deserve to be brought back into general discussion.

Empires in the Abstract

When we think of empires the image at the front of our minds is that of great strength. This is largely the result of the mental image created by the

---

[2]   This judgement applies even to N. Mouzelis's *Back to Sociological Theory*, Macmillan, London, 1990. This does theorize the political successfully, but only at the cost of taking us from Marx to Weber.

[3]   M. Weber, *The Agrarian Sociology of Ancient Civilisations*, New Left Books, London, 1978.

[4]   A. Smith, *The Wealth of Nations*, Oxford University Press, Oxford, 1976, especially Book 3; D. Winch, *Adam Smith's Politics*, Cambridge University Press, Cambridge, 1978.

monuments and records of arbitrariness empires have left behind; this image has been formalized by Wittfogel, whose view of hydraulic empires stresses their total control of their societies.[5] A moment's reflection must make us doubt all this. It is always dangerous to take written records at face value, and this is especially true in pre-industrial empires where the demands of ideology and myth-making are great. We know that such empires could not have been so strong: economically they remained segmentary, unless there was water transport, since large-scale transportation over land was impossible, and this in turn logistically limited the means of military power.[6] All this is more than confirmed by what we know of limits to the powers of emperors themselves.[7] In the later Roman Empire, for example, the emperor was quite incapable of seeing every paper sent to him. He threatened all administrators who prepared or submitted illegal rescripts. But he openly admitted his impotence by declaring invalid in advance any special grants in contravention of the law, even if they bore his own signature.[8]

Those who have written about empires have tended to stress one or the other of these factors. In fact both were present: the paradox of empire is that its great strength – its monuments, its arbitrariness, its scorn for human life – is based upon and reflects social weakness. Put thus, this sounds a straightforward contradiction rather than a paradox, but that this is not so can be seen by identifying two distinct faces of power.

One view of power has always seen it in terms of command, of the ability to get people to do something against their will. But there is a different view, which has stressed that power is an enabling means, created by an agreement about what is to be accomplished. Something follows from this: social capacity is likely to be enhanced if agreement can be reached. The argument to be made is that a contrast can be drawn in terms of this dimension between a capstone state, strong in arbitrary power but weak in its ability to penetrate its society, and a more organic state, deprived of arbitrary power but far more capable of serving and controlling social relations within its territory. We can now turn to explaining this variation.

[5] K. A. Wittfogel, *Oriental Despotism*, Yale University Press, New Haven, 1957.
[6] D. Engel, *Alexander the Great and the Logistics of the Macedonian Army*, University of California Press, Berkeley, 1978.
[7] S. Eisenstadt, *The Political Systems of Empires*, Free Press, New York, 1969.
[8] A. H. M. Jones, *The Later Roman Empire*, Basil Blackwell, Oxford, 1973, p. 410.

Splendours and Miseries of the Chinese Imperial State

Marx's theory of history posited that capitalism would follow feudalism. At first glance this theory receives decisive refutation from the Chinese case, for a long period of feudalism was ended in 221 BC when one border kingdom, that of the Chi'n, making use of large citizen armies and acting with a brutality of Assyrian intensity, united all China in an empire. It is important to note that despotism had little to do with water control of any sort: arbitrary rule of a military type came from the west of China, where no water control was needed: the empire was in place before much advantage was taken of the loess soils of the great river valleys; and, more generally, the bureaucracy *never* planned or managed irrigation works, for reasons to be noted.[9] Where does all this leave marxism? One commendably blunt retort is that given by Witold Rodinski in a recent history of China:

> The political structure of the Chou era clearly and unambiguously deserves to be referred to as feudal; confusion ensues when some historians, who restrict the meaning of this term to political phenomena, see in the creation of a centralised, absolute monarchy, beginning with Chi'n and Han, an end to feudalism in China. In reality, in its socioeconomic sense, it was to be present up to the middle of the twentieth century.[10]

This is a very bold statement indeed; it says, in effect, that the fact of empire made no real difference. And the same argument underlies the refusal to allow the military factor any real autonomy in Chinese history. It may well be that an army is not always exploitative: Michael Mann has argued that the creation of an empire, by establishing peace, allows for an expansion of regular economic activity, a process sometimes aided directly by the state.[11] But the marxist position does lead us to ask not just about the creation of empires (often, by means of booty, 'cost free') but about the continued maintenance of such military power. What were the relations between state and society? Did the former have any substantial autonomy over the social classes of the larger society?

There is no doubt that there is much to be said for the marxist-inspired scepticism about the power of the state. All pre-industrial regimes must

---

[9]   I learnt much about this from a paper given by M. Elvin at LSE, 1982.
[10]   W. Rodinski, *The Walled Kingdom*, Flamingo, London, 1983, p. 23.
[11]   M. Mann, 'States, Ancient and Modern', *European Journal of Sociology*, vol. 18, 1977.

tax through local notables, and China, despite having a historically large bureaucracy, was not different in this respect. We can see that Wittfogel's thesis of a state exercising 'total power' over its society is a fantasy by looking at simple figures. The first Ming emperor in 1371 sought to have but 5,488 mandarins in government service. This number did expand, yet in the sixteenth century, the last of the Ming dynasty, there were still only about 20,400 in the empire as a whole, although there were perhaps another 50,000 minor officials.[12] As a very large number of these were concentrated in Peking, an official in one of the 1,100 local districts might well have managed 500–1,000 square miles with the aid of only three assistants. Weber's comment remains apposite:

> The officials' short terms of office (three years), corresponding to similar Islamic institutions, allowed for intensive and rational influencing of the economy through the administration as such only in an intermittent and jerky way. This was the case in spite of the administration's theoretical omnipotence. It is astonishing how few permanent officials the administration believed to be sufficient. The figures alone make it perfectly obvious that as a rule things must have been permitted to take their own course, as long as the interests of the state power and of the treasury remained untouched . . . [13]

All in all, the Chinese state simply did not have the means by which to exercise the total control envisaged in Wittfogel's picture. Of course it sought, as did other imperial states, to gain such autonomy, and the use of eunuchs – supposedly biologically loyal to the state – is one index of this. Importantly, the mandarinate was always jealous of eunuchs, since it was aware that an increase in central power would be at its own expense. When the state was strong, most usually when it had just been founded, decentralizing tendencies were strongly counteracted. Land was shared out, taxes were collected and abuses corrected; at the accession of the Ming in 1371, over 100,000 members of the gentry were executed. Moreover, individual members of the gentry always had something to fear from the arbitrary exercise of state power; thus the making of a fortune in state service was best followed by a discreet withdrawal to the country, where profits could be enjoyed in peace. Nevertheless, arbitrary action against individuals was counterbalanced by a fundamental inability of the state to go against the gentry class as a whole. Reformer after reformer tried to establish a decent land registry as the basis for a proper taxation system, but all were defeated by landlord refusal to

---

[12] R. Huang, *1587*, Yale University Press, New Haven, 1981, ch. 1.
[13] M. Weber, *The Religion of China*, Free Press, New York, 1964, p. 134.

cooperate. Chinese society thus witnessed a 'power stand-off' between state and society, a situation of stalemate that led to the inability to generate a large sum of societal energy.

The mechanism of this power stand-off can be seen at work in the dynamic process of Chinese history already noted, that is in the cyclical pattern, well known to the mandarins themselves, whereby disintegration of the empire was followed by imperial reconstitution. Naturally, each historical case had its peculiarities, but it is nevertheless possible to detect a habitual pattern. A newly established dynasty sought to create a healthy peasant base for both its tax and military potential. To this end, seeds were distributed and some attempt made, usually with striking success, to promote agricultural development, not least through the printing of agricultural handbooks. Yet even without internal or external pressures, the state tended to lose control of society. The local power of the gentry was transformed into the ability both to increase their estates and to avoid taxation. But pressures were in any case usually present. Internally, prosperity led to an expansion of population, by no means discouraged by the gentry, and this eventually caused land hunger and peasant rebellion.

Externally, the nomads on the borders found the empire more and more attractive as its prosperity waxed in front of their eyes. There is some scholarly debate as to whether such nomads invade of their own will, or whether they are forced into such action by mercantilist policies of the state itself, keen to keep its riches to itself and loath to treat with nomads for whom trade is virtually a necessity.[14] Whatever the case, nomads do not often, as Hollywood representations might suggest, come into empires intent on loot, rape and destruction – although these were precisely the aims of the Mongols. Barbarians wish to possess the benefits of civilization and prove increasingly capable of getting them. For barbarians are often employed as mercenaries by empires in their later days and, as a result, they learn military techniques that, when allied with their inherent military resource of great mobility, make them a formidable force.

In these circumstances, the imperial state is, of course, forced to increase taxation, and it is at this moment that the power stand-off between state and society proves to be important. Many landlords choose to shelter peasants who refuse to pay such increased taxation, and thereby increase their own local power. The combination of feudal-type disintegration and overpopulation led to a constant decrease in the number of taxpaying peasant smallholders. Rodinski cites as one

---

[14]   I owe this point to O. Lattimore.

example of this process the census of 754, which showed that there were only 7.6 million taxpayers out of a population of 52.8 million.[15] In such circumstances the state is forced to tax even more heavily where it can, and is driven to arbitrary action of all types; this in its own turn fuels peasant unrest.

This situation of breakdown and division could, as noted, last for a long time, but a new dynasty was established in the long run, usually in one of two ways. Nomads succeeded in establishing only two dynasties that united all of China, namely those of the Mongols and the Manchu, although they ruled various segments of northern China on several occasions. Other dynasties resulted from peasant revolt. It is worth nothing that peasants were not able to link their laterally insulated communities horizontally, so that successful and non-local revolt often depended upon the help of *déclassé* mandarins, members of millenarian groups or discontented gentry. The leaders of such revolts, when they proved successful, eventually cooperated with the gentry and founded a new dynasty—which again began the cycle of Chinese history.

This has been a long description of the perpetual cycle of Chinese civilization, and certain points at issue in it need to be spelt out. In so far as nomad pressure ran according to its own logic, it is inappropriate to say that the whole cycle of Chinese history can be seen in internal class terms. The empire was, to borrow a famous description of the Fall of Rome, at least sometimes 'assassinated' from the outside. But sophisticated marxist analyses have important points to make, and these have been made, for a different empire, with marvellous acuity by Geoffrey de Ste Croix in his *Class Struggle in the Ancient Greek World*.[16] Such analyses powerfully draw our attention to the thoroughgoing class nature of the imperial state and to the extreme selfishness of the upper classes in refusing to place the situation of their civilization above their own personal liberties. Had this class domination been absent, it is argued, nomadic pressure could have been dealt with since, after all, a mere 10,000 nomads on one occasion overran the Chinese state. I think it is unlikely that this debate over the primacy of external military or internal class factors, whether in Rome or China, is ever going to be finally resolved, largely because both approaches do emphasize certain features of social reality. But even were some ultimate primacy to be given to class factors when considering the fall of empires, it remains the case that the classical marxist canon would remain badly dented.

[15] Rodinski, *The Walled Kingdom*, p. 78.
[16] Duckworth, London, 1981.

At an abstract level, marxist concepts depend upon classes being dynamic, that is conflicting in such a way as to lead to a higher mode of productive relations. The developmental aspect of class was missing in China; the situation can be aptly captured in the words of Marx, as historian rather than theorist, to the effect that 'both classes went to their common ruin'. This point can be put in more technical terms, borrowed from Mann.[17] Where class conflict in the modern world sees organized groups of owners confronting equally organized groups of workers, the segmented nature of the pre-industrial economy meant that class conflict took on a very different form. Most typically, conflict is avoided by the disintegration of society that results from landlords protecting peasants from the taxing powers of the central state. The theoretical point to be made is simple: it looks very much as if social progress does not result from internal class factors only.

All this downplays the importance of the empire by stressing its weakness. But this is not the whole story, as we can see by asking why it was that time and again the empire was restored. The collapse of Rome led to a type of treason, to be noted later, amongst one section of that elite. The mandarins, in contrast, held together and remained true to the imperial ideal. On a number of occasions barbarians tried to rule without them, partly because they wished to maintain their own cultural identity, and partly because the mandarins were wont to stay away from a dynasty that did not respect the fundamentals of Confucianism.

A famous example of this was that of the Mongols, one of the two sets of nomads to conquer all of China and to establish a new dynasty, who tried to turn north China into pasture for their horses. This phase did not last long. They wished to be civilized and, in order to become so, had to adopt and adapt to the imperial form. Any consideration of the rather small numbers of the elite shows that an enormous confidence trick was played on the gentry. They remained loyal to the state, but the paucity of their numbers is evidence that they did not do all that well from it; indeed a well-known social problem in Chinese history was that of the downward mobility of those members of the gentry who failed in one way or another. Furthermore, there was, as noted, great insecurity attached to office holding. This is not, it must be stressed, to resurrect the notion of totalitarian strength on the part of the state. This did not exist and in most matters and for most of the time the scholar-gentry class could block imperial initiatives, although individuals amongst its number did suffer in one way or another. So the argument here is that there is, in

17   Mann, 'States, Ancient and Modern'.

Chinese history, a definite autonomy of the state, of the political, because the state was strong enough to force class relations into a particular pattern. Of course, this pattern was maintained by the acquisition of solid profits, via state service and by cultural indoctrination stressing imperial loyalty; and the latter was much reinforced by the Chinese ideograph, which increased cohesion amongst the elite largely by making their monopoly of literacy, as is historically rare, firm and immovable. It is a remarkable fact that this loyalty survived during periods of disunity, and especially during the long first period of disunity of the empire, about which much too little is known. Perhaps the mandarins were prepared to wait for the material incentive of renewed state profit, but a further part of the explanation may be found in the monolithic nature of Chinese culture.

The more cosmopolitan world of the Middle East allowed for different ideological options; the centrality of Confucianism in China meant that alternative ideological options were much harder to come by, and in this manner ideological residues probably exerted a certain force. But whatever the exact explanation for the loyalty, its importance is clear: it largely explains the power of the empire to reconstitute itself. However, this merely returns us to the central questions: given the presence of the empire, in what ways, if any, did it have deleterious effects upon the Chinese economy?

Bureaucracy and Capitalism

A number of theoretical questions need to be highlighted at the start of this section. If greater taxation and control of landlord classes was one way in which empires would, in principle, have been able to counteract barbarian invasion, another method, again much discussed by marxist writers, would have been to increase state revenue by means of an expanding and improving economy. This brings to mind Max Weber's contention that the bureaucracy of pre-industrial empires killed off capitalist developments within their territories. Is there any truth in this view?

If much real light is to be thrown upon this question it is as well to concentrate our attention. It is not just easy but also perhaps tempting to do so; for there was a highly notable efflorescence of economic advance in medieval China from the tenth or eleventh century to the fourteenth. There are obvious indices of economic progress in this period. A striking revolution in water transport occurred, and this was of course a necessary precondition for greater economic interchange. Shiba Yoshinobu has shown in pioneering studies how deeply the commercial spirit penetrated society, with predictable results in the nature of business and financial organization.[18] The government provided a sound copper currency; as a result, where only 4 percent of taxes had been paid in money in 750, about 50 percent were so paid in 1065.[19] Perhaps the most impressive achievement is that drawn to our attention in a series of articles by Robert Hartwell.[20] Most of these deal with the iron and steel industry, and they demonstrate that Sung China, producing at least 125,000 tons of iron in 1078, easily led the world in the production of this basic commodity. But, in the end, this fabulous start did not lead to any 'take-off', and we must ask why this was so.

The first point to note is that the greatest expansion took place during a period when the empire was disunited. The Northern Sung did, supposedly, rule all of China from 960 to 1127, but even in that period they were faced with the militant nomadic Jurchen, who conquered their capital Kaifeng in 1127. After that, the Southern Sung (1127–69) were always faced with competitors to the North, first Jurchen and then Mongol. The fact of disunity is exceptionally important. It encouraged the Southern Sung to build a navy in order to man all waterways that stood between them and their northern competitors. This construction produced techniques and skills that proved beneficial to the economy as a whole and, most spectacularly so, to the Chinese voyages of discovery of the fourteenth century. Further action of this sort was forced on the Sung by the presence of real competitors. One of the greatest of all sinologists, Etienne Balazs, was wont to argue that the market and cities gained some autonomy precisely during the period of disunity in Chinese history, and this finding has received support from later research.[21] Elvin notes that the quality of coinage provided by states tended to improve during this period for the simple reason that traders would not return to or trust

[18] S. Yoshinobu, *Commerce and Society in Sung China*, University of Michigan Press, Ann Arbor, 1970.

[19] L. J. C. Ma, *Commercial Development and Urban Change in Sung China*, University of Michigan Press, Ann Arbor, 1971, p. 17.

[20] 'Markets, Technology and the Structure of Enterprise in the Development of the Eleventh Century Chinese Iron and Steel Industry', *Journal of Economic History*, vol. 7, 1966; 'A Cycle of Economic Change in Imperial China: Coal and Iron in Northeast China, 750–1350', *Journal of Economic and Social History of the Orient*, vol. 10, 1967; 'Financial Expertise, Examinations and the Formulation of Economic Policy in Northern Sung China', *Journal of Asian Studies*, vol. 30, 1971.

[21] E. Balazs, *Chinese Civilisation and Bureaucracy*, Yale University Press, New Haven, 1964.

governments that manipulated the coinage too much for their own ends.[22] The general principle is clear. 'Competition between equals, whether the Southern Sung and the Mongols, or the contestants in the Japanese civil wars, or the states of early modern Europe, is an indispensable condition of progress in military technology.'[23]

There is something like conclusive proof of this point. Much of the interest shown by the Sung in military matters resulted from their nomadic neighbours in fact having the edge over them. Thus the Mongols made the greatest use of gunpowder: this forced the Sung into making use of it as well. Yet once the empire was firmly reunited under the native Ming dynasty it proved possible for many decades to *downplay* gunpowder. The nomads to the north, even when they continued to use gunpowder, could always be defeated by sheer logistical weight; and it was best that gunpowder was controlled since it could all too easily aid the further disunification of the empire. Only an empire, free of rivals of equal status, could afford this sort of policy; in Europe it would have spelt destruction, probably within a single generation.

But once imperial rule was securely established, most clearly under the Ming, market forces began to be controlled. This can be seen clearly in urban affairs, cities again becoming centres of government and thereby losing their autonomy. Very little is known about the causes for the collapse of the iron and steel industry of Sung China, but it is plausible, perhaps likely, that imperial interference in pricing policy, with an eye to revenue gains, undermined this spectacular success story. However, there is sufficient information available to be fairly definite when discussing the collapse of the other great Sung achievement, its naval strength. The navy retained some strength even under the Mongols, but the foundation of a native dynasty together with an improved Grand Canal, no longer requiring ocean-going transport from south to north, led to a series of edicts that undermined its position. Most obviously, between 1371 and 1567 all foreign trade was banned. This is not to say that trade in fact ceased; instead it was organized by 'pirates', often of Japanese origin, in conjunction with local gentry, who thereby gained considerable profit. But such a ban must have had a great effect; certainly the ban instituted in 1430 against the construction of further ocean-going ships led eventually to technological amnesia.

However, the most spectacular way in which politics could affect the economy concerns the fate of the explorations undertaken by the

[22] M. Elvin, *The Pattern of the Chinese Past*, Stanford University Press, Stanford, 1971, ch. 19.
[23] Elvin, *The Pattern of the Chinese Past*, p. 97.

eunuch admiral Cheng-Ho in the 1430s. As befitted an empire, these expeditions to the Pacific and Indian oceans were mounted on a large scale. They were, moreover, entirely successful, and they placed China in a position in which she could have reaped the benefits that were shortly to fall to the Portuguese, Dutch and British. But the character of politics in China, in this case largely court politics, determined that none of this was to happen. The mandarins were always extremely jealous of the emergence of sources of power alternative to their own, and were thus naturally opposed to Cheng-Ho precisely because he was a eunuch whose cause was promoted by the eunuchs at court. They had good reason for their opposition; eunuch generals had recently led the army to defeat in Annam, while sudden renewed nomadic pressure on the northern frontiers allowed them to argue that resources had to be spent to meet a more immediate problem. In a centralized system relatively minor conflicts and pressures could thus have important effects.

Let us return to Max Weber's dictum that bureaucracy killed off capitalism in the pre-industrial world. Certain reservations must be made about such a blunt formulation. On the one hand, this view tends to underplay economic advance within empires, in particular agricultural advance, to which the state did, so far as its limited resources allowed, sometimes contribute. On the other hand, Weber's formulation occasionally gives the impression that the state was all powerful, and that bureaucratic interference in pre-industrial and industrial societies is somehow of the same character. In fact, as noted, he was well aware that bureaucracy in pre-industrial societies was puny and that, as we shall see, a stronger state might have been able to foster economic advance.

Ultimately, however, Weber's argument gains support from the Chinese case. It is true that there is one undeniably intangible point. The Ming were perhaps unusual compared with other empires in history in, as it were, stepping backward by abandoning coinage and creating a purely natural economy. Had they continued along the path laid down by the Sung, it is possible that greater tax revenues could have enabled them to provide the greater social infrastructure their society needed for economic take-off. Perhaps the character of the Ming was historically peculiar and specific, and certainly that character was possible only in an extremely isolated geographical context. But there seem to be plenty of factors suggesting that the habitual character of imperial politics was exerting its sway.

Such politics deserve to be labelled 'capstone' in character. The interest of the mandarinate/state lay in preventing horizontal communication of any sort between the series of laterally insulated areas on the top of which it sat. It sought control rather than efficiency. This was true in many areas. The mandarins undermined the positions of generals, Buddhist monasteries, eunuchs and capitalists because they felt that their power was dependent upon social passivity, rather than upon social mobilization. This can be seen particularly clearly by means of a brilliant analysis of Ming taxation. The main task of the administration of the Ming was that of imperial cohesion: 'As the Ming administrators saw it, to promote those advanced sectors of the economy would only widen the economic imbalance, which in turn would threaten the empire's political unity. It was far more desirable to keep all the provinces on the same footing, albeit at the level of the more backward sectors of the economy.'[24] Of course, this meant that they would seek their revenue in taxation from the land. The Ming initially sought to have this taxation paid mostly in kind, as noted, and to that end did not provide a sound copper currency. Probably the fundamental reason for this change was political. The Ming did not wish monetary supplies and surpluses to be located at any single point where they could be seized and thus support rebellion. 'The empire's fiscal operations were so fragmented as to make them virtually safe from capture, and the mere knowledge of this fact was sometimes sufficient to discourage potential rebels.'[25] It is worth remembering that the empire founded by the Ming, and continued by the Manchu, lasted from 1371 to 1911, and that this represents the longest period of uninterrupted imperial rule in history. The capstone system *did* remove all alternative bases of power and there were *no* successful internal revolts for half a millennium. The Ming and Manchu had learnt how to perfect capstone government.

Chinese capstone government blocked the fully fledged emergence of intensive capitalist relationships, but this is not to say that the impact of the state upon capitalism must always be negative. On the contrary, a different type of state, the European organic state, proved capable, once capitalist relationships were established, of providing crucial services for this type of economic system. It is very noticeable that Chinese capstone government was incapable of providing equivalent services, and again Huang firmly offers what should now be a familiar explanation for this. The Ming aim was to create a stable agrarian state based on a healthy peasantry. This was the traditional Confucian view, which considered that the land was the provider of all that was meritorious, and perhaps

---

[24] R. Huang, *Taxation and Governmental Finance in Sixteenth Century Ming China*, Cambridge University Press, Cambridge, 1974, p. 2.
[25] Huang, *Taxation and Governmental Finance*, p. 321.

the origin of the Ming in a peasant rebellion helped ossify this view. But the fixing of once-and-for-all equal tax revenues at the beginning of the dynasty proved, in this connection, to be a terrible mistake, especially given that the administration was initially conceived on such a small scale. The trouble proved to be that the administration was underfinanced, and thus too weak to take advantage of such expansion of the population as took place. The image of a strong peasantry could only have been achieved had the state been powerful enough to establish decent currency and credit arrangements, instead of allowing the peasantry to be exploited at will by money-lenders and gentry; the dynastic cycle resulted in part because the state taxed too little rather than too much. The weakness of the government can be seen in other ways:

> It must be pointed out that in the late Ming most of the service facilities indispensable to the development of capitalism were clearly lacking. There was no legal protection for the businessman, money was scarce, interest rates high and banking undeveloped. Such an environment was hardly favorable to industrial production and the efficient circulation of goods. At the same time merchants and entrepreneurs were hindered by the frequent road blocks on the trade routes, government purchase orders and forced contributions, the government's near monopoly of the use of the Grand Canal and active involvement in manufacturing. On the other hand, the security and status of land ownership, the tax-exemption enjoyed by those who purchased official rank, and the non-progressive nature of the land tax increased the attractions of farming to the detriment of business involvement.[26]

Nor could the state play much of a role in helping recovery from those natural disasters that so plagued Chinese ecology.[27] The weakness of the government is beautifully caught in a dilemma in which they found themselves when administering the salt monopoly. Quotas for salt had initially been set without an eye to expanding consumption, and the government simply had no machinery by means of which it could itself increase production, even though it would thereby have made substantial profits. Merchants did start new production, and they were soon able to undercut government-produced salt. When government revenue fell, the state decided to clamp down on private production, even though this caused widespread hardship.[28]

[26]   Huang, *Taxation and Governmental Finance*, pp. 318–19.
[27]   E. L. Jones, *The European Miracle*, Cambridge University Press, Cambridge, 1981.
[28]   Huang, *Taxation and Governmental Finance*, ch. 5.

Trahison des Clercs

It is now possible to develop the rest of the argument with greater speed. There is not sufficient space to consider the origins of Christianity, although it is worth emphasizing that the Roman state felt nervous about it precisely because it was based on a non-official, horizontal communication channel. However, it is necessary to describe briefly the concordat reached between church and state between the conversion of Constantine and the fall of the Empire. How well did both sides do from this new relationship?

The church gained enormously from *détente*. It became extremely rich. More importantly, its very form of organization, the hierarchy of bishop, deacon and presbyter, was modelled on that of the secular state. The church also called upon the state to help it in its battles. Throughout the fourth century it pushed the state towards a position increasingly hostile to traditional paganism, even though such paganism was especially strong amongst the traditional landed and Roman aristocracy. Augustine had no compunction whatever in using the secular arm to hunt out those he considered to be heretics; Christian persecution to establish a single church organization rapidly took the place of the earlier persecution of Christians.

But what of the state? How well did it do from the bargain? The hugely interesting answer is that it did very poorly indeed out of the deal: it is proper to talk only of an attempted takeover of the church, since that attempt in fact failed.

One imagines that Constantine himself might have had some disquiet by the end of his reign. In the course of the two decades after the adoption of Christianity he found himself in a hornet's nest of controversy. Donatism in North Africa asserted that those who had apostatized during the persecutions should not be accepted as leaders of the church. This might seem a trivial point but a very great deal was involved in it. The Donatists wished to emphasize the purity of the church community – that is they wished to remain a sect opposed to a world that would sully their purity; perhaps in this Donatism was a rallying cry for disaffected provincials tired of Rome's overlordship. Constantine also found himself deeply involved in the long-running squabble between Arius and Athanasius as to whether Christianity was to be rigidly monotheist or not. Constantine attempted to compromise at the Council of Nicaea between those who believed God had made Jesus (and was thus the only *true* God himself) and the Trinitarians, by saying that Jesus, God and the Holy Spirit were 'essentially of the same substance':

but this did not resolve the conflict, which indeed continued in the Middle Eastern provinces, in the form of monophysitism, until the Islamic conquests.

But are these matters not theological in another sense entirely, that is trivial and unimportant to most Christians? Even more important, was not the empire beginning to gain loyalty from the church? Certainly Eusebius of Caesarea positively welcomed his role as an adviser in a sort of Caesaropapist doctrine centred on Constantine, and it seems that some Western bishops were also rallying to the empire. Augustine, after all, fiercely attacked the Donatists and did so with some success.[29] Yet we must note the arguments he used against the Donatists. He accused them of lacking imagination in wishing to be a sect, an anti-society. He was quite as puritanical as they were, but insisted that a much greater historical opportunity lay in front of them: the church could *become* society rather than merely constitute an opposition to it. So if the church integrated people into society, it is vital to insist that the society in question was Christian rather than Roman. There is a distinct difference here between East and West, caused perhaps by the fact that the emperor spent so much more time in the Eastern provinces, and finally of course cemented by the fact that the emperor *did* save the Eastern empire. And Augustine was one of the socially mobile provincials, who came first to Rome and then to Milan, where he was elevated to a Professorship of Rhetoric. The influence of St Ambrose upon him in Milan led him to abandon the service of the empire, and to retreat to private study, first in Cassiacum and then in North Africa, before becoming a servant of the church. Of course, his *City of God*, perhaps the single most important theological work in medieval Christendom, famously argued that God's kingdom could not be associated with the destiny of Rome. God's timetable was his own, and should not be conflated with the destiny of Rome. This was a remarkable, indeed foolhardy, judgement given that, at the time, the basic infrastructure of the church – that is literacy–was not yet provided by the church but was the general product of Roman civilization.

In the West the church moved from ingratitude to, and scorn for, the state to a realization that it could in fact do without it. It was the church that negotiated with the barbarians at the walls of most cities, and arranged for them to be saved rather than destroyed. Where Chinese intellectuals refused to serve barbarians until they accepted the imperial form, and thus put themselves on the road to assimilation, in Western Christendom exactly the opposite was the case. The elite broke ranks.

[29]   P. Brown, *St Augustine*, Faber, London, 1967.

The intellectuals went out to the barbarians and provided services for them as well as the promise of universal salvation. For the chiefs of tribes, the church, as the bearer of literacy, proved invaluable in allowing legal codification. Thus Gregory the Great's mission to England landed in 597, and by 616 more than ninety laws had been written down. Much the same story could be told of the codification provided for the Lombards and the Franks. But perhaps underlying all this is something much simpler. The church, as Anderson stresses, wore the mantle of Rome: it was civilization and the hope of a better life.[30]

So the City of God came to be dissociated from the imperial structure, a fact pregnant with consequences. In China and Rome, a large geographical space was chained together by political/military means. But in Christian Europe, as in Islam and in the land of the Brahmans, cultural identity was more extensive than the political order.[31] Latin Christendom held together an extensive space until approximately 1100 but, lacking its own political theory, it then provided the shell within which organic states could develop. The manner in which this took place concerns us below. But one contention necessary to the rest of the argument must be made first. It is now something of a commonplace amongst medieval historians to note that great technological breakthroughs occurred in European history in the years between 800 and 1000, that is precisely in those years in which Europe was held together culturally but not, in the fullest sense of the word, governmentally.[32] The extensive area of Latin Christendom created a market, and helped the restoration of trade.[33] Further, the egalitarian nature of Christian belief, so much in contrast to classical Hinduism, perhaps proved to be an energizing force. Crucially, the fact that the Christian church was not a full-blooded government meant that property relations could set without state interference. This is extremely important. Where Confucian mandarins could look to the state for money, it became quite clear early on that medieval

[30] P. Anderson, *Passages from Antiquity to Feudalism*, New Left Books, London, 1974, pp. 128–44

[31] For an analysis of Islam and Hinduism in the light of this chapter, see J. A. Hall, *Powers and Liberties*, Basil Blackwell, Oxford, 1985, chs. 3–4.

[32] C. Cipolla, *Before the Industrial Revolution*, Methuen, London, 1976; G. Duby, *The Early Growth of the Medieval Economy*, Weidenfeld & Nicolson, London, 1974; M. M. Postan, *Medieval Economy and Society*, Penguin, London, 1975.

[33] I owe this point to M. Mann, *Sources of Social Power*, vol. 1: *A History of Power from the Beginning to A.D. 1760*, Cambridge University Press, Cambridge, 1986. I am in debate with this masterpiece throughout this chapter, differing from Mann particularly in my relatively negative view of empires.

landlords – and peasants, particularly of the kulak variety – had to look to their estates for increased income. The exact causes of the intensive and capitalist turn of the European economy do not concern us here.[34] What is important is to see the relationship between a pre-existing civil society – for this is what the prior establishment of property relationships, cities and churchly power (that is the emergence of strong and autonomous social groups) amounted to – and a particular type of state.

The Organic State in the State System

The argument to be made has three parts: a counterfactual proposition; a characterization of the organic state; an appreciation of the role of state competition. These parts are mutually supporting, and all centre on the undoubted fact that European society did not, despite the attempts of Charlemagne, Frederick Barbarossa, Charles V, Napoleon and Hitler, develop an imperial structure after the collapse of Rome.

At first sight some of the statements in the preceding paragraph may seem slightly overblown. Surely, it might be objected, the church did develop a political theory, and did seek to establish a real imperial papacy. By the middle of the eleventh century a reforming spirit, originating in Cluny, swept the church and created a drive for power seen most clearly in the papacy under Gregory VII, Innocent III and Boniface VIII – that is between approximately 1050 and 1300. In this period the papacy had, to oversimplify the matter somewhat, certain doubts about the wisdom of crowning Charlemagne Holy Roman Emperor in 800, and it sought to qualify this. Most dramatically, the papacy humiliated the emperor Henry IV who, famously, had to ask penance of the pope at Canossa. The origin of this argument between pope and emperor was the right to grant clerical appointments. Formally the pope won, and it is such victories that help account for the creation of the papal governmental and juridical machine at this period. The church grew ever richer and more powerful. But did it manage to establish a new primacy sufficient to give it something like an imperial status? The answer to this question must be no. The papacy never possessed its own army, while the various kings of Europe very plainly did. Thus it was never able to establish a priestly imperial structure.

It is now time to turn to the other side of the coin. If the drive to an imperial papacy was defeated as much by the presence of diverse states as

---

[34]   For further details, see Hall, *Powers and Liberties*, ch. 5.

by anything else, how did those states come into being in the first place? Specifically, what role did the church itself play in the creation of such states? The church played a notable role in making empire impossible. It refused to serve as second fiddle in an empire equivalent to those of China and Byzantium and thus did not create a Caesaropapist doctrine in which a single emperor was elevated to semi-divine status. Very much to the contrary, the church's habitual playing of power politics encouraged the formation of separate states whose autonomy eventually led to the failure of its own imperial drive. This whole process was symbolized in 1312, when the Emperor Henry VII asked the pope to send Robert of Sicily, the pope's vassal, to the imperial court at Pisa. Clement V issued the bull *Pastoralis Curia*, in which he argued that a king owed no duties to the emperor, and was instead master in his own realm. This was not the only way in which Christianity provided the best shell for the emergence of states. The church provided those numinous aspects of kingship – the coronation and the singing of the *Laudes Regiae* – that made a king more than one amongst equals. Even more important was its attack on extended kinship systems. In other civilizations, above all in Islam, the lower classes could often rely upon kinship systems as a means of protection and mutual aid; the removal of this weapon made the European peasant that much better fodder for state formation.

With these background comments in mind, the first argument can be presented. Imagine what European history might have been like had the Roman Empire somehow been reconstituted, or had any imperial form taken its place! We have seen that empires are too centralized for their logistical capacity, and thus have produced capstone government based on their appreciation that secondary organizations are dangerous. Empires usually sought to encourage the economy, but this form of government has historically never ultimately allowed sufficient leeway to the economy for it to gather self-sustaining momentum. Why should an imperial Europe have been any different? One notable characteristic of the Christian tradition is its adaptability to different types of power – from trying to establish its own empire, to supporting a secular emperor briefly, to acceding eventually to the principle of *cuius regio, eius religio*. If there had been a European empire, it is extremely likely that the Christian church would have provided it with an ethic that distrusted economic gain quite as much as did Confucianism.

This counterfactual can be put in a rather different manner. My contention was that a decentralized market system came into place between 800 and 1000 when there was no state that could interfere with its workings, but an organization that nevertheless gave people a sense of belonging to a single civilization. An imperial form would very probably have sought to control such 'natural' processes. The point is perhaps best illustrated by a consideration of the Europe city. Historians think Max Weber correct in the more materialist part of his theory about the rise of the West, namely in his contention that only in Europe did the city gain full autonomy. It invented a new civilization, that of the Renaissance, whose political theory contributed vitally to the rest of European history; it provided a space in which the merchant was king and in which bourgeois values could solidify.[35] We live in the world created by this civilization. With a matter of such import, it is essential to ask how this autonomy occurred. One part of the answer is that the crucial north Italian cities wedded their monetary might with new military techniques to provide a powerful combination that gave them protection until the invasion of the French at the end of the fifteenth century. It was precisely this combination – of money and military means – that Chinese capstone government so wisely sought to undermine. Nevertheless, the more satisfying answer is that the northern Italian cities were themselves the result of the absence of a single centre of power in Europe. Specifically, they gained their autonomy as the result of a power vacuum between pope and emperor, such that they were able, as is often the case in Third World countries today, to get the best for themselves by opportunistically chopping and changing their allegiance.[36] How much they owed to their freedom from interference is simply seen: once they become part of the Spanish mini-empire they contributed virtually nothing new to European civilization. The same point can be made by indulging in a 'thought-experiment': had Philip II created a long-lasting empire based on his new Spanish possessions, what would have happened to the social experiments taking place in the United Provinces and England? It seems likely that social experiments at the periphery would have been ruled out.

It might at first sight seem contradictory to say that the organic state, the second characteristic of the European polity to be discussed, *helped* in economic development after the largely negative comments made about empires. But my argument is in fact that no simple view of the state is of much use, for there are *different* types of state in different historical and social circumstances. Two general principles about the relations of government to the economy seem valid. Firstly, the absence of *all* government is disastrous, because it encourages localism, and thus prevents trade; and the point made already about the service provided by Christianity in

35   J. Baechler, *The Origins of Capitalism*, Basil Blackwell, Oxford, 1975.
36   This point (apparently drawn from J. Burckhardt) is made by P. Burke in his splendid 'City States', in J. A. Hall, ed., *States in History*, Basil Blackwell, Oxford, 1986.

holding Europe together shows that no such anarchist vision is encouraged here. Secondly, however, what I have referred to as capstone imperial government, characteristically distrusting secondary organizations and indeed all uncontrolled participation by its citizens, was indeed hostile to endogenous economic development. In one sense, as noted, it is a mistake to call such government strong, since it was based on weak infrastructural penetration of the society: indeed its arbitrariness results in part from that weakness. This gives us the clue to the distinctiveness of the European state: a limit to arbitrariness combined with, indeed in part caused, considerable and ever increasing infrastructural penetration. Two such limits are important.

The first limit is straightforward. The European state evolved slowly and doggedly in the midst of a pre-existing civil society. It was no capstone organization in large part because it was not a conquest state. Rather its history is typified by the cautious policy whereby, for example, the King of France was slowly able to expand from his own domains in the Île-de-France and gradually to achieve domination of the larger region we know today as France. This process took a very long time, and it was not fully completed by the time of the Revolution. This can be put in a different way. One other uniqueness of the West is the role that parliaments played in its history: indeed so unique has this role been that German historians have considered the *Standestaat*, the representation of the three functional estates, church, noble and burgher, to be a particular stage in world history.[37] It is quite clear that the prominence of such assemblies owes a great deal to the church. Since it owned so much land it was as jealous as any noble of the powers of the crown to tax. Hence it generalized two tags of canon law – 'no taxation without representation' and 'what touches all must be approved by all' – and these became crucial to these estates. It is proper to speak of a civil society that pre-existed the monarch: his only way of gaining money was to cooperate with this society.

The paradox of this situation is that restraint on government in the end generated a larger sum of power. Perhaps the most important mechanism in this process was the King's decision to make money by providing a certain infrastructure to the society.

This is most clearly seen in the field of justice. The lawyer has a very central place in European society, and this results from the King's desire to gain profits from justice. Fees were charged for every legal transaction, and these came to provide an important part of the revenue of most

[37] A. R. Myers, *Parliaments and Estates in Europe to 1789*, Thames and Hudson, London, 1975.

monarchs after about 1200. This is not of course to say that the law was equally open for all to use; but it was present.

Increasingly European states provided other sorts of infrastructural help. They became good at managing disasters of various sorts; by the eighteenth century, for example, considerable help was available to the victims of earthquakes, whilst disease was quite rigidly controlled by quarantine laws.[38] And they sought to encourage economic growth. The internal colonialism whereby Scots, Irish and Welsh were integrated into a single community, a process repeated elsewhere in Europe, created a single market. In the more advanced European states, though *not* in France until after 1789, this process went hand-in-hand with the removal of internal tariff barriers, and this was an incentive to trade. Rulers had encouraged such trade for a long time because a disproportionate part of their revenues came from customs and excise. So they did all they could to attract traders; a typical piece of legislation in this matter was Edward I's *Carta Mercatoria* of 1297.

It is worth trying to summarize the general spirit at work here. It is not being claimed that 'society' had suddenly come to include everybody, although the degree of literacy and the eventual creation of national tongues do witness to the emergence of what is properly called the nation state. What is apparent is that large sections of the powerful in society proved prepared in the long run to give quite high taxation revenues to the crown because they realized that their interests were usually being served. Conflicts of course occurred, and they make up much of European history. But the more important fact remains the organic quality of the state. It can be summed up in the single, oft-mentioned point that so impressed Tocqueville on a visit to England. Where many aristocracies, Chinese, Roman and some European, hid their wealth from the state and refused to do its bidding, the English aristocracy and gentry manned local government and taxed itself. There was no fundamental power stand-off between state and society because the state *was* capitalist in character. Hence the level of infrastructural support and penetration was high. A Confucian bureaucrat who moved away every three years simply could not know enough about local conditions to serve a particular area well; representations to a central assembly by local aristocrats from that area could create a different result.

The argument here is essentially that of Adam Smith in *The Wealth of Nations*. Smith sought to explain a particular connection between

---

[38]   Jones, *The European Miracle*, ch. 7.

commerce and liberty by showing that commercial development came *before* the full emergence of the European state and, as a result, gave that state a particular form. His posited connection seems empirically justified, especially when it is remembered that he is not claiming that opulence and liberty always go together: his highly critical comments on China show clearly that he realized that capstone-style government could simply deliver the poor into the hands of the rich. He is not as antipathetic to government as some contemporary ideologists would have us believe; his notion of the rule of law was by no means negative. Despite all this, his account must be qualified by remembering Durkheim's criticism that consensus stands behind contractual market relationships. Consensus, or rather the enforcing of contracts, came to be provided by the state; but a sense of mutual trust provided by the Christian shell had been necessary for the European market to emerge in the first place.

The second general restraint on arbitrariness is also the third general point to be made about the European polity. Individual states did not exist in a vacuum. They were, rather, part of a competing state system, and it was that system, particularly the military organization it engendered, that played a considerable part in determining the character of individual states. Political competition proved beneficial to economic progress. Why was this?

Perhaps the most obvious fact about a state system is that it leads to a high degree of emulation. This can be seen in European history most spectacularly in the history of art. The invasion of Italy by the French in 1492 spread the styles of the Italian Renaissance around Europe, and thereafter rivalry and status-seeking ensured that what was fashionable abroad had to be copied at home. In fact, this emulation was not at all confined to artistic matters but extended, for example, to the establishment of various scientific clubs in eighteenth-century France in conscious imitation of their English rivals. Such emulation is ultimately only possible between states that recognize each other as of more or less similar standing; empires do not tend to copy the culture of small neighbours – mere barbarians!

Moreover, the reference to empires brings out other facts about a state system that prove beneficial for economic growth. A state system always has an inbuilt escape system. This is most obviously true in human matters. The expulsion of the Jews from Spain and the Huguenots from France benefited, and was seen to benefit, other countries, and this served in the long run as a limitation on arbitrary government. Capital was equally mobile. Thus Philip II's abuse of Antwerp led within a matter of years rather than decades to the rise of Amsterdam. In a brilliant passage making this point, W. H. McNeill has shown that time and again Philip II wanted to behave like an autocrat but the mobility of capital sapped his ambition.[39] This was particularly true of his relationship with Liège, the foremost cannon producer of late-sixteenth-century Europe. When Philip pressed too hard, artisans and capitalists simply upped and left. A certain measure of decent and regularized behaviour was ensured by these means. However, perhaps the fundamental mechanism at work was that of military competition. Mann's striking reconstruction of the figures for English state finance shows with great clarity that the major expenditure of the British state was on warfare and that jumps in levels of expenditure were occasioned either by wars or by the need to invest in new miliary technology – the necessity for Italian wall defences against gunpowder, and so on.[40] The impact of the slaughter of the First World War on our image of war has been so great that in a sense we are now all opposed to war. But it is very important to remember that it was a normal, and usually acceptable, form of behaviour for European states in history. War in European history, *pace* John Nef's famous thesis, served as a source of social and economic progress.[41] A revolution in military technology had to be adopted very quickly by neighbouring states, on pain of dismemberment – something that notoriously happened to the Polish state at the end of the eighteenth century.

The positive impact of competition on European society can most dramatically be seen in the modern world. The revelation of German industry applied to war in 1870, for example, sent a ripple of anxiety and countermeasures throughout European capitals; states were forced to rationalize their societies to survive. Yet state competition was responsible for rationalizing European societies *before* to the age of industry. Consider again the German case. Dramatic defeat by Napoleon was not ascribed to greater industrial development, but to the impact of an ideologically motivated citizen army. The reform group around Hardenburg (including Scharnhorst and Gneisenau, and with Clausewitz as their greatest intellectual figure) realized that serfs could not provide such an army; the reforms of 1807, 1811 and 1818 changed the Prussian social structure at a stroke. The purpose of such changes was military but the commercialization of agriculture that

[39] W. H. McNeill, *The Pursuit of Power*, Basil Blackwell, Oxford, 1982, ch. 1.
[40] M. Mann, 'State and Society, 1130–1815: an Analysis of English State Finances', in M. Zeitlin, ed., *Political Power and Social Theory*, vol. 1, JAI Press, Connecticut, 1980.
[41] J. U. Nef, *War and Human Progress*, Harvard University Press, Cambridge, 1950.

resulted was economically beneficial. This mechanism was at work in Europe roughly from 1100 when the multi-state character of Europe finally crystallized. Throughout the middle ages there was a breeding race to provide heavier, more effective cavalry, and changes as great were associated with the rise of bowmen and pikemen, the adoption of gunpowder and the consequent need for new Italian defences, the vast increase in army size in the seventeenth century, and the creation of a citizen army during the French Revolution. Each of these changes required money, and it was the search for funds that had the king calling his estates and raising funds by providing the infrastructures mentioned.

As noted, the European state became able to generate far more power than its imperial rivals: thus the France of Louis XIV probably had as large and effective an army as Ming China even though her population was only 20 million, not about 150 million. This raises an interesting and important question. The organic quality of the European state arose from its having to accept and cooperate with other elements in civil society. Why was it, however, that the more powerful European state did not turn inwards in order to establish something more like an imperial system? Roughly speaking, European absolutism represents just such a move, and it is important to stress how unsuccessful it was. It is conventional to compare absolutist France with England in order to give the impression of France's greater strength. This is mistaken, since English society generated more power *without* absolutism; it proved this by defeating France in war on every occasion bar one in which they met in the eighteenth century.

This returns us to the question of competition. No state could afford to go it alone without risking defeat. It is very significant that by the middle of the eighteenth century France was sending its intellectuals to England and was in other ways trying to copy her secrets. All this suggests that there must be a prime mover among the states in order to get competition to work in the first place. In fact there were several prime movers in European history, the torch of progress being passed from Italy to Holland and to England. It seems no accident that England possessed a powerful and, crucially, *centralized* estates system which insisted on the state remaining organic during the absolutist period. It is important to stress this since the reaction to the discovery that imperial strength hides feet of clay has been to say that the European state was always more powerful.[42] Put like this the statement is misleading. Power operates on two dimensions and the real contrast is between arbitrary capstone

---

[42]   B. Turner, *For Weber*, Routledge & Kegan Paul, London, 1981.

government generating little power and civil society/organic government generating a great deal.

Conclusion

Let me conclude by trying to avoid two misunderstandings that might arise. Firstly, my argument does stress the effects, largely seen as beneficial, of competition; but few conclusions can really be drawn from this. On the one hand, the argument has stressed positive roles played by Christianity and by the organic state that militate against any automatic *laissez-faire* philosophy of history. On the other hand, and more importantly, modern circumstances are such as to rule out any repeat of the historical pattern noted.

Secondly, my argument does not seek to revive the hackneyed view that politics always holds primacy over economics; it merely suggests that political forms, on occasion, have an independent impact upon social evolution. This should be obvious as, when discussing the rise of the West, I have pointed to the remarkable interplay of state and capital; states existed within larger capitalist society, and the security of the latter would be undermined by the emergence of any single controlling polity. This complex relationship remains with us still, but here too one significant change is worth remarking upon. Since 1945 capitalist society has benefited because the United States has shouldered certain regulatory tasks for the system as a whole. This contribution has not been, however, neutral: rather it has privileged the particular interests of a great power, as has become obvious to many Europeans. Much future social evolution will depend upon whether a new way of regulating the larger capitalist system can be discovered.[43]

---

[43]   On this topic, see ch. 7.

2

A CURIOUS STABILITY?

One staple of Western thought has been an assumption that democracies lack coherence and so are essentially unstable. The taproot of this view can be found in Greek thought. If Plato's distrust of the people probably reflects the position of a threatened aristocrat, Aristotle's endorsement of this position had as background the destruction of autonomous Greek city states by Macedonian imperialism. The links between democracy and war proved to be especially important in the revival of Greek thought. Machiavelli argued, as do modern historians of the ancient world, that democracy depended upon service in a citizen militia – and to that end inveighed against the practice of his fellows, made lazy by affluence, of hiring mercenaries.[1] The link made here, between riches and corruption, was at the centre of Rousseau's thought. Given an insistence that the individual was weak and easily distracted by fashion's positing of alternative social selves, it was scarcely surprising that Rousseau insisted that the authentic life could only be assured by a return to Spartan simplicity.[2]

---

[1] N. Machiavelli, 'The Art of War' and 'Discourses on the First Decade of Titus Livius', in *Machiavelli: The Chief Works and Others*, three volumes, trans. A. Gilbert, Duke University Press, Durham, 1989. A useful overview of the relation between infantry warfare and Greek democracy is provided by J. Bryant, 'Military technology and socio-cultural change in the ancient Greek city', *Sociological Review*, vol. 38, 1990.

[2] J. Shklar, *Men and Citizens*, Cambridge University Press, Cambridge, 1969, especially ch. 1. Cf. C. Blum, *Rousseau and the Republic of Virtue*, Cornell University Press, Ithaca, 1986.

Much eighteenth-century thought, particularly in Britain, assailed this general position. Most obviously, there was less reason to worry about corruption, as Gibbon stressed, because high taxes meant that technology–above all the use of guns – could compensate for the military fitness of outsiders; Europe was at last safe from barbarian incursions.[3] Adam Smith shared this position, and then went much further, placing wealth above virtue. One reason for this was that the provision of wealth meant that the sufficiency of the many would be great; differently put, he refused to share the admiration of the classical world on the ground that its benefits, anyway for the few, rested on slavery.[4] More fundamental to Smith was the fact that money-making brought in its train softer politics based on the rule of law. The key characteristic of the superlative third book of the *Wealth of Nations*, which makes this argument, is its stress on the role of unintended consequences. The irony with which Smith viewed the emergence of commercial society extended to its essential mechanism. In the sixth book of his earlier *Theory of Moral Sentiments*, Smith had famously remarked that human beings were deceiving themselves when imagining that power and riches brought absolute benefits: 'They keep off the summer shower, not the winter storm, but leave [man] always as much, and sometimes more exposed than before, to anxiety, to fear, and to sorrow; to diseases, to danger, and to death.'[5] Nonetheless, Smith argues that 'it is well that nature imposes on us in this manner'.[6] The beneficial side-effect of the vast majority within commercial society seeking to keep up with the Joneses, to endlessly run up a moving escalator, is nothing less than social peace. But Smith was slightly ill-at-ease with this, his principal argument, and encouraged the state to add to a naturalistic process a measure of citizen training through education and service in a militia.

Despite a sympathy for labour, Smith remained an eighteenth-century thinker in presuming that it was normal for those at the bottom to seek to imitate their betters. The escalator of social life was, in other words, naturalistically grounded. This view was challenged by the French Revolution. Obviously, on one side thereafter stood Marx and his followers, possessed of a theory that at one and the same time described and endorsed the coming triumph of the proletariat. Not surprisingly,

[3]   E. Gibbon, *The History of the Decline and Fall of the Roman Empire*, seven volumes, Oxford University Press, Oxford, 1906, especially vol. 4, pp. 191–202.
[4]   I. Hont and M. Ignatieff, eds, *Wealth and Virtue*, Cambridge University Press, Cambridge, 1983.
[5]   A. Smith, *The Theory of Moral Sentiments*, Oxford University Press, Oxford, 1976, p. 183.
[6]   Smith, *The Theory of Moral Sentiments*, p. 183.

bourgeois or liberal theorists felt the need to ensure that commercial society had positive rather than accidental sources of social cohesion. Even those we think of as the absolute apostles of individualism, that is the 'lights of liberalism' of nineteenth-century Britain, had at the centre of their thought the need to create noble and altruistic motives, for the newly enfranchised workers quite as much for the middle classes: accordingly, reading Wordsworth would help to ensure social stability.[7]

The most distinguished twentieth-century British liberal, Maynard Keynes, noted early in his career that the attempt to provide positive endorsement to capitalism, on the part of different social classes, had failed. His analysis of nineteenth-century social peace stresses unintended consequences quite as much as had that of Adam Smith. He finds stability curious:

> . . . this remarkable system depended for its growth on a double bluff or deception. On the one hand the labouring classes accepted from ignorance or powerlessness, or were compelled, persuaded, or cajoled by custom, convention, authority, and the well-established order of society into accepting, a situation in which they could call their own very little of the cake that they and nature and the capitalists were co-operating to produce. And on the other hand the capitalist classes were allowed to call the best part of the cake theirs and were theoretically free to consume it, on the tacit underlying condition that they consumed very little of it in practice. The duty of 'saving' became nine-tenths of virtue and the growth of the cake the object of true religion. There grew round the non-consumption of the cake all those instincts of puritanism which in other ages has withdrawn itself from the world and has neglected the arts of production as well as those of enjoyment. And so the cake increased; but to what end was not clearly contemplated.[8]

Keynes insisted, of course, that this mentality had come to debilitate capitalism and thereby to undermine liberalism, and accordingly sought to save European society from both fascism and bolshevism by replacing a faulty mechanism with inspired intelligence.[9] For a while, many observers, including marxists, believed that Keynesianism worked, that

[7] C. Harvie, *The Lights of Liberalism*, Allen Lane, London, 1976; S. Collini, *Public Moralists: Political Thought and Intellectual Life in Britain, 1850–1930*, Oxford University Press, Oxford, 1991, especially ch. 2; P. Corrigan and D. Sayer, *The Great Arch*, Basil Blackwell, Oxford, 1985.

[8] J. M. Keynes, *The Economic Consequences of the Peace*, Macmillan, London, 1971, pp. 11–12.

[9] R. Skidelsky's biography in progress – *John Maynard Keynes*, vol. 1: *Hopes Betrayed, 1883–1920*, Macmillan, London, 1983; vol. 2: *The Economist as Saviour, 1920–1937*, Macmillan, London, 1992 – makes this particularly clear.

liberalism was assured because capitalism had been made to work sufficiently smoothly to ensure social peace by means of economic growth
and full employment. But the resurgence of class conflict in the late 1960s
and the seemingly related spread of inflation and cessation of economic
growth led many to think that Keynes had not so much saved capitalism
as staved off – and perhaps added to – its final crisis. The left naturally
welcomed such militancy, but did rather little to plan for a new age.[10]
Rather different and more disturbing was the view of many on the right,
whose talk of a generalized crisis of ungovernability had as an all-too-
realistic implication the need to increase authority.[11] In these circumstances, much attention was focused on corporatism – that is a system
which would assure social and economic stability by taking workers in
from the cold so that they could form an estate of the realm.[12]

The argument of this essay is occasioned by a simple empirical finding.
Democracies in the modern world have not been particularly unstable –
or, more precisely, the combination of liberal democracy and capitalism
(for the former has not existed without the latter, which is not to say that
commerce always and automatically creates liberty) does not lead to
political disaster. Waves of democratization, most notably after 1918,
1945 and 1989, have slowly increased the absolute numbers of democracies, despite the retreats to fascism and communism in the inter-war
period and to bureaucratic-authoritarianism in the 1970s – and, one
must add, the likely failure of some of the regimes established in the
euphoria of 1989.[13] Of course, figures of democratization are often
highly flawed: for example, Mexico is sometimes considered to be democratic, sometimes authoritarian, without there being any significant
change in its social structure. None the less, what probably counts
most is power: given that both Japan and Germany have now consolidated their democracies, this criterion supports measured optimism. But

---

[10]   A particularly striking analysis, centring on the collapse of capitalist profit-
ability, was given by A. Glyn and B. Sutcliffe, *Capitalism in Crisis*, Random
House, New York, 1972.
[11]   M. Crozier, S. P. Huntington and J. Watanuki, *The Crisis of Democracy*,
New York University Press, New York, 1975.
[12]   E. Gellner, 'A Social Contract in Search of an Idiom: the Demise of the
Danegeld State', *Political Quarterly*, vol. 46, 1975 was highly representative of
this mood. The chief theorists of corporatism include J. Goldthorpe, C. Maier, C.
Crouch and F. Hirsch: all have important papers in F. Hirsch and J. Goldthorpe,
eds, *The Political Economy of Inflation*, Harvard University Press, Cambridge,
1978.
[13]   I rely for much of the rest of this paragraph on S. P. Huntington, *The Third
Wave: Democratisation in the Late Twentieth Century*, University of Oklahoma
Press, Norman, 1991.

what matters more for the purpose of this essay is a more particular point that emerges from the figures. Most breakdowns of democracies occur in newly established and correspondingly fragile regimes. The collapse of the Weimar Republic is typical. Further, most of the breakdowns that have occurred after, say, a quarter-century of democratic rule have taken place in countries in the developing world. Accordingly, the precise claim to be made is that the advanced part of the capitalist world does not witness the breakdown of historical liberal democracies. To say this is not for a moment to suggest that countries so blessed are always free from 'disloyal oppositions'.[14] Nor should it be forgotten that such settled regimes can be corrupted by affluence: thus democratic France was not prepared to take on Hitler early enough in the 1930s, while the current Western retreat from active intervention in the face of ethnic cleansing is, if not as dangerous, scarcely inspiring.[15] None the less, the extreme stability of Western liberal democracy is a brute fact. Surely we cannot help but see this given the obvious contrast with the collapse of state socialism.

Such stability, so much counter to the expectations of the mid-1970s, needs explanation. I begin by outlining the views of Fred Hirsch's *Social Limits to Growth*.[16] The central reason for concentrating on Hirsch is that his treatise offered, in my view, the most original statement of the view that the West's curious combination of social inequality and political freedom had become unhinged.[17] The analysis of Hirsch's views that follows thus comes quickly to rest on the brilliant analysis, at once destructive and creative, of Michael Smith's *Power, Norms and Inflation*.[18] This account of the postwar inflation has at its centre a refusal to accept 'the sociological argument', that is the marxisant insistence that pressure from below caused inflation, and an endorsement of the categories of traditional economic theory follows in consequence. But

---

[14] This useful concept is that of J. Linz, *The Breakdown of Democratic Regimes: Crisis, Breakdown and Reequilibration*, Johns Hopkins University Press, Baltimore, 1978.
[15] Particularly pertinent comments along these lines can be found in R. Aron, *Democracy and Totalitarianism*, Weidenfeld & Nicolson, London, 1968, ch. 9.
[16] Routledge & Kegan Paul, London, 1977. For critical commentary on Hirsch, see the essays in A. Ellis and K. Kumar, eds, *Dilemmas of Liberal Democracy*, Tavistock, London, 1983.
[17] A more personal reason for writing about Hirsch is to distance myself from an earlier essay, 'The Conscious Re-legitimation of Liberal Capitalism: Problems of Transition', in Ellis and Kumar, *Dilemmas of Liberal Democracy*. That earlier critique had naively accepted rather too many of those presuppositions of the age to which Hirsch gave such striking expression.
[18] Aldine de Gruyter, New York, 1992.

Smith's arguments suggest a theory of liberal politics, and this comprises a third section of this essay. This move from economics to politics, from the capitalism to the democracy of the omnibus term 'capitalist democracy', draws on arguments from the second volume of Michael Mann's *Sources of Social Power*.[19] There are interesting differences between Smith and Mann, and reflections on these entail a return to Hirsch in the conclusion.

Social Limits to Growth

The force of Hirsch's arguments combined with their having been taken from widely different disciplines has made it hard to unpack his principal theses with exactness. I believe that his account of the putative crisis of liberal capitalism can be summed up in three points.

1   Some 'goods' are positional, i.e. they are positions that can only be occupied or that gain their value from being occupied, by a single person. There can typically only be one prime minister or president or king. However, affluence is beginning, according to Hirsch, to make it clear that social goods are of the same character. A single summer house by a lake is a positional good destroyed when a second dwelling is built. Thus Hirsch is led to argue that growth cannot make us all happy.

2   The political action of large groups of people is now being influenced by the frustration consequent on this first limit to growth. Hirsch's words are important here:

> But in the late 1960s the issue of who gets what returned in strength. This reemergence could not be attributed to the collapse of economic growth – as had happened so abruptly in 1929 – or even to its decisive deceleration. The inflationary crisis that pushed Western economies into their most severe postwar recession in the mid-1970s can itself be seen as, in part, a result of the surfacing of political and economic pressures by the poor to get what they saw as their fair share. In the quarter century following the end of World War II, the leading economies showed an exceptional performance in growth of national product. Why then did the intractable, divisive issue of economic equality return to centre stage?[20]

[19]   M. Mann, *Sources of Social Power*, vol. 2: *The Rise of Classes and Nation-states, 1760–1914*, Cambridge University Press, Cambridge, 1993.
[20]   F. Hirsch, *Social Limits to Growth*, Routledge & Kegan Paul, London, 1977, p. 174.

The discovery that growth does not, as had been expected, bring satisfaction breeds frustration. But instead of blaming this frustration on the inherent scarcity of positional goods, social actors continue, and in fact increase, their demands. Hirsch sees this process as self-defeating, illusory, and the origin of crisis. Frustration was powerful enough, let it be noted once again, to start giving liberal capitalism problems even before growth had in fact collapsed.

3 Liberal capitalism is also seen as suffering from a declining moral legacy. One central presupposition of Keynesianism and so apparently of our political economy as a whole, at least according to Hirsch, is that the elite will act in the interests of economic rationality. Keynes's Bloomsbury background gave him an unfettered contempt for the stupidity of capitalists who preferred, in time-honoured Victorian manner, to save rather than to spend, and he believed that the enlightened behaviour of the mandarins could so adjust capitalism as to prevent its having dangerous troughs. This view Hirsch rightly insists is comprehensible only when we remember that the English mandarinate to which Keynes belonged was the world of Lord Reith, Oxbridge, and Royal Commissions manned by 'the great and the good'. This is to say that this elite was responsible. But in time the English mandarinate/political establishment learned, if learning was necessary, that economic irresponsibility could help to buy votes. Perhaps the behaviour of the mandarins is in any case in part a response to the undermining of another presupposition of Keynes's system, namely that the working class would be sufficiently deferential to accept the wise guidance of their leaders, secure in the knowledge that this would lead to benefits for them as well. Hirsch believes that such deference has gone for good, that the elite can no longer exercise authority. Capitalism has been all too successful in encouraging selfish motivations; trade unionism, in this view, is, as Bernard Shaw had it, 'the capitalism of the proletariat'.

A part of the brilliance of Fred Hirsch's argument lies in the fact that it is subject to different readings. One reading was given by Ralf Dahrendorf in a lecture to the Royal Society of Arts in 1980. Hirsch's importance for Dahrendorf lay in the demonstration via the thesis of positional goods that growth cannot solve the social problems that now confront us, and perhaps for this reason there is a notable hostility to growth in Dahrendorf's analysis. Broadly speaking, I would dub this interpretation of Hirsch conservative: the moral explicitly drawn by Dahrendorf is that life is hard, that it would be better for us to learn to accept our condition rather than to kick vainly against the pricks.[21] Now there is no doubt but that Hirsch himself lends support to this interpretation in varied passages in his work. At the end of the book, for example, he encapsulates his position thus: 'This book has suggested that the prime economic problem now facing the economically advanced societies is a structural need to pull back the bounds of economic self-advancement.'[22] But this exceptionally fertile book does not fit entirely within this schema. For there is a fundamental ambiguity about the concept of social limits to growth: does it mean that society has finally limited growth (and a good thing too) or could it mean that if we change some social institutions then (heaven be praised) the growth process can be restored? Dahrendorf's interpretation of Hirsch seems to me to have been typical in stressing the former of these, and I would guess that this derives from the fact that Hirsch's thesis is popularly associated with the concept of physical limits to growth. It is worth recalling that Hirsch was aware of the criticisms of the celebrated Club of Rome report, criticisms which can only be increased when we note that its author, Denis Meadows, came to admit that he had only 0.1 per cent of the information necessary for his model.[23] In contrast, the conclusion pays some attention to the second possible interpretation of Hirsch's position, essentially because of a bias in favour of economic growth.

Frustration Unbound? The Sociology of Inflation

At first sight Hirsch's argument about positional goods has something of the quality of a logical proof. Personally, however, I follow Jonathan Gershuny's argument to the effect that a second, third, and even fourth house by a lake still leaves the original summer-house as a desirable enough good in itself.[24] Perhaps once it was more pleasant to be rich, but I do not believe we should overburden ourselves with the tribulations of our betters.

However, there is a further, more important consideration that should make us sceptical of the salience of positional goods in Hirsch's argument. Hirsch's view of economic and social goods is

---

21   R. Dahrendorf, 'The Limits of Equality: Some Comments on Fred Hirsch', *Journal of the Royal Society of Arts*, June, 1980.
22   Hirsch, *Social Limits to Growth*, p. 190.
23   J. Gabler, 'Alternatives to Growth?', paper presented at the Joint Seminar of the Universities of Frankfurt and Southampton, 1982.
24   J. Gershuny, 'Technical Change and "Social Limits"', in Ellis and Kumar, *Dilemmas of Liberal Democracy*.

simplistic and absolute. The summer-house by the lake is a typical example in this respect since it stresses how an absolute 'good' can be destroyed. But a look at some principal and well-founded theses in the sociology of fashion can demonstrate that his view is overstated, and indeed naive.

The foremost English writer on the sociology of fashion, Quentin Bell, describes its characteristic process thus:

> Novelty, audacity, and above all exclusiveness, the bright badge of social enterprise brings a fashion in , and when a hat or shoe has lost its social appeal, when everybody is wearing it, it dies of popularity. Such seems to be the fate of elitist art in our society, the social impulse that made it fashionable with the few ends by making it vulgar with the many whereupon the elite must look for something else.[25]

Bell is a disciple of Veblen, whose book *The Theory of the Leisure Class* appeared, it should be noted, in 1899. And the same points have long been known in France. One of the most notable books on the subject was Edmond Goblot's *La Barrière et le niveau*, in which he demonstrated the exceptional ability of the rich to establish new positional areas in order to prevent themselves being swamped by the masses.[26] This same thesis is neatly summed up in the title of Pierre Bourdieu's *La Distinction*.[27] But perhaps the clearest summary in the whole matter has been provided by a French sociologist of literature, Renée Balibar.[28] Her striking empirical work on the schoolbooks of French children in the later nineteenth and early twentieth centuries shows, for example, that just as soon as a broad spectrum of the population began to understand Zola, the elite changed its interests to symbolism and surrealism; that is secondary schools began to teach these authors. The analytic point that follows is straightforward. If the crux of class is the business of distinction rather than the possession of absolutely scarce goods, then there is reason to doubt Hirsch's argument. Bluntly, Hirsch severely underestimates the capacity of the rich to dream up new goods and thereby to establish new scarcities. Some time ago a television programme explored the way very rich Japanese were able to spend their money. Notoriously Japan itself is short of summer-houses by deserted lakes, and perhaps it is for this reason that the wealthy

[25] Q. Bell, *A Demotic Art*, University of Southampton Press, Southampton, 1976, p. 8.
[26] Presses Universitaires de France, Paris, 1967.
[27] Éditions de Minuit, Paris, 1979.
[28] R. Balibar, *Les Français Fictifs*, Hachette, Paris, 1974.

choose to take their meals below the water in submersibles. These looked hot, cramped, and generally uncomfortable, but they doubtless served the function of distinguishing the rich from the less well-off.

The cynicism of the negative argument that has been made needs correction if a balanced view is to be created. Fashion is not just idle frippery; nor is it just fun. Rather, fashion allows human beings to try out different personalities, and thereby to experiment with the very selves they wish to create.[29] Rousseau had recognized and inveighed against this. There are good reasons to reject his position. By and large, the sense of freedom of individuals in advanced societies depends upon their ability to play and to pretend, to control the information about themselves that they wish to give off. In so far as the ability to involve oneself in a society of images depends upon economic growth, there is everything to be said against the puritanism implicit in Hirsch's call to 'pull back the bounds of economic self advancement'.[30] This is one justification for a bias in favour of economic growth.

These points have relevance for Hirsch's claim that the smooth workings of capitalism depended upon a prior moral legacy – and upon the claim of many authors that some new shared morality is necessary if capitalism is to function again.[31] Let us recall Adam Smith's view of the mechanism of capitalist stability, namely that the endless chasing of the person or position immediately above helps to get away from the politics of absolute confrontation, for all the contentiousness that it involves. Striking evidence produced by Garry Runciman many years ago showed that comparison does tend to be limited, that is that ambition is limited to immediate steps rather than to absolute ascent.[32] Given the falsity of Hirsch's claim about positional goods, there seems no reason to presume that stability by means of the endless catching up with the Joneses has to come to an end.

The point being made is, in a sense, that there is a continuing shared culture of comparison. But most notions of 'shared moral community', whether of the past or planned for the future, tend to be fuller and more total than this and, in particular, to stress the role of ideology in curtailing demand. Yet empirical work on the role of ideology in history, and

---

[29]   J. A. Hall, 'Sincerity and Politics: the "Existentialists" versus Goffman and Proust', *Sociological Review*, vol. 25, 1977.
[30]   Hirsch, *Social Limits to Growth*, p. 190.
[31]   D. Bell, *The Cultural Contradictions of Capitalism*, Heinemann Educational Books, London, 1978.
[32]   W. G. Runciman, *Relative Deprivation and Social Justice*, University of California Press, Berkeley, 1966.

particularly amongst the Western working classes, has thrown a great deal of doubt upon the view that capitalism was ever maintained by an ideology of this sort, whether shared or imposed.[33] Thus the Victorians, who had believed that such ideological cohesion was in place, were very shocked by the census of 1851, which showed not only that the lower orders were not religious but that they could not have been so, in the sense of attending church, for the simple reason that there were insufficient churches to accommodate them. Similarly, modern Japan, the one liberal capitalist country that does sometimes look as if it rests upon some sort of moral consensus, apparently owes its success at least in part to hidden but effective social controls. It may be the case that Japanese organizations are womb-to-tomb in character but apparently someone who leaves such an organization is thereafter branded as 'not a company man', a dangerous reputation most wish to avoid. This discovery of coercion behind seeming consensus should put us more generally on our guard. There is no doubt that at least some of the myriad calls for renewed community come from thinkers wishing to extend liberalism.[34] But the theory and practice of such statements tend to be terribly vague. Given the historical fact that the demand for shared morality has occasioned massively illiberal coercion, in industrial circumstances even more than in the agrarian world, there seems as yet everything to be said for steering clear of modern communitarian ideals.[35]

If there is no sense to Hirsch's claims about the nature of a positional good and about the impact of a declining moral legacy, all that is left of his general position is the much more traditional view that workers endanger social stability by causing inflation. The simplest version of this general view stresses demands for higher wages, whilst a more complicated version, that of the theory of political business cycles, argues that finance ministers are virtually forced into causing inflation by the knowledge that 'priming the pump' will secure their parties' election. As the

---

[33] N. Abercrombie and B. Turner, 'The Dominant Ideology Thesis', *British Journal of Sociology*, vol. 29, 1979.

[34] A representative thinker here is Charles Taylor, whose views are very clearly stated in 'Cross Purposes: the Liberal–Communitarian Debate', in N. Rosenblum, ed., *Liberalism and the Moral Life*, Harvard University Press, Cambridge, 1989.

[35] S. Holmes, 'The Permanent Structure of Antiliberal Thought', in Rosenblum, *Liberalism and the Moral Life*; J. A. Hall, *Liberalism*, Paladin, London, 1988, chs 3 and 7. A striking analysis of the endemic coercion of traditional societies admired by many communitarian thinkers is D. Phillips, *Looking Backward*, Princeton University Press, Princeton, 1993; the force of this book gains from the fact that its author *shares* with communitarians a dislike of the 'disenchantment' of the modern world.

reverse side of this coin stands the contention that countries that integrate workers by means of corporatist institutions are best able to ensure the basic health and success of their economies.

It is no exaggeration to declare bluntly that these views can no longer be entertained after Michael Smith's assault upon them. An exemplary and high-powered review of the evidence finds little support for the view that workers caused inflation, either directly by seeking higher wages or indirectly as a result of politicians' seeking to purchase votes.[36] If limitations of space make it impossible to restate this part of Smith's destructive case, attention can be given to some of his reasoning. The huge literature on corporatism is correctly held to have been vitiated by a failure to agree about what makes a country corporatist – a failure that renders most of the supposed empirical support for the corporatist case more or less useless.[37] This failure followed from using the general label of corporatism licentiously; if the crucial notion was that of agreements between states, workers and capitalists, it was further presumed that this would lead to Keynesian demand management and the maintenance of the welfare state.[38]

But few countries embraced this complete package deal. Germany never accepted every element of the package, despite the fact that most studies placed it high on their scales of corporatism: a historic fear of inflation ensured that the independence of the Bundesbank – mandated to fight inflation – was never challenged. Further, the supposed corporatism of many other smaller countries scarcely counted given their decision to tie their currencies to the Deutschmark, thereby effectively accepting the discipline provided by the Bundesbank.

More powerfully still, Smith is able to make use of hindsight to point to the undoubted fact that the main contentions of the sociological argument have been utterly disproved by events. One example of this is that supposed long-term secular process of the maturation of working classes, made much of by Goldthorpe, which is considered to make it impossible to pursue deflationary policies.[39] Evidence showing that at crucial moments unions have become extremely unpopular, not least amongst

---

[36]   Smith, *Power, Norms and Inflation*, pp. 45–53, 104–18.
[37]   Smith, *Power, Norms and Inflation*, chs 6 and 7.
[38]   Similar sloppiness was shown about the related notion that 'Keynesianism' was part of the post-war settlement. For an exemplary analysis of the varied acceptance of Keynesian ideas, see P. Hall, ed., *The Political Power of Economic Ideas: Keynesianism across Nations*, Princeton University Press, Princeton, 1989.
[39]   Smith, *Power, Norms and Inflation*, pp. 114–15.

union members themselves, fits ill with this argument; so does the notable recent decline in union membership in many advanced capitalist countries. More bluntly still, the fact of the matter is that deflationary policies were pursued for more than a decade in most countries without there being any serious threat to social peace. This was made possible (at least in part), in Smith's eyes, by the sophistication of voters – who understood the dangers of inflation and the mechanics of the political business cycle, and who accordingly chose, time after time, to elect politicians prepared to offer them hard medicine.

The razor-sharp scepticism of Smith's analysis makes it tempting to stay with the destructive side of his argument. This would be a mistake. For quite as remarkable is the positive case that is being made. The great post-war inflation seems to have resulted from the conjunction of several factors. Hirsch is indeed right to say that inflation began to take hold in the 1960s but quite wrong to ascribe this to pressure from below. The prime mover of post-war inflation was the United States. Lyndon Johnson refused to raise taxes to pay for the simultaneous costs of the Great Society programme and the war in Vietnam, preferring instead to cover expenses by printing money. Given the hegemonic power of the United States within the world political economy, above all in providing the means of international exchange, it proved possible to pass on some of these costs to other countries. Europeans were forced to hold dollars they did not want; put differently, Europe imported inflation from the United States.[40] If the abuse of the Bretton Woods system caused inflationary problems, its final collapse none the less made eventual recovery from inflation particularly hard. Inflationary countries had been forced by the Bretton Woods system to change policies so as to protect their currencies; floating rates removed this discipline, effectively allowing endless competitive realignments. Advanced capitalism was thus in the worst possible condition to handle the two great oil shocks of the 1970s. Continued loyalty to full employment in combination with a refusal to 'tighten one's belt' caused inflation to get out of control.

None the less, inflation *was* eventually controlled in the core of advanced capitalism. If this sheer fact went against sociological expectations, so too did the pattern by means of which control was imposed. The growth of employment and of the economy more generally has been higher in the United States, after the severe deflation imposed by Paul

[40]   This analysis has been made over many years by D. Calleo, most strikingly in *The Imperious Economy*, Harvard University Press, Cambridge, 1982. Cf. Smith, *Power, Norms and Inflation*, pp. 33, 63.

Volcker, than in 'corporatist Europe'. Of course, the notion of a single European political economy is a nonsense. But within Europe, it seems that the level of corporatism does not relate strongly to degree of economic success, with German prosperity owing everything to its refusal to place full employment above price stability. In summary, inflation either never got out of hand or was quickly controlled in countries blessed with an independent central bank and with elites not interested in, or quickly prepared to drop, Keynesian norms. The dominance of Keynesian ideas amongst the British policy making elite combined with the dependency of the Bank of England to ensure that inflation was particularly rampant in the 1970s.

Smith's argument might be misunderstood, and it is accordingly important to highlight what is being said – not least because this will then encourage further generalization. Misunderstanding might result from the clear finding that economic theory explains the great post-war inflation better than does 'the sociological argument' – that is that inflation was the result of bad economic policy far more than of worker pressure. Further, the fact that Smith seems as pleased by the recovery from inflation as many of those proffering the sociological argument had been by the prospect of capitalism's collapse may suggest to some that he is an economist rather than a sociologist.[41] Hence the important point to be made is that Smith explains *sociologically* that political irresponsibility which created bad policy: what mattered were the seigniorage rights of the United States, the depth of the addiction of different policy-making elites to Keynesian norms and the degree of autonomy of the central bank. What is implied here is that capitalism, when left to itself, will work according to the logic of the hidden hand – with international pressures accordingly being such as to severely curtail the autonomy of national economic policy.

But what matters for our purpose is that political stability is likely to be enhanced by letting capitalism alone. It is now apparent, against the clear expectations of most social theory, that governments do not face more unrest from deflationary policy than they do from following the corporatist logic of incomes policy. State involvement in and responsibility for the economy positively encourages political action; in contrast, deflationary policies can be blamed on the market and in any case assail the old, the

---

[41]   I am influenced here by the way in which a more recent paper by Smith was subjected to almost wilful misinterpretation: M. Smith, 'What is New in 'New Structuralist' Analyses of Earnings' and A. Sorensen, 'Throwing the Sociologists Out? A Reply to Smith', both in *American Sociological Review*, vol. 33, 1990.

non-unionized unemployed and the young (for whom special provision can easily be made) rather than organized labour.[42] The principle at work is simple. Conflict diffuses into society when it is not concentrated by the state; differently put, the more liberal a polity, the more likely it is that political stability will be maintained – which is not to deny that there may be high levels of *social* conflict, there being, of course, differences of interest between capitalists and workers. Smith's concentration is on a particular moment at which the governments of advanced capitalism discovered that they could increase stability by shedding certain burdens they had shouldered.[43] But if we are to understand fully why the combination of capitalism and democracy is not at all curious, it is necessary to widen the historical range so that further generalization is allowed.

But before doing so it as well to sound a cautionary note. The emphasis placed on the way liberalism diffuses conflict should not be taken as implying that more traditional factors do not matter. Economistic considerations may not be complete, or even crucial, but they still have their importance. Prolonged and dramatic reductions in living standards may eventually undermine liberal governments; there is plenty of evidence to suggest that growth (which slowed rather than stopped for most countries in the 1970s, with improved rates thereafter) does help to ensure social cohesion – not least by allowing for that endless running up the moving escalator of social comparison. More generally there seems no reason to reject the notion, derived from eighteenth-century thought, that money-making takes people's minds off political struggle.[44] This is a second reason for a bias in favour of growth. Additional support for it can be gained if we think – as Hirsch never really did – of a society without growth. Consider a thought experiment. Clearly transition to a no-growth economy would require revolutionary changes in the economic structure. Not only the industrial sector, but the structure of jobs, education, and the regional structure of the economy would have to change. Investment goods industries would, of course, have to shrink very markedly, and their redundant workers would have to be absorbed elsewhere without a cushion of growth to make the process palatable.

---

[42]   Smith, *Power, Norms and Inflation*, p. 115 properly cites the pioneering argument of K. Bradley and A. Gelb, 'The Radical Potential of Cash Nexus Breaks', *British Journal of Sociology*, vol. 31, 1980.

[43]   A rather similar point can be made about state ownership of industry. Often this increased the lobbying power of failing industries, thereby diminishing the state's room for manoeuvre and creating severe political pressures. Privatization can enhance state powers, as argued below, by leaving it free to act in other areas.

[44]   A. Hirschman, *The Passions and the Interests*, Princeton University Press, Princeton, 1977.

This sounds as if it would be very much a war of all against all. And matters are really much worse than this. Zero growth would have to be enforced. This means that there could be no individual freedom to invest, nor could there be a free movement of labour. If we did not want to keep present consumption patterns, as is likely, it would be necessary to compensate growth in one sector by a reduction in another. If we ask who could oversee such processes, and with what standards, we must surely come to worrying conclusions. Analogously, the German marxist thinker Wolfgang Harich has argued forcefully that the creation of a 'green economy' would require a highly authoritarian regime – a regime his critics dubbed a kind of ecological neo-Stalinism.[45]

Liberalism as a Form of Politics: Conflict no Catastrophe

The way in which liberalism allows conflict to be defused rather than concentrated can be better understood, and its historical conditions more fully appreciated, by means of a key finding of modern historical sociology.[46] Let us concentrate on the different levels of working-class militancy within the capitalist mode of production in the years before the First World War, and then offer more general reflections upon liberalism as a form of politics. The analysis at all times draws, as noted, on the second volume of Mann's *Sources of Social Power*.

At one pole of a typology of class feeling stands the figure of Samuel Gompers, the accommodationist leader of the American Federation of Labour: he disliked socialism and warmly endorsed 'the American way of life', as have many American workers thereafter. Such loyalty is scarcely surprising. American white males had the vote as early as the 1830s, making them citizens almost from the start of American history. But if the position of Gompers won out in the United States, it did not do so without a fight.[47] Before 1914 radical syndicalism and reformist socialism were also present, in the 'Wobblies' and in the socialist party

---

[45]   W. Harich, *Kommunismus ohne Wachstum?*, Rowolt, Frankfurt am Main, 1975, cited in Gabler, 'Alternatives to Economic Growth?', p. 19.
[46]   There is now a large literature on this point: see, *inter alia*: D. Geary, *European Labour Protest, 1848–1945*, Methuen, London, 1984; R. McKibbin, *The Ideologies of Class*, Oxford University Press, Oxford, 1990; I. Katznelson and A. Zolberg, eds, *Working Class Formation*, Princeton University Press, Princeton, 1987; T. McDaniel, *Capitalism, Autocracy and Revolution in Russia*, University of California Press, Berkeley, 1988. As noted, I draw most on Mann, *Sources of Social Power*, vol. 2.
[47]   Mann, *Sources of Social Power*, vol. 2, pp. 635–59.

of Eugene Debs. The radicalism of these organizations was created by the viciousness of capitalists in the United States, prone to use lock-outs and to employ Pinkerton detectives – something which accounts for the several *hundred* deaths of American labour history. Accordingly, the broadest generalization to be made about the American case is that there was no socialism less because of some essentialist peculiarity of the United States than because workers, faced with the stick of labour violence yet blessed with citizenship, found that their best avenue to increased security lay in coming to terms with capitalists.

This generalization is reinforced by a consideration of Britain. Chartist militancy was certainly defeated by a clear-sighted regime that joined together repression with increasing liberalism: genuine radicals were deported whilst the rest were offered more political space in which to create that respectable unionism symbolized by Robert Applegarth.[48] All the same, British workers were not given full citizenship and they accordingly gained a sense of common identity in their struggle to achieve it. A particularly important part of that identity came as the result of the regime's retreat, albeit very brief, from liberalism: British workers began to demand labour representation because of restrictions imposed as a result of the Taff Vale court decision. All the same, the British working class was not too bothered by politics, having an entirely autonomous life of its own based on football, pigeons and gambling.[49] It fought loyally in the war, and there is not much sign that many harboured notions of the nation of great distinctiveness. During the war, the trade unions became very embittered by those middle-class socialist pacifists who criticized a conflict in which their members were dying. Thus when the Labour Party finally produced a constitution and became capable of gaining political power, it was no accident that the unions ensured, through instituting the block votes of unions at party conferences, that they, rather than the middle classes or the socialist societies, would control the ultimate destiny of their party.[50] This control has never been relinquished, and the Labour Party has remained true to its name. Class loyalty never became politicized class consciousness.

At the other pole of this typology stand the Russian workers of St Petersburg and Moscow. Such workers could be more radical than their leaders, the Bolshevik Party at times following rather than leading – and this despite Lenin's accusation, in *What is to be Done?*, that

[48]   Mann, *Sources of Social Power*, vol. 2, ch. 15.
[49]   McKibbin, *The Ideologies of Class*.
[50]   R. McKibbin, *The Evolution of the Labour Party, 1910–24*, Oxford University Press, Oxford, 1974.

they were merely economist. Genuinely socially revolutionary feelings resulted from autocracy. The Tsar had always sought to be father of his people, and so was extremely suspicious of every intermediary organization and grouping. At the end of the nineteenth century, however, the Russian state prevaricated between this loyalty to autocracy and the acceptance of the intermediary organizations necessary to capitalism. The westernisers introduced capitalism but were unable, despite several government reports, to introduce the basic union organization that might have limited class conflict to the workplace. A vital point about such limitation is that it would have coopted the workers into a routine existence, thereby making them visible and accountable. On the occasions when this policy was tried, most notably immediately after the 1905 Revolution, it seemed as if it was likely to succeed: scarcely surprisingly, the political opening tipped the balance from the revolutionaries to the reformists.[51] However, this policy was not consistently maintained. The traditionalists tried to integrate the workers directly into the state, particulary in the Zubatov movement. One important consequence of the failure of this movement was that the workers, whose hopes had been raised by politicians, blamed the state rather than employers or the market. This was one factor explaining why autocracy eventually moved towards a policy of total repression, a policy that produced workers with revolutionary political consciousness. Such workers had little choice: they had to destroy autocracy before anything else could be done.

The bureaucratic authoritarianism of Wilhelmine Germany was quite different from this. The German state never tried to undermine the hierarchical principles upon which capitalism depended; it had none of the monarchist populism that so raised the expectations of Russian workers. It could therefore afford, after the experiment with anti-socialist laws, to take the state out of industrial relations, that is to hand them back to the capitalist class. A consequence of this was that the German working class, politically aware though it was, did not really develop the revolutionary political consciousness that had once seemed possible. All the same, the state remained authoritarian, and this created a Social Democratic Party with political and industrial wings. Max Weber's comments on this situation retain all their perceptiveness.[52] Speaking as a sort of democratic Machiavelli, he insisted that the greater political liberalism he

---

[51]   McDaniel, *Capitalism, Autocracy and Revolution in Russia.*
[52]   Weber made his views particularly clear in his wartime reflections on the historical sociology of Wilhelmine Germany. See M. Weber, 'Parliament and Government in a Reconstructed Germany', in *Economy and Society*, trans. G. Roth and C. Wittich, University of California Press, Berkeley, 1978, p. 1391.

advocated would increase rather than dilute social cohesion: the more workers felt themselves to be part of society, the less likely they would be to embrace radicalism.[53]

This typology can be seen in terms of Tocqueville's later work. Social movements are not pure, deriving simply from socio-economic relations; rather their character is influenced by the states with which they interact. More precisely, classes quite as much as nations have to be imagined.[54] In both cases, minds are concentrated and imaginings undertaken principally in reaction to the state. I suspect that this tells us something about human nature (or, rather, reminds us of the forgotten insight of eighteenth-century social theory): political arbitrariness causes far more resentment and so mobilizes more strikingly than mere difference in income level. Furthermore, liberal states allow workers to become reformists and to seek gains at the industrial level, thereby diffusing conflict through society; in contrast, authoritarian and autocratic states exclude workers from participation in public life, so making it necessary to take on the state – to act politically. Differently put, capital and labour by themselves can quite easily coexist. So too can other classes, which are far more capable of cooperation, as Tocqueville realized, than crude notions of material interest allow; only in this way, after all, is it possible to explain Scandinavian social democracy, distinctively the result of peasant–worker alliance.[55] Difficulties in the relations between classes come, as Dahrendorf rightly stressed, when religious, political or national divisions are superimposed on each other: such superimposition leads to intensification of feeling, and so to violence.[56]

None of this, it should be stressed, is to deny that there can be much conflict in society within liberal politics. But such conflict is not likely, as Marx had it, to polarize two great forces against each other. Very much to the contrary, capitalism produces whole sets of divergent interests, both within and between classes. The interests of the propertied and the meritocratic can, for example, be quite as diverse as those between

---

[53] It might be objected that the United States and Britain could afford liberalism because of their level of socio-economic development, whereas Germany and Russia were so poor that control of popular forces was a functional prerequisite for democracy. Various considerations go against this view, most importantly the fact that the German economy overtook that of Britain just before the First World War.

[54] See ch. 6 for an analysis of nationalism.

[55] G. Esping-Anderson, *Politics against Markets*, Princeton University Press, Princeton, 1984.

[56] R. Dahrendorf, *Class and Class Conflict in Industrial Society*, Stanford University Press, Stanford, 1959.

craftsmen and the unemployed. If politics does not concentrate matters, civil society is likely to entertain endless contention and comparison. Such conflicts are unlikely to lead to political instability. Rather, social conflict may well be less a catastrophe than a means of social integration – as any follower of Simmel should know.[57]

Three cautionary notes must be issued at this point. Most immediately, it is important to point out that the terms of reference of this essay have been subtly biased. For much of the time the implicit question has been as to whether working-class interests would destabilize a seemingly curious combination of capitalism and democracy. We can now see that working-class militancy is but a reaction to old regime intransigence: put another way liberal capitalist nation states have been made more politically stable mainly by the removal of old regime and radical right political actors and their replacement by Christian Democrats after the Second World War. Further, there is much truth in the argument that workers have pushed for democratization and that they have remained more loyal to it than have middle classes, as was true in the Weimar Republic.[58] All in all, there remains sense in Chesterton's view that the poor are likely to appreciate government rather than anarchy: 'The poor man really has a stake in the country. The rich man hasn't: he can go away to New Guinea in a yacht.'[59]

Secondly, any self-satisfaction about liberalism as a form of politics should be diluted by the discovery that coercion has regularly been used against those seeking to challenge the very notion of private property relations. If there is relative softness within the liberal polity, distinct harshness has been meted out to those wishing to create alternative worlds.

Finally, it is important to stress that the concentration in this essay on the behaviour of classes should not be taken as a denial of entirely different sources of stability within modern democracy. The most important of these is simply that a system of checks and balances encourages rational calculation. This matters crucially in connection

[57]   G. Simmel, *Conflict and the Web of Group-affiliations*, Free Press, New York, 1955. Cf. L. Coser, *The Functions of Social Conflict*, Free Press, New York, 1956.

[58]   D. Rueschemeyer, E. Stephens and J. Stephens, *Capitalist Development and Democracy*, Polity Press, Cambridge, 1992. I would add, however, that the rhetoric of socialism of the German Social Democrats was unwise: it was not meant, and it cut off potential alliance with middle-class elements. For further elaboration of this point, see ch. 5.

[59]   G. K. Chesterton, *The Man Who Was Thursday*, Penguin, London, 1962, p. 129.

with geopolitics. Fascism might have been a more or less viable means of running an industrial society – except for its inability to control the geopolitical adventurism of its leaders. This is not to suggest that democratic statesmen always make good geopolitical judgements. That the Versailles settlement was far less efficacious than the American system that followed the end of the Second World War suggests a generalization: capitalism prospers within the confines of settled geopolitical rules, with the inter-war economic collapse being consequential upon geopolitical failure.

Conclusion

The main argument of this essay amounts to saying that the stability of the combination of social inequality and political democracy is not really curious after all. Liberal politics diffuse pressures through society. This applies to religion and nation, just as much as it does to class.[60]

It might be objected that this view is unduly complacent about contemporary capitalist democracy. Certainly capitalism faces real problems. The discipline of Bretton Woods has indeed gone, whilst the predatory behaviour of the United States is likely to cause greater reactions now that the Cold War is over. But many other considerations point towards stability. Meetings of the G7 powers attest to a desire to continue multilateralism, whilst there is no real sign that either Europe or Japan is prepared to challenge the geopolitical dominance of the United States. Still more importantly, the development of capitalism has diminished the size of the working class and rendered it ever less effective. In addition for capitalists now clearly inhabit a global society, leaving their workers more nationally caged than ever.

This raises a further consideration. Is the descriptive argument, that political stability results from the separation of politics and economics, morally callous? While there is much to be said for sociologists trying to tell it like it is rather than placing their hopes above analysis, disagreement between Smith and Mann does at least provide room in which a reasoned normative point can be made. Smith tends to a robust defence of the market against social democracy; in contrast, Mann's democratic socialism calls for the international rules of capitalism to be changed, not least since he judges national social democracy to be in great

---

[60]   For an application of this principle to nation, see ch. 6.

difficulties.[61] I doubt whether much change in international rules is possible, and anyway place a higher valuation on the market – believing, for example, that opening our markets is the best way to help Eastern Europe, the developing world and, therefore, in the long run ourselves.

But saying all this does not entail complete correspondence with the views of Michael Smith. To the contrary, Adam Smith's sympathy for labour still recommends itself. Swimming in the market, especially in late-industrial circumstances, depends heavily on human capital being improved by intelligent state action: industrial success for the advanced world cannot be based on a cowed nineteenth-century type of workforce. If there is much to be said for the state retreating from the management of industries and incomes, there is nothing to be said for its retreat from education. Further, there is evidence that if workers' rights are strong – which might be seen as a useful part of the corporatist bargain – this can lead to efficiency by creating human capital. The ability of Anglo-Saxon management to hire and fire at will stands in great contrast to the practice of Japanese management; unable to dismiss, the latter is forced to retrain.[62] All this can be put in different words. A very good case can be made that social democracy remains, despite the views of both Smith and Mann, a powerful option for national life within capitalist society: high levels of citizen training in conjunction with openness to the market – that is the precise opposite of democratic socialism's putative alternative to capitalism – may well yet ensure economic success. If the demand for this policy from below has weakened, realization amongst the elite, particularly in small trading states, has sometimes – and I hope this is analysis rather than mere hope – increased.

A radical reading of Hirsch's *Social Limits to Growth* can serve as a final conclusion. Throughout this essay, growth has been favoured because it allows consumers freedom and avoids the politics of redistribution within nations; this bias would be much increased by considering the difficulties of redistribution between nations. Perhaps this bias cannot, in the face of ecological problems, be sustained. Even if that is so, even if, that is, fusion power does not again revolutionize our productive relations, there remains a very great deal to be said for an

---

61   Mann has expressed his views on this matter on two occasions: 'Nationalism and Internationalism in Economic and Defence Issues', in J. A. G. Griffith, ed., *Socialism in a Cold Climate*, Allen & Unwin, London, 1983 and 'Nation-states in Europe and Other Continents: Diversifying, Developing, Not Dying', *Daedalus*, vol. 122, 1993.
62   R. Dore, *Flexible Rigidities*, Athlone Press, London, 1987.

argument of Hirsch's that has been unduly neglected. The particular proposal worth underscoring concerns the uncoupling of the traditional linkage of status with reward. Hirsch suggests that those with jobs with intrinsic rewards, that is autonomy, greater leisure time and responsibility, might continue to work without gaining the highest salaries. Monies saved could instead by used to integrate those with poorer quality jobs, as well, it can be added, as those with the negative power to disrupt the economy. This is to suggest a creative use of the market, either to restart the growth machine or to make life without it more manageable. It would prove possible to fill university posts with still further reductions in salary. One suspects that any systematic varying of the link between status and reward could only be implemented by a supremely intelligent elite in the dead of night. For widespread discussion of such a programme might kill it, whilst it would anyway have a very much greater chance of success in a climate of some economic growth; further, this policy would 'take on' the most powerful sectors of the professional world. None the less, fewer jobs remain at the end of every recession experienced by the advanced economies, and Hirsch's bold thought may yet have relevance.

3

AN ABSOLUTE COLLAPSE

It is useful to begin by recalling, if only briefly, the extent to which socialism was seen, to put it mildly, as a viable option of modernity. If it is scarcely surprising that adherents felt this, it is worth recalling the fervour of their beliefs. Thus Trotsky insisted that the coming of socialism would ensure that 'man would become immeasurably stronger, wiser, freer, his body more harmoniously proportioned, his movement more rhythmic, his voice more musical, and the forms of his existence permeated with dramatic dynamism'.[1] More generally, in the 1930s the putative crisis of liberalism meant that the Soviet Union was seen by many as the hope of mankind – as 'a new civilisation', at once scientific and just, 'a future that worked'.[2] If for many that view faded with the Hitler–Stalin Pact and for still more with the invasion of Hungary in 1956, the view of socialism as one of the possible organizational options of modernity most certainly did not disappear. Thus Raymond Aron, the supreme analyst of

[1] Cited (without reference) in D. Bell, *The End of Ideology*, Harvard University Press, Cambridge, 1988, p. 275.
[2] Reference here is of course to S. and B. Webb, *Soviet Communism: a New Civilisation?*, Longmans, Green and Co, London, 1936 and to L. Steffens, *The Autobiography of Lincoln Steffens*, Harcourt, Brace and World, New York, 1931. D. Caute, *The Fellow Travellers*, Weidenfeld & Nicolson, London, 1973 remains the best account of Western illusions about socialism put into practice.

the different polities of the industrial era,[3] argued ever more firmly in his last years that no change was possible inside the communist world.[4] An element of truth can most certainly be read into what had become pessimism of almost Manichean hue. Rigidity meant brittleness, a tendency to snap, far more than it meant effective strength. The inability to act as reformers turned many into dissidents; strikes did not, as in liberalism, diffuse conflict through society but necessarily concentrated it, turning simple disputes into challenges to the regime.[5]

But Aron did not have that sort of consideration in mind: he was impressed rather with the power capacity of this sort of regime, its ability to continue to rule whatever the cost. These views came to seem still more convincing to many in the 1970s and 1980s when, in the aftermath of the oil shocks, the Western combination of social inequality and democracy was judged to be none too stable. A crisis of governability was deemed to exist, the most important consequence of which was difficulty in running Western economies.[6] Although there was already recognition of a slowdown in economic growth under socialism, many held that its capacity to avoid inflationary policies – a single party having no need to print money in order to ensure election – might in the long run give its social system decided comparative advantage.[7] It is important to note, finally, that these sorts of views were not confined to a particular generation wedded to anti-communism. Interestingly, the greatest sociologist of the current generation conceptualized matters in much the same way as late as the mid-1980s – and this despite clear leftist political persuasion: the Soviet Union was seen as joining to its despotic power the infrastructural

---

[3]   R. Aron, *Democracy and Totalitarianism*, Weidenfeld & Nicolson, London, 1968. On Aron in this context, see G. Ionescu, 'Raymond Aron: a Modern Classicist' in A. de Crespigny and K. Minogue, eds, *Contemporary Political Philosophers*, Methuen, London, 1975 and J. A. Hall, *Diagnoses of Our Time*, Heinemann Educational Books, London, 1981, ch. 6.

[4]   R. Aron, 'On Liberalisation', *Government and Opposition*, vol. 14, 1979. This view was much debated in the Reagan years, after it had been popularized by Jeanne Kirkpatrick, most notably in 'Dictatorships and Double Standards', *Commentary*, vol. 68, 1979.

[5]   These points were realized very clearly by R. Dahrendorf in his *Class and Class Conflict in Industrial Society*, Stanford University Press, Stanford, 1959. But Dahrendorf did not really follow through on the logic of this argument. On the contrary, he was impressed by the façade of strength, and came up with *ad hoc* reasons explaining why socialist regimes would not in fact become unstable. For an account of Dahrendorf's thought, see Hall, *Diagnoses of Our Time*, ch. 5.

[6]   For a discussion of this belief, see ch. 2.

[7]   This view lies at the back of E. Gellner, 'A Social Contract in Search of an Idiom: the Demise of the Danegeld State', *Political Quarterly*, vol. 46, 1975.

capacities that came with the modern means of communication in such a way that its stability was ensured.[8]

Now it is entirely comprehensible that much current attention is devoted to trying to delineate the contours of the world after the Cold War. One notes further the habit of being less interested in decline than in rise to power. None the less, the absence of sustained attention given to the collapse of state socialism is an appalling dereliction of duty. The events associated with 1989 are of definite world historical importance and require thorough investigation on that count alone. More immediately it was not, as we have seen, that most social scientists did not *expect* the collapse of the socialist power system: they deemed it impossible. This cognitive failure must be confronted; it should not be swept under the carpet. It is worth adding that the generalized marxist reluctance – with one honourable and notable exception[9] – to confront the utter confounding both of expectation and hope is almost certainly a sign of complete intellectual bankruptcy.

I will go to some length to explain why I did not share the main thrust of the views described.[10] This is not done in order to suggest that a hunch that things would change allowed me to predict accurately what in fact happened. On the contrary, my surprise at the way events unfolded was just about total, perhaps especially because I had let myself be convinced that the desire for a cordon sanitaire would ensure the retention of East Germany within the Soviet sphere. So this chapter must take the form of an autocritique. An initial description of expectations is followed by a look at communism in the light of brute post-communist reality before then offering an account of the collapse. Two cautionary words should be borne in mind throughout. First, the height of my ambition is that of pointing to what needs to be explained about the socialist collapse; sufficient evidence is not as yet available for definitive conclusions – most particularly, in my opinion, because we have no reliable knowledge of calculations made inside the Kremlin. Secondly, in the analysis of socialism and its demise, description and prescription often go hand in hand: some attempt to face up to the troubling moral conundrums that result from this concludes the chapter.

---

[8]   M. Mann, 'The Autonomous Power of the State: its Origins, Mechanisms and Results', *European Journal of Sociology*, vol. 25, 1984
[9]   A. Callinicos, *The Revenge of History: Marxism and the Eastern European Revolutions*, Polity Press, Cambridge, 1991.
[10]   J. A. Hall, *Powers and Liberties*, Basil Blackwell, Oxford, 1985, ch. 7 and 'Classes and Elites, Wars and Social Evolution', *Sociology*, vol. 22, 1987.

Great Expectations

Visits to socialist states in the last ten years of their existence convinced me that these regimes were far from being the monoliths imagined by many in the West. It was certainly possible to detect elements of socialism at work. Artists were often paid highly, some becoming heroes of their republics; they benefited from rights to travel and had access to good housing. On the one hand, this was a legacy of the social background of the marxist intelligentsia, of the utterly unquestioned presupposition – held against mounting evidence[11] – that workers would eventually prefer opera to Dallas; on the other hand, it was the product of a Leninist voluntarism that Marx himself would surely have rejected, in which artists were favoured because they were pathfinders to a new form of socialist consciousness. Against such elements had to be set entirely different realities. On my first trip to Eastern Europe, I often asked historical sociologists about the way in which 'the Asiatic mode of production' was viewed, but elicited few responses. On one occasion, this led me to recommend the undoubted thoroughness and characteristic verve of the investigation of the concept by the British marxist Perry Anderson.[12] No interest was shown in this; rather a certain hostility was evident. They had suffered under marxism, and certainly did not wish to hear about additional varieties of the disease. More generally, it was in fact rather difficult to *find* genuine marxists, although some establishment members were recognizably old bolsheviks. But it was often very hard to know exactly how to take this, to work out what the real rules of the societal game were. Orthodoxy on the part of the head of an academic institute sometimes went hand in hand with extraordinarily radical thoughts in his staff; at times this seemed far from accidental, the orthodoxy serving, consciously or not, as a cover for novelty. Only very occasionally did people let themselves talk freely, and at last on one of those occasions I was told bluntly how it felt to have the Red Army on one's national soil.

---

[11] My own personal impressions of the narrow social base for artistic consumption in socialist society received much support from a series of surveys conducted in the late 1970s by Elemér Hankiss in Budapest. These neatly paralleled findings for Western societies, most notably those of P. Bourdieu and A. Darbel, *L'Amour de l'Art*, Minuit, Paris, 1969.
[12] P. Anderson, *Lineages of the Absolutist State*, New Left Books, London, 1984, pp. 462–549.

Life was hard, and it was so in many ways. Essentially middle-class people, from doctors to academics, paid relatively less in their societies in comparison with their equivalents in capitalist societies, were clearly engaged in a desperate struggle to maintain the educational standards of their children. There was a rigour and a discipline about some of their behaviour that was very striking. This was true of parts of private life and most particularly of the attention given to deep personal friendships, which served as a sort of oasis free from any reference whatever to the public sphere. Still more admirable was much of intellectual life. Ideas mattered, and just beneath the surface of orthodoxy was debate so vital that it shamed Western visitors: questioning after a seminar could run for hours, whereas in the freedom of the West it was quickly curtailed once the pubs were open. None the less, the process of daily life meant that most people had to make many compromises. The state had considerable – but *never* total – knowledge of one's private life: the drawings of one's children in kindergarten in East Germany, for example, were used to reveal whether one watched West German television. If it was true that the midnight knock on the door had gone, considerable pressures – the removal of the ability to teach, the denial of one's children's right to learn a foreign language – could still be exerted by the regime. If some were impossibly brave and absolutely clean, and others absolutely corrupt, many necessarily had hands that were slightly dirty. How could it have been otherwise when blackmail involved the fate of one's children? One was glad not to have to make choices like that, and aware of a deep resentment about it that lurked just below the surface. One indicator of this lay in humour – bitter, dry and sophisticated ironies at the expense of the party-state and its leaders, clearly Russian to many in East Central Europe rather than socialist.

This was a world without legitimacy, as was so graphically demonstrated in 1956, 1968 and 1981, and it seemed to me likely that it would somewhere, somehow, sooner or later change – which is not, let me repeat, to claim for a moment any special prescience about the speed or manner of the eventual collapse. The position I had arrived at stressed that change was likely for essentially socially evolutionary reasons. The heroic period of Bolshevism had managed to industrialize, albeit in a brutal manner, but it was clearly proving to be less and less effective in economic terms as a transition to a third industrial age took place. The nature of computers seemed to make the point most effectively. Widespread possession of printers quite as much as the machines themselves was surely necessary if a society was to thrive in the late industrial era, and this seemed to make a new social contract necessary. Gone would be the days when the attempt to break the bounds of censorship involved spreading samizdat documents by retyping them using ten carbon papers at a go!

Crucially, it was possible to see in most ruling parties of socialist societies a positively schizophrenic gap between the technocrats and the bolsheviks, between those who wished to give the party new life by assuring economic growth and those who were prepared to maintain socialism as an ideocracy, a power system based on an unsullied and unquestioned total ideology. In a sense, the moment in 1968 when Kadar, himself imposed by the Russians in 1956, announced that the rules of the system had changed – so that not to be against the system was acceptable and to endorse it enthusiastically at every moment was not required – signalled the formal start of softer political rule. Liberalization was already under way and the era of high totalitarianism accordingly finished. It seemed very likely that liberalization would continue. Modernizing leaders might be able to work with the technically competent, who had enough sense of international comparison to know that their mobility had been blocked, to create a more vigorous economy in tandem with softer political rule. Ernest Gellner put the case as a whole with characteristic verve:

> . . . an advanced industrial society requires a large scientific, technical, administrative, educational stratum, with genuine competence based on prolonged training. In other words, it cannot rely on rigid ideologues and servile classes alone. It is reasonable to assume that this kind of educated middle class, owing its position to technical competence rather than to subservience, and inherently, so to speak professionally, capable of distinguishing reality and thought from verbiage and incantation, will develop or has developed the kind of tastes we associate with its life-style–a need for security, a recognition of competence rather than subservience, a regard for efficiency and integrity rather than patronage and loyalty in professional life . . . This class is large, and it cannot be penalised effectively without a cost to the economy which may no longer be acceptable.[13]

If all of this was based in modernization theory, the position as a whole was not held in an utterly naive manner. Great skill would be needed to make the most of favourable opportunity, to ask for reasonable change so that alliances could be made between frustrated educated labour in society and technocrats inside the ruling elite; put differently, to ask too much too fast ran the risk that an endangered and reunified elite would call in Russian tanks. There seemed here an overlap with the burgeoning literature of the early 1980s on transitions from authoritarian capitalist

---

[13]   E. Gellner, 'Plaidoyer pour une libéralisation manquée', *Government and Opposition*, vol. 14, 1979, pp. 63–4.

rule.[14] This literature always emphasized the need to make pacts so as to reassure the powerful that change would not be at their expense. More recently, a brilliant argument by one of the leading proponents of this school has noted that successful transitions from authoritarian capitalism have been those initiated and controlled from above; transitions initiated by pressures from below have tended to fail.[15] The nature of socialism – the fact that domination was so concentrated, that is that different regimes had single parties rather than a dominant landed class and, crucially, that the fate of those regimes depended absolutely upon perceptions in Moscow – seemed to make an emphasis on liberalization rather than democratization still more necessary. Processes of reassurance seemed especially necessary given that liberalization had been defeated in Hungary, Czechoslovakia and Poland precisely when liberalizing reforms, often in the economy, had come to call the party-state into question.

All this can be summarized by saying that no allegiance was being given to convergence theory. Pressure was certainly being placed on socialism because it was failing in world market terms, but the best way to respond seemed not to be that of demanding full-blooded Western liberal democracy. Nor was my position as a whole completely at one with theories of civil society that became popular in the 1980s. Change depended most of all upon a liberalizing elite, for all that it might seek support outside its own ranks. Further, some of the criticisms directed against this view do not really seem justified. It is not really true that the theory was made both weak and unfalsifiable by saying that liberalization was most likely where the economy was (at least within the socialist bloc) of a high standard *and* in crisis. On the contrary, all that was being maintained was Tocqueville's fully developed view, which precisely combined analysis of rising expectations with an insistence on the damage done if these were suddenly blocked.[16] And whilst it is true that insufficient attention was given to the impossibility – stressed so powerfully then and since by Janos Kornai[17] – of reforming the market mechanism without a great deal of privatization, China's

---

[14]   G. O'Donnell, P. Schmitter and L. Whitehead, eds, *Transitions from Authoritarian Rule*, Johns Hopkins University Press, Baltimore, 1986.
[15]   T. Karl, 'Dilemmas of Democratisation in Latin America', *Comparative Politics*, vol. 23, 1990.
[16]   J. A. Hall, 'Trust in Tocqueville', *Policy Organisation and Society*, vol. 5, 1992.
[17]   J. Kornai, *The Socialist System*, Princeton University Press, Princeton, 1992. Cf. J. Merquior, 'Thoughts on Liberalisation', in J. A. Hall and I. C. Jarvie, eds, *Transitions to Modernity*, Cambridge University Press, Cambridge, 1992.

current economic success seems to show that the route as a whole was not doomed to failure.

It is as well to own up to the fact that these considerations led me to warm endorsement for Gorbachov. It was very noticeable that he was not forced into his course of action by popular pressure from civil society. Very much to the contrary, he had to make rigorous and continuous use of the mass media in order to try to raise consciousness sufficiently to allow for reform. It was scarcely surprising that this was necessary, given that many feared that a turn in the political wind would bring back the prison camps. Above all, Gorbachov seemed the perfect technocrat, keen to admit that he had been impressed by Western standards of consumption, and with a wife whose abilities in that area were not open to serious question. It was quite clear that Gorbachov's purpose was to strengthen a moribund system, but that pill was sugared by the promise of liberalization. Further, the geriatric and worried elite had by the late 1970s lost their greatest virtue, that of considerable circumspection in foreign policy.[18] The fact that Gorbachov seemed prepared not just to leave Afghanistan but to let Eastern Europe go turned endorsement into something stronger. A consequence of this position was a certain reserve shown to the nationalists of the Baltic states. To give up Soviet territory might endanger the whole process of change. This seemed wildly irresponsible given that these states were being offered something like Finlandization – that is much greater autonomy provided they served as conduits of Western technology.

Reflections on Communism in the Light of Post-communist Reality

It must be said loudly and clearly that liberalization failed. For a short period it seemed as if round-table discussions leading to various types of pacts, habitually creating electoral rules designed to reassure the elite, were part of the classical scenario for controlled liberalization. But this was merely a stage, and a very short one at that. What followed was an absolute and fundamental collapse. The long round-table talks in Poland produced rules designed to keep the party in power, but these were invalidated utterly by the very first election. In Eastern Europe the removal of the Russian card generally meant that regimes simply

---

[18] J. Snyder, *Myths of Empire*, Cornell University Press, Ithaca, 1991.

crumbled. Once deprived of the capacity to repress their own people, party-states fell apart – with the notable exception of Romania, where much blood was shed in the process of removing Ceauşescu.

All of this is to say that the name of the game suddenly became that of democratization rather than liberalization. One way to highlight this is to recall that some academics began to make jokes saying that the attention given to the transitions to democracy literature would be replaced by a return to a previous literature concerned with the breakdown of democratic regimes.[19] Such pessimism was engendered by the hunch that were everyone able to demand everything immediately there would be such an overload to the new system that it would be bound to collapse. One pithy formulation suggested that the East was likely to become the South.[20]

But this last comment misleads. For one thing, the South has itself changed: the fact that Menem came to power on the basis of Peronist populism has not led, for example, to a return to protectionism. More generally and importantly, post-communist society possesses a unique social character.[21] One way to make this point is by recalling a conversation that took place with Britain's brilliant leading marxist before the first election in reunified Germany. Sophisticated reasons were adduced – the Protestant background, historical loyalties to the SPD, the impact of communism itself – for insisting that the addition of the Eastern Länder would inevitably lead to defeat for Chancellor Kohl. But it seemed to me that all of this was beside the point: it failed to recognize that distaste for the old regime was positively visceral. Of course, it could be argued that Kohl's eventual triumph was largely instrumental, that the Easterners would have voted for any Chancellor who promised them a substantial amount of material benefits. But this rather cynical view does not capture the mood of the time. In the immediate aftermath of 1989 there was much discussion of post-communist societies finding a 'third way', perhaps somehow based on the Swedish model. Such a route would doubtless have been well beyond the means of any country in the region. But what is really striking is that the route was scarcely sought: on the contrary, the mere allusion to social objectives in a party's name tarred it with socialism – and electoral disaster. The clearest way some members of the old regime have survived is by self-transmutation, that is by

---

[19]   J. Linz and A. Stepan, eds, *The Breakdown of Democratic Regimes*, Johns Hopkins University Press, Baltimore, 1978.
[20]   A. Przeworski, *Democracy and the Market*, Cambridge University Press, Cambridge, 1991, conclusion.
[21]   J. A. Hall, 'After the Fall: an Analysis of Post Communism', *British Journal of Sociology*, forthcoming.

becoming nationalist leaders. The extent to which a ruling elite has been deposed is historically incredible. It reflects far more than that this elite had no large landed estates to which it could retreat. Rather there has been on overwhelming desire for a completely new start, and it is this that accounts for the adoption of the crudest free-market doctrines – taken, one might note, like a new religion and imposed, yet again, by revolution from above. But it is quite as mistaken to make much of the possession of a new doctrine. For the baseline of the situation in post-communist society is that of sheer vacuum. A whole moral order has collapsed, leaving many like the living dead, utterly unsure as to what makes sense let alone what their best interests are. It is this that underlies the astonishingly low turn-out for elections in many post-communist societies.[22]

The rejection of the old order is so astonishingly complete that it suggests – perhaps demands – sustained theoretical reflection. The benefits of hindsight suggest that there were very great problems within the very essence of socialism that went well beyond the noted limitations of central economic planning. Recalling three famous anatomies of communism will sharpen analysis, allowing clearer appreciation of sociological realities.

It is impossible to understand the enormous influence exerted by Karl Marx's thought without a proper appreciation of the way in which it combines prescriptive and descriptive categories. Marx was deeply influenced by romanticism and, above all, by the view that human beings should be complete and unitary. This is made crystal clear in the famous characterization of communist society:

> . . . the division of labour offers us the first example of how, as long as man remains in natural society, that is, as long as a cleavage exists between the particular and the common interest, as long, therefore, as activity is not voluntarily, but naturally, divided, man's own deed becomes an alien power opposed to him, which enslaves him instead of being controlled by him. For as soon as the distribution of labour comes into being, each man has a particular, exclusive sphere of activity, which is forced upon him and from which he cannot escape. He is a hunter, a fisherman, a shepherd, or a critical critic, and must remain so if he does not want to lose his means of livelihood; while in communist society, where nobody has one exclusive sphere of activity but each can become accomplished in any branch he

---

[22]   Particularly good accounts are available for the Polish case: L. Kolarska-Bobinska, 'Civil Society and Anomy in Poland', *Acta Sociologica*, vol. 33, 1990 and G. Ekiert, 'Peculiarities of Post-communist Politics: the Case of Poland, *Studies in Comparative Communism*, vol. 25, 1992.

wishes, society regulates the general production and thus makes it possible for me to do one thing today and another tomorrow, to hunt in the morning, fish in the afternoon, rear cattle in the evening, criticise after dinner, just as I have a mind, without ever becoming hunter, fisherman, shepherd or critic.[23]

It was once popular to believe that this early humanism was left behind, to be relaced by 'scientific' socialism.[24] Recent scholarship has gone against this view, arguing instead that these early attitudes lie behind and remain implicit in later thought. One way in which this is true concerns the vital question why we should jump onto the historical bandwagon, that is why we should accept the various historical stages identified by Marx's materialist conception of history rather than seek to delay their coming. The answer to this question is surely that the earlier thought reveals an essential human nature that existed before class society, thereby assuring us that the process of history is creating something that is not just inevitable but also practicable and desirable. More generally, Marx's thought bases itself on the presumption of cooperation and sharing – although this is interestingly contradicted by the solitary nature of the pursuits listed in this passage. The historical process itself cannot be understood without paying allegiance to this. Pre-modern communism is certainly seen as being rooted in communal practices, and the same fundamental principle applies to the working class– indeed, economic performance in socialism will improve upon that in capitalism as cooperation takes the place of competition.

Durkheim formally wished to distinguish himself from Marx, and gave lectures on early socialism that can be seen as an attempt to draw his students away from what he regarded as a false trail. He regarded a distinction between communism and socialism as of crucial import:

> One school labels as antisocial everything which is private property, in a general way, while the other considers dangerous only the individual appropriation of the large economic enterprises which are established at a specific moment in history. Therefore, their significant motives are not at all the same. Communism is prompted by moral and timeless reasons; socialism by considerations of an economic sort. For the former, private property must be abolished because it is the source of all immorality; for the latter, the vast industrial and commercial enterprises cannot be left to themselves, as they affect too profoundly the entire economic life of society. Their conclusions are so different because one sees the remedy in

[23]   Karl Marx and Friedrich Engels, '*The German Ideology*', in R. W. Tucker, ed., *The Marx-Engels Reader*, 2nd edn, Norton, New York, 1978, p. 160.
[24]   L. Althusser, *For Marx*, New Left Books, London, 1969.

a suppression, as complete as possible, of economic interests; the other, in their socialisation.[25]

Durkheim suggests that the social carriers of communism are dreamers, that is isolated intellectuals unrepresentative of any broader social current. In contrast, he takes socialism much more seriously: it may well be that socialist ideas are produced by intellectuals, but their appeal is wide because the working class is not properly integrated into modern society. Nevertheless, Durkheim insists that socialism is no answer to their very real suffering because it stands far too close to the world that it putatively seeks to replace. In particular, it seeks merely to spread material goods around, and so fails to regulate appetites. This is a recipe for disaster:

> . . . it is a general law of all living things that needs and appetites are normal only on condition of being controlled. Unlimited need contradicts itself. For need is defined by the goal it aims at, and if unlimited has no goal – since there is no limit. It is no true aim to seek constantly more than one has – to work in order to overtake the point one has reached, with a view only to exceeding the point . . . an appetite that nothing can appease can never be satisfied. Insatiable thirst can only be a source of suffering. Whatever one does, it is never slaked . . . In its normal state sexual desire is aroused for a time, then is appeased. With the erotomaniac there are no limits.[26]

Some commentary on this is required immediately. Durkheim's ideas are extremely interesting and thought-provoking. This is particularly true of the distinction drawn between socialism and communism – a contrast that parallels that drawn by Élie Halévy between freedom and organization.[27] Certainly some socialists, most notably the Webbs, were keener on the extirpation of waste than on freedom; and it is quite correct to say that modern socialism does habitually take the problem of organizing the industrial machine very seriously indeed. But if we grant these differences, it is noticeable that Durkheim is largely wrong. Modern socialism in the end is an example of communism: socialism is in the end inconceivable without the emphasis on solidarity, equality and sharing. More generally, socialism proved in practice to be a hugely Durkheimian affair – as might have been guessed when realizing that the Webbs were driven by moral

[25] E. Durkheim, *Socialism*, trans. C. Sattler, Collier Books, New York, 1967, p. 75.
[26] Durkheim, *Socialism*, pp. 239–40.
[27] É. Halévy, 'The Policy of Social Peace in England' and 'The Problem of Worker Control', both in É. Halévy, *The Era of Tyrannies*, trans. R. K. Webb, Anchor Books, New York, 1967.

purpose far more than by a penchant for economic planning. The purpose of socialism was exactly that of creating a new moral order.

Marx and Durkheim have much in common, seeing social processes as being for the most part derived from the bottom up.[28] With Max Weber we enter an entirely different world, as can be seen in negative and then in positive terms.

Negatively, Weber did not feel that there was an inevitable link between the working class and socialism. In so far as the working class had embraced socialist ideals, and this was by no means total, this was due to anti-socialist policies of the state, which prevented industrial organization – so making it necessary for workers to 'take on' the state. Weber accordingly recommended that the state should observe liberal neutrality: if workers were left alone, it was unlikely they would have any particular political ideas – beyond, perhaps, loyalty to the nation, in whose primacy Weber himself of course believed utterly.[29] Weber makes a very similar argument about the peasantry at various points in *Economy and Society*. Thus he noted that the communist ideas of Donatists, Taborites and seventeenth-century English radicals were 'possible only on the basis of an already existing ethical religion which contained specific promises that might suggest and justify a revolutionary natural law'.[30] In general, and particularly outside the occidental tradition, peasants were not blessed with an ethical religion, that is a religion favouring abstract law over power and tradition, and accordingly had no capacity for fundamental projects of social reform, including all forms of communism:

> Hence, manifestations of a close relationship between peasant religion and agrarian reform movements did not occur in Asia, where the combination of religious prophecy with revolutionary currents, e.g., as in China, took a different direction altogether, and did not assume the form of a real peasant

[28]   I have in mind here the way in which Marx and Durkheim believe that alienation and anomie can be avoided, albeit on different time scales, whereas Max Weber considers disenchantment to be an ineluctable fate. An influential discussion of Marx and Durkheim – S. Lukes, 'Alienation and Anomie', in P. Laslett and W. G. Runciman, eds, *Philosophy, Politics and Society*, Basil Blackwell, Oxford, 1967 – is of particular relevance here.

[29]   Weber's views about the German working class are contained in his wartime 'Parliament and Government in a Reconstructed Germany', in his *Economy and Society*, trans. C. Wittich and G. Roth, University of California Press, Berkeley, 1978. For the context of these views and for Weber's loyalty to the nation as a whole, see W. Mommsen, *Max Weber and German Politics, 1890–1920*, Chicago University Press, Chicago, 1984.

[30]   Weber, *Economy and Society*, p. 469.

movement. Only rarely does the peasantry serve as the carrier of any other sort of religion than their original magic.[31]

Weber's positive case includes the notion that modern communism is economically rational: it seeks to manage the economy rather than to abolish it. He further argues in a Durkheimian spirit that, in general, communism is fundamentally 'indifferent to calculation' and hence oblivious to any 'consideration of means for obtaining an optimum of provisions'; what matters instead is 'direct feelings of mutual solidarity'.[32] But his analysis as a whole has a different spirit from that of his French contemporary. In particular, he specifies three social bases for premodern communism. The bases in question are household communism, military communism and the love and charity characteristic of a religious movement. The first of these is, so to speak, natural, and he held it to exist in some large financial houses even in his own day.[33] This form of communism prevents any communistic practices concerning women,[34] and it is certainly no model for a whole society. This is not true of military communism, about which Weber wrote with great power.[35] But it is the third type that really matters for Weber. This is the sharing of a religious group. Everything here depends upon charisma. More particularly, such communism seems to be accepted because it is a temporary necessity. This leads Weber to make a characteristic judgement when writing about early Christianity:

> Work attained dignity much later, beginning with the monastic orders who used it as an ascetic means. During the charismatic period of a religion, the perfect disciple must also reject landed property, and the mass of believers is expected to be indifferent toward it. An expression of this indifference is that attenuated form of the charismatic communism of love which apparently existed in the early Christian community of Jerusalem, where the members of the community owned property 'as if they did not own it'. Such unlimited, unrationalised sharing with needy brothers, which forced the missionaries, especially Paulus, to collect alms abroad for the anti-economic central community, is probably what lies behind that much discussed tradition, not any allegedly 'socialist' organisation or 'communist' collective ownership. Once the eschatological expectations fade, charismatic communism in all its forms declines and retreats into monastic

---

[31]   Weber, *Economy and Society*, p. 470.
[32]   Weber, *Economy and Society*, p. 153.
[33]   Weber, *Economy and Society*, p. 300.
[34]   Weber, *Economy and Society*, p. 363–4, here at p. 364
[35]   Weber, *Economy and Society*, p. 1153.

circles, where it becomes the special concern of the exemplary followers of God.[36]

Of course, the fact that egalitarian sharing was encoded in one of the crucial documents of the Western tradition matters greatly from a Weberian point of view: it provides a moral legacy absent elsewhere, which was, as noted, available for later European radicals. None the less, if Marx was but one of a long line of intellectuals to make use of that legacy, Weber's case remains that the generalized appeal of socialism in the modern world derives, as noted, from old regime politics – rather than being, as both Marx and Durkheim believed, an expression of society.

The historical record lends far more support to Weber's position than it does to Durkheim's or Marx's.[37] Sharing did and does occur inside charismatic communities, whether in Roman Palestine, fifteenth-century Tabor, sixteenth-century Munster or twentieth-century Korea: in all these cases, the belief that the world was about to end led many to burn or sell their houses, and to share what they possessed with others of the elect until the final entry into bliss.[38] Further, Weber was right to note that a division of labour occurred in the West, whereby the tradition of communism was maintained by monks – although, their practice was not accepted by, but probably necessary to, a wider society in which private property rights were enshrined in law and custom.[39]

Military communism is equally recognizable, but it is much rarer. Its archetype is of course Sparta, a peculiar society in which the discipline of a small elite had to be maintained at all costs – not least so that it would be capable of waging war on its own helots once a year.[40] This system

---

[36]   Weber, *Economy and Society*, p. 1187.
[37]   My knowledge of this record derives very largely from a conference on 'Pre-modern Communism' that I organized with Patricia Crone in 1992. I am deeply grateful to her and learnt much from all the participants, some of whom are cited below. Patricia Crone and I intend to write systematically on this subject in the near future.
[38]   A particularly striking account of the career of John of Leyden in Munster is offered by N. Cohn, *The Pursuit of the Millennium*, 2nd edn, Harper, New York, 1961. I am indebted in general to a brilliant paper by R. Scribner, 'Practical Utopias: Pre-modern Communism and the Reformation', paper for the 'Pre-modern Communism' conference, 1992.
[39]   R. I. Moore, 'Property, Marriage and the Eleventh-century Revolution: a Context for Early Medieval Communism', paper for the 'Pre-modern Communism' conference, 1992.
[40]   P. Cartledge, 'Utopias in Ancient Greece: Fact or Fantasy?', paper for the 'Pre-modern Communism' conference, 1992.

was glorified by Plato, and his influence thereafter ensured a favourable hearing to the Spartan tradition.[41]

It is worth making a generalization here about the attraction of intellectuals to communist ideals; that is we need to go beyond Durkheim's realization that dreamers produce communist ideas to explain why this should be so. In Plato's own case, modern scholarship has gone some way to supporting Popper's contention that Plato was attracted to a closed world as the result of sheer dislike of the way the advent of democracy undermined the aristocracy from which he sprang.[42] Similar displacements may explain the attraction of other intellectuals to communism. This is most obviously the case with Thomas More, the most famous of all idle dreamers. He had been deeply influenced by the monastic ethos and in a sense disliked the secular world in which he was forced to operate. He may well be representative of a type of intellectual displaced by the Reformation's assault on monasticism. More generally, one of the features of modern social thought has been the extent to which intellectuals have lost much of their status as literacy has become universalized: this status insecurity may go some way towards explaining the anti-capitalist nature of most modern social thought.[43] Finally, it is worth remarking that modern historical sociology has reached something like consensus in support of Weber's view that industrial workers are attracted to socialism only when they are excluded from political participation.[44]

I have no wish to assert that there is some essential human nature, some sort of universal 'species being'. On the contrary, it is entirely

[41] M. Schofield, 'Communism in Plato and the Stoics', paper for the 'Pre-modern Communism conference', 1992; E. Rawson, *The Spartan Tradition in European Thought*, Oxford University Press, Oxford, 1969; D. Dawson, *Cities of the Gods*, Oxford University Press, Oxford, 1992.

[42] K. R. Popper, *The Open Society and Its Enemies*, 4th edn., vol. 1, Routledge & Kegan Paul, London, 1962. Popper's view is effectively supported by E. M. Wood and N. Wood, *Class Ideology and Ancient Political Theory*, Oxford University Press, Oxford, 1978. Dawson, *Cities of the Gods*, ch. 2, offers cautionary words on this interpretation and provides a balanced account.

[43] M. Mann, 'The Ideology of Intellectuals and Other People in the Development of Capitalism', in L. Lindberg, R. Alford, C. Crouch and C. Offe, eds, *Stress and Contradiction in Modern Capitalism*, D. C. Heath, Lexington, 1975.

[44] D. Geary, *European Labour Protest, 1848–1945*, Methuen, London, 1984; R. McKibbin, *The Ideologies of Class*, Oxford University Press, Oxford, 1990; M. Mann, 'Ruling Class Strategies and Citizenship', *Sociology*, vol. 21, 1987; I. Katznelson and A. Zolberg, eds, *Working Class Formation*, Princeton University Press, Princeton, 1986; T. McDaniel, *Capitalism, Autocracy and Revolution*, University of California Press, Berkeley, 1987. For full discussion of this point, see ch. 2 in this volume.

correct to say that every part of our social world is culturally constructed, with behaviour that might seem outlandish from the outside 'making sense' to the actors themselves.[45] However, some cultural patterns are harder to maintain than others, as Weber realized when insisting that a religion needed social rules quite as much as a theodicy.[46] It seems as if pure altruism is particularly hard to maintain: practices which make sense when the millennium is expected prove contentious once it is necessary to live within a continuing social world. This is not to deny that such practices can be maintained by a virtuous elite, but it is to insist that whole societies have difficulty supporting such generalized enthusiasm for very long. This surely goes some way to explaining, in general terms, the collapse of state socialism. The regime placed excessive demands on its citizens: continual sharing requires too much effort.

It is well worth noting that other scholars are beginning to offer explanations for the ideological weakness of communism. A particularly powerful account, interestingly different from that proposed here, stands at the heart of Ernest Gellner's most recent thoughts on socialism. Even though it made much sense to see marxism as a secular religion, the nature of its demise is very unlike that of the great faiths: no loyalists are left, prepared to fight to the bitter end. This lack of staying power is held to have something to do with Marx's eminently bourgeois emphasis on the importance of work:

> . . . this means that a Marxist society is left with no humdrum sphere of the profane into which to escape during periods of diminished zeal and enthusiasm. Other faiths, even if they circumscribe the economic zone with religious rules, nevertheless do not elevate and sacralize it. Marxism did, and perhaps this constituted its undoing. Faith survived random and massive terror, and indeed found a confirmation in it: the final, total transformation of the human condition was confirmed in blood. But faith did not survive the squalor in the economic sphere. The vision of the *nomenklatura* murdering each other was acceptable, but that of its bribing each other was not. The squalid, gray, sleazy inefficiency of the productive process in the Brezhnev era really eroded faith.[47]

---

[45]　For a profound meditation on culture and nature, see P. Crone, *Pre-industrial Societies*, Basil Blackwell, Oxford, 1989, ch. 5.

[46]　Weber explains the failure of Buddhism to replace Hinduism in terms of its inability to develop rules for daily life in *The Religion of India*, Free Press, New York, 1951.

[47]　E. Gellner, 'Homeland of the Unrevolution' *Daedalus*, vol. 122, 1993, pp. 146–7.

In many ways this overlaps with what has been argued: special privileges for the party elite, for example, seemed sleazy and arbitrary because of the emphasis placed on sharing. A notable merit of this account is, however, that it seeks to be historically specific, that is it implicitly explains why collapse occurred at a particular historical moment. The question of timing is indeed absolutely crucial, and it is time to confront it directly.

Accounting for Collapse

Barbara Misztal has recently argued that Western social science conceptualized socialist society by means of four models.[48] We have already seen that the concept of totalitarian society was replaced by modernization theory, one version of which emphasized the possibility of liberalization. Where these theories concentrated on elite politics, those that gained popularity in the 1980s tended to give priority to social forces operating from below. This was most obviously true of the notion of civil society, of the putatively increasing capacity of varied types of groups to organize themselves in opposition to the state. But theorists who posited a crisis of the party-state depended quite as much on the notion of social forces becoming more powerful and harder for the regime to handle: this underlay their claim that it was becoming ever more difficult to arrange compacts between state and society.

This is a useful and accurate account of Western social science. But we must ask which model, or combination of models, helps us best to understand the collapse of the socialist project – an additional advantage of which will be to establish the proper weight to be lent to the analysis of the ideological weakness of socialism. Let us begin with the view from below before returning to the theories of liberalization and totalitarianism.

There is some truth to the view from below. If civil society was a much desired dream, the theory as a whole was not purely a matter of prescription. Bluntly, Solidarity provided the descriptive 'beef' of the concept. In seeking to establish free trade unions this movement from below directly challenged the party-state. This extraordinary movement, based on Christian mission and Polish destiny, changed the history of Eastern Europe as a whole – or, in a different formulation, Eastern Europe

---

[48]   B. Misztal, 'Understanding Political Change in Eastern Europe: a Sociological Perspective', *Sociology*, vol. 27, 1993.

owed its freedom at least in part to the glorious Poles.[49] It undermined the socialist project by leading to martial law, thereby removing any pretence that socialism was popular. That military rule was imposed by Poles rather than by Russian tanks presumably reflects the Kremlin's calculation that the Poles would have been prepared to engage in armed struggle, whatever the cost. Equally, there is some truth in the notion of a crisis in the party state: there is a continuing history of attempts to bridge the gap between state and society by entering new social contracts. In a sense, the socialist system tried force, persuasion and bribery in turn, leaving it bereft of viable new options. Further, it is almost certainly true that the introduction of bribery – that is clientelism, nepotism and patronage in addition to sheer graft – did a great deal to discredit the party-state in its last decade.[50]

But if the view from below has some truth, its general direction misleads. Most obviously, Solidarity had been controlled by the mid-1980s, albeit at very great cost in terms of legitimacy, whilst no regime other than that of Poland was seriously threatened by its civil society. Moreover, the lack of positive new initiatives should not be taken to mean that socialist regimes were bound to break down: a very long and messy period of 'muddling through' would surely have been possible before unfavourable social trends gained real bite. Most generally, legitimacy had long been absent, and one doubts very much whether increasing disillusion suddenly so tipped the scales that the regime collapsed. The analysis of the ideological weakness of socialism already offered is far more use in helping us to explain why a social world was not and is not likely to be reconstituted than in explaining why breakdown occurred in the first place.

It is important to recall once again the actual pattern of collapse. One feature of the collapse, that it was like that of a house of cards, with events in one place imitating – at ever greater speed – those in another, follows from the fundamental lack of legitimacy: once the Russian card had been withdrawn, as it was when the Kremlin allowed Hungary to open its borders for East Germans wishing to go West, regimes began to crumble. Forces from below did not so much cause collapse as occupy political space once it became available. The crucial question accordingly becomes that of the motivation of actors inside the Kremlin. These actors were definitely not faced by any hint whatever of popular uprising, and it

[49] L. Kolakowski, 'Amidst Moving Ruins', *Daedalus*, vol. 121, 1991.
[50] G. Ekiert, 'Democratisation Processes in East Central Europe: a Theoretical Reconsideration', *British Journal of Political Science*, vol. 21, p. 304.

accordingly becomes vital to try and reconstruct their position. The methodology involved in answering this question must in part be that of imputing motives, for the simple reason that we have little reliable knowledge of debates within the highest echelons of the Soviet state. This analysis of motivation must involve some consideration of Gorbachov's own personality, his desire to be seen as a world peace-maker, but very much more than that is involved. For Gorbachov's liberalizing role had first been contemplated by Andropov – whose replacement by the old bolshevik Chernenko suggests that this party was as internally divided as others in the socialist bloc. What sort of considerations seem to have been important?

The most obvious considerations of the Soviet leaders have already been stressed. Gorbachov wished to renew socialism by formally replacing the stick of Stalinism with the carrot of economic growth. Awareness of the economic achievements of the West, not least as the result of his own experience in Canadian supermarkets, made him well aware that the socialist bloc was losing the economic competition with its rival. If the system could be softened sufficiently to call forth the willing consent of more of its citizens – above all of its educated labour – then the regime might emerge with its authority enhanced rather than diminished. But this reform path could only be taken if the costs of empire were controlled.[51] The boldest of all Gorbachov's actions were accordingly geopolitical; he sought to create sufficient space to allow for the possibility of economic reform. The cornerstone of this policy was of course *détente* with the United States, that is those varied moves – from nuclear policy to the retreat from Afghanistan – that made Gorbachov the darling of the West. This *rapprochement* increased security sufficiently to allow him effectively to let the satellite countries go and, stunningly, even to accept German reunification. A great deal of this policy was immensely intelligent, with many released countries, well aware of continuing geopolitical and geoeconomic realities, pursuing policies of caution and moderation. Even at the time, however, it seemed as if Gorbachov was making a mistake about the most obvious nationalist movements within the Soviet Union. It might have been possible to divide and rule, to declare the incorporation of the Baltics to have been illegal so as better to hang on to the Ukraine.

---

[51] V. Bunce, 'The Empire Strikes Back: the Transformation of the Eastern Bloc from a Soviet Asset to a Soviet Liability', *International Organisation*, vol. 39, 1985; R. Collins, 'The Future Decline of the Russian Empire', in R. Collins, *Weberian Sociological Theory*, Cambridge University Press, Cambridge, 1986. Both these authors deserve commendation for predicting, on the basis of geopolitical realities, fundamental change in Eastern Europe.

The fact that Gorbachov was worried about questions of territorial integrity makes it necessary to give attention to perhaps the main institutional structure of Soviet society. The attempt to reform must have received support from the leaders of the armed forces and, more probably, from the military-industrial complex as a whole. Why would such a conservative force contemplate reform? Most importantly, the Soviet Union was massively stretched by arms spending. If there could be at least some doubt about the claim of the United States that its economy was being hurt by defence spending greater than that of many of its allies,[52] the fact that Soviet expenditure took perhaps three times as large a proportion of national product – that is at least a quarter of the total – unquestionably hurt the economy. Crucially, it seemed as if this economic debilitation was beginning to have negative consequences even for the military. While scepticism may have been shown to the complete claims of Reagan's Star Wars initiative, the fears that American high technology would have military applications that could not be imitated were very real indeed. In this connection, it was very noticeable that the Russian military watched the Iraqi use of their weapons in the Gulf War very closely – and that they were shocked to see major deficiencies. Perhaps the military had also come to realize that the huge expansion of interventions abroad in the Brezhnev era – in the face of economic and ideological weakness – was likely to be self-defeating.

All of this added up to a single strategy. The elite decided to try to liberalize, very much according to the expectations outlined at the start of this essay. Put differently, one of the general views identified by Misztal, namely the imperative of modernization, does have to be taken very seriously. But the elite was not, as noted, able to carry out a successful liberalization. Whilst errors of judgement were certainly made, the fundamental reason that liberalization could not work in socialist society was that civil society had been destroyed.[53] Let us see why this destruction took place, and then begin to note its consequences.

States throughout history have been nervous about channels of communication they can scarcely see. Accordingly, it has been very common to find many states that ban horizontal linkages in civil society so as to privilege their own offical means of communication and power networks. The reply of a Roman emperor to his governor in Palestine as to whether to allow that local organization of a fire brigade is revealing: such organization should not even be contemplated, insisted the emperor, for once

---

52   For a defence of this view, see ch. 7.
53   R. Bova, 'Political Dynamics of the Post-communist Transition: a Comparative Perspective', *World Politics*, vol. 44, 1991.

gathered together minds will drift from fires to politics. In fact, in the long run, perhaps because of the cosmopolitanism inherent in its empire, Rome could not control those horizontal channels of Christians to which it had reacted so harshly – and so sought to go with what it could not control.[54] In contrast, China did perfect low intensity rule in the agrarian era.[55] The spirit of such rule was neatly captured by Tocqueville:

> Any independent group, however small, which seemed desirous of taking action otherwise than under the aegis of the administration filled it with alarm, and the tiniest free association of citizens, however harmless its aims, was regarded as a nuisance. The only corporate bodies tolerated were those whose members had been hand-picked by the administration and which were under its control. Even big industrial concerns were frowned upon. In a word, our administration resented the idea of private citizens' having any say in the control of their own enterprises, and preferred sterility to competition.[56]

Such sterility, together with the weakness it causes, was always, characteristic of socialist society. But if we wish to understand the modern destruction of civil society in Russia, attention must be given quite as much to autocracy as to totalitarianism.[57] Tsarism had been just as suspicious of civil society, being utterly opposed to capitalism and the rule of law: what mattered was the possibility that isolated individuals might be able to approach their Great Father. As is so often the case, a revolution merely intensified existing social patterns: secret police, government inspectors, atomization, boredom and privatization were familiar to late nineteenth-century Russians, albeit in infinitely milder form.

Transitions to democracy depend completely upon the striking of bargains, above all upon a reforming elite seeking to give a little, to receive in return a signal that this has been understood and accepted, so that more can be given without fear of any complete loss of position. It takes but a moment's thought to appreciate that what is involved here is a sort of partnership in which forces from below discipline themselves so as to reassure those at the top. This whole strategy was ruled out of court in

[54] M. Mann, *Sources of Social Power*, vol. 1: *A History of Power from the Beginning to 1760 AD*, Cambridge University Press, Cambridge, 1986, ch. 10.
[55] Hall, *Powers and Liberties*, chs 2 and 5. See also ch. 1 of this book.
[56] A. de Tocqueville, *The Old Regime and the French Revolution*, trans. S. Gilbert, Anchor Books, New York, 1955, p. 64.
[57] McDaniel, *Autocracy, Capitalism and Revolution in Russia*, chs 2 and 3.
[58] Bova, 'Political Dynamics of the Post-communist Transition'.

the Soviet Union: the absence of partners in society made liberalization impossible. One interesting speculation has suggested that the absence of discipline at the bottom reflects more than the simple destruction of civil society.[58] Had the forces at the top been organized and united, the threat of their return to power might have been so obvious as to create some discipline in society. But the elite was not at all like that. Very much to the contrary, party members – at least, in *some* countries, most notably Hungary – had clearly decided before 1989 that the most secure access to privilege had come to be through the economy rather than through political position.[59]

Three further points about the destruction of civil society are supremely relevant in the context of this chapter. First, the manner of collapse, the fact that it was so sudden, was very much the result of the absence of intermediate structures – exactly as had had been the case, in Tocqueville's eyes, in the French Revolution: once the head was removed, the absence of alternate organizing structures was revealed. Secondly, the weakness of civil groupings helps explain the paltriness of attempts to reimpose authoritarian rule: beneath the surface gloss of power was emptiness as much as organized interest. Finally, one cannot help but note how strange has been the rule of both Gorbachov and Yeltsin: both have sought to create civil society from the top, by fiat and command. They are right to appreciate that a strong civil society increases the capacity of a state to rule, but this scarcely lessens the obvious self-contradiction at the core of their programme.

The analytic point being made is that the theory of totalitarianism has a great deal to tell us. Expectations of liberalization were thwarted by the absence of civil society; differently put, insufficient attention was given to the long-term effects of totalitarianism. This cognitive failure suggests re-examination of Tocqueville's ideas, on which the theory of totalitarianism was largely based. Tocqueville disliked administrative centralization, but he considered that the deepest reason for the destruction of cooperative relations lay elsewhere. It was the divide and rule tactics of the old regime that most fundamentally sowed seeds of distrust in society. His judgement on this point has enormous power, and is hideously relevant to post-communism:

---

[59]   E. Hankiss, *East European Alternatives*, Oxford University Press, Oxford, 1991. For an analysis of the 'political capitalism' that resulted, see J. Staniszkis, *The Dynamics of the Breakthrough in Eastern Europe*, University of California Press, Berkeley, 1991.

It was no easy task bringing together fellow citizens who had lived for many centuries aloof from, or even hostile to, each other and teaching them to co-operate in their own affairs. It had been far easier to estrange them than it now was to reunite them, and in so doing France gave the world a memorable example. Yet, when sixty years ago the various classes which under the old order had been isolated units in the social system came once again in touch, it was on their sore spots that they made contact and their first gesture was to fly at each other's throats. Indeed, even today, though class distinctions are no more, the jealousies and antipathies they caused have not died out.[60]

The lack of trust, the desire of the smallest units to separate from larger corporations, has proved to be endemic in post communism, and it does much to account for the peculiar vacuum that characterizes the region. But the main property of a vacuum is that it soon becomes filled. In this context, it is very noticeable indeed that the renewal of self-organization has proved to be much faster on national than on civil society lines.[61] Such nationalist organization led to Gorbachov's demise, most importantly because Yeltsin was prepared to turn to the nationalities in order to oust his great rival.

This brings us to a final point about liberalization and collapse. Tocqueville long ago made us aware that liberalization is extremely difficult, and his viewpoint has been expanded by Przeworski, who goes so far as to say that it is just about impossible – at all times rather than, as argued here, in societies that have suffered under totalitarianism.[62] Expectations tend to to increase and to run ahead of the ability to deliver them: the paradox of the situation is that the new regime may fall even though it is in fact more legitimate than the old one. Certainly, Gorbachov felt these pressures. But it is important to note that he was by no means, as Western commentators imagined, the absolutely skilful politician, making the very best of the small amount of room for manoeuvre available.

The worst possible conduct, during the liberalization process, as Tocqueville stressed when examining the policies of Louis XVI, is to dither systematically: to raise expectations and then dash them lends energized people virtually revolutionary feelings. What is necessary is consistency, a clear and absolute outlining of priorities, a listing of

---

[60] Tocqueville, *The Old Regime and the French Revolution*, p. 107.
[61] E. Gellner, 'Nationalism and Politics in Eastern Europe', *New Left Review*, no. 189, 1991.
[62] A. Przeworski, 'The Games of Transition', in S. Mainwaring, G. O'Donnell and S. Valenzuela, eds, *Issues in Democratic Consolidation*, University of Notre Dame Press, Notre Dame, 1992.

areas where change is permissible and of areas where it is not, and absolute determination not to retreat from announced reform when difficulties arise. It is necessary, in other words, to take the long view, to realize that an increase in liberalism will eventually diffuse conflict: in the politics of decompression it is vital to do what one annouces and to be sparing in what one announces.

So it was particularly mad illogic on Gorbachov's part to offer much to the Baltic states, and then to threaten them: some part of the nationalities problem was created by Gorbachov. More generally, it is worth remembering that nationalism flourishes in circumstances of political exclusion, making exit thereby an attractive option; loyalty results from the possession of voice. The legacy of distrust in the Russian socialist empire was, of course, extremely high, and any move to greater openness thus likely to be treated with scepticism. But the very difficulty of these circumstances meant that the only potential route for success lay through greater rather than lesser boldness. Early calling of union elections, which Gorbachov could not stomach, was vital.[63]

To say this returns us, of course, to the question of democracy. Was not democratization rather than liberalization inevitable if the nationalities question were to be solved? It is crucial at this point to make a distinction. There is all the difference in the world between the democratization that follows collapse, that is the chaotic vacuum whose prevalence in the region makes Hobbesian calls for a state comprehensible, and the democratization willingly given so as to ensure the continuity of some structures that may thereby be shored up. Voluntary renunciation of power enables more of it to be retained: a firm, planned move towards elections could have been part of a liberalization strategy. In a sense, the handling of the nationalities question was the worst possible. There might have been logic in letting the Baltic states go and being strict elsewhere; what was disastrous was to pretend to be tough on the Baltic states and then let them go, thereby giving a precedent to other regions whose nationalisms up to that point had been very weak.

Conclusion

In general, I hold to the view that moral judgements are best considered not just by means of formal argument but quite as much in terms of what

[63]   J. Linz and A. Stepan, 'Political Identities and Electoral Sequences: Spain, the Soviet Union and Yugoslavia', *Daedalus*, vol. 121, 1992. For a fuller argument on this point, see ch. 6 in this volume.

is sociologically possible. Liberalization in state socialism had accordingly been endorsed because it was judged to be the best option available: less than complete democracy was being recommended – to spell out unease present even at the time – for others, even though this would not have been judged acceptable at home. How should the experience of having been wrong about the possibilities of liberalizing state socialism make me feel?

There are very difficult issues involved here, some of which I still find too hard to handle. In one sense it was fortunate that proper sociological understanding was *not* available. The crucial sociological discovery detailed in this essay, that totalitarianism had so destroyed civil society as to all but rule out any careful decompression, amounts to saying that it was nearly inevitable that socialist leaders would lose control. Had this been known in advance, it would have encouraged such bunker mentality that no change would have been attempted. Gorbachov destroyed state socialism perfectly because he was blind. The incredible difficulty of trying to do everything at one time, to undertake nation-building, accept the market and move towards softer political rule at one and the same moment, also makes my moral discomfort less than total. I judge the chances of long-term change in China to be better because the tasks of reformers may be easier, most obviously because an improving economy may eventually create civil society partners for a liberalizing elite.

There is another way of looking at the whole matter. It may well be, horrible though it is to say so in advance, that the likelihood of making a transition between socialism and democracy is very small indeed.[64] One sociological moral that has been drawn from this is that greater boldness was required in the liberalization process for it to have had any chance of success. A more general moral point is that awareness of difficulty should occasion greater help from the outside. The fate of the new democracies is very largely outside Western control, but the small margin where aid and consideration can matter needs to be seized, not least since monies spent now are nothing compared with those that either increased ethnic rivalries or a return to authoritarianism will certainly require.

[64] For a fuller argument on the possibilities of consolidating democracies, see ch. 5.

4

STATE POWER AND PATTERNS OF LATE DEVELOPMENT

(WRITTEN WITH DING-XIN ZHAO)

Turmoil in world politics occasions the reflections of social scientists. Clearly, the absolute collapse of the socialist project in Eastern Europe calls for fresh thought about the relations between states and markets. Such thoughts should not be, as now tends to be the case in the United States, naive:[1] it will not do to replace love of the state with adulation for the market–principally because these two sources of power habitually intertwine and sometimes depend upon each other. The thesis of this chapter is that sustained success in late development depends upon the actions of states with 'bounded autonomy', that is states with some independence from domestic social forces yet firmly oriented towards participation in the international market economy.

The most cursory of glances at the historical record suggests the sense of the line of argument to be pursued. The initial triumph of commercial capitalism in north-west Europe would most certainly not have been possible without the benefit of state action. If the most obvious contribution of the state was that of the protection of property rights, perhaps as important – in the eyes of Adam Smith quite as much as in reality – was the infrastructural support that led to the control of disease, the amelioration of communication and eventually the planned improvement of

---

[1] The outstanding example is F. Fukuyama, *The End of History and the Last Man*, Free Press, New York, 1991.

human capital.[2] Beyond this it is now almost a truism to insist that economic development was allowed by, in part caused by, and always in relationship with the geopolitical competition characteristic of a multipolar world.[3] There is a great difference between this initial pattern, taking place over centuries, based on petty technology, and very much the result of accident rather than design, and the planned and forced industrializations occasioned by uneven development.[4] States sponsored such late development largely to enhance their security,[5] and they did so in the belief that mere dependent peripheralization within capitalism would be their fate if they left everything to the market.[6] Such late industrialization changed the historical record. And if the collapse of the socialist project has revealed the eventual limits to industrial revolutions seeking to *escape* the market, there can be no doubt about the fabulous success of a few state-led industrializations *within* capitalist society. Scepticism must be shown to the dictums of narrow-minded neo-classical economics.[7] The first part of this chapter seeks to explain how certain states gained the 'bounded autonomy' that allowed them to create effective late development.

Identification of the ways in which states with bounded autonomy help development allows an escape from the crisis in the sociology of development identified by Mouzelis.[8] At the root of crisis, in Mouzelis's eyes, was the marxisant economism of dependency theory – that is the pessimistic *alter ego* to the equally implausible triumphalist liberal economism that, as noted, is currently dominant in the United States. The position

[2] A. Smith, *The Wealth of Nations*, Oxford University Press, Oxford, 1976, especially book 5. Cf. E. L. Jones, *The European Miracle*, Cambridge University Press, Cambridge, 1981; J. A. Hall, *Powers and Liberties*, Basil Blackwell, 1985; M. Mann, *Sources of Social Power*, vol. 1: *From the Beginning to 1760 AD*, Cambridge University Press, Cambridge, 1986.
[3] C. Tilly, *Coercion, Capital and European States*, Basil Blackwell, Oxford, 1990.
[4] A. Gershenkron, 'Economic Backwardness in Historical Perspective', in B. Hoselitz, ed., *The Progress of Underdeveloped Areas*, Chicago University Press, Chicago, 1952.
[5] G. Sen, *The Military Origins of Industrialisation and International Trade Rivalry*, Frances Pinter, London, 1984.
[6] D. Senghaas, *The European Experience: a Historical Critique of Development Theory*, Berg, Leamington Spa, 1985; R. Szporluk, *Communism and Nationalism*, Oxford University Press, Oxford, 1988.
[7] A striking example of this is D. Lal, *The Poverty of Development Economics*, Hobart Paperback 16, London, 1983.
[8] N. Mouzelis, 'Sociology of Development: Reflections on the Present Crisis', *Sociology*, vol. 22, 1988.

articulated here can be seen as meeting Mouzelis's demand for that specification of a non-reductionist view of 'the political' that would allow analysis of differential patterns of development. This can be put more bluntly: a 'Third World' doomed to a single fate by the power of capitalism clearly no longer exists. The second part of this chapter outlines the logic of some political economies within the late-developing and underdeveloped world, in the belief that doing so suggests a way in which the sociology of development can regain momentum.

Explaining Bounded Autonomy

Perhaps there is at least this to Lévi-Strauss's notion of binary opposition: it is extremely hard not to think in either/or terms, that is with stark polar contrasts at the forefront of attention. But proper sociological understanding, with an awareness that conflict can sustain consensus and that a prior consensus is necessary if conflict is to have function, has always resisted binary thinking. Certainly advances in state theory in recent years have resulted precisely from escaping the total opposition between society and statist theories occasioned by the initial desire to 'bring the state back in'.[9] Accordingly, the analysis of bounded autonomy that follows is in effect that of two sides of a coin.

Some degree of autonomy from societal pressures is necessary in order to organize and rationalize a society so that it may undertake the immensely painful and difficult transition to industrialism. A series of factors, singly or in combination, create such autonomy.

1 **Geopolitical factors** The geography of politics has often affected the economic prospects of weak and small countries in a wholly negative manner. For example, central European and Balkan states owe much of their historical backwardness to their status as buffers between the great powers, a situation that may again face most of them in the coming years.[10] None the less, the *Pax Americana* increased the autonomy and the opportunities of states at the edge of the defence perimeter established by the United States. The societal grip of extreme right and left on West Germany and Japan was destroyed. Less noticed

[9]   J. A. Hall and G. J. Ikenberry, *The State*, Open University Press, Milton Keynes, 1989; P. Evans, D. Rueschmeyer and T. Skocpol, eds, *Bringing the State Back In*, Cambridge University Press, Cambridge, 1985.
[10]   D. Chirot, ed., *The Origins of Backwardness in Eastern Europe*, California University Press, Berkeley, 1989.

was the fact that the states of South Korea and Taiwan gained autonomy over their societies thanks to immense loans given for geopolitical purposes. Such capital helped development, not least by preventing multinationals dominating the national economy. The contrast with Latin America, which received few such geopolitical favours, is very striking.

2 **Old regime structures** The persistence of old regime structures has negative consequences on the state's capacity to implement economic development. There remains much to be said for Barrington Moore's insistence that the destruction through revolutionary processes of disabling social structures is a precondition of economic development.[11] A *tabula rasa* can equally be created by war, natural disaster or foreign occupation. In this vein, it has become conventional to compare the fundamental land reform pushed through by the Japanese in parts of their colonial empire with the continuity of highly inegalitarian land holding patterns of Latin America.[12] This accounts for the marked difference in income distribution between East Asia and Latin America.[13]

3 **Nationalism** Nationalism makes citizens readier to undergo sacrifice and to accept the state's leading role in creating economic development to ensure national security. Most late-developing countries, with China, Japan and Korea as obvious exceptions, lack a common base to encourage imagined community.[14] Firstly, these countries usually lack a common language, religion, culture and ethnic base to sustain a solid nationalistic ideology. Secondly, most of the countries are without a history of a uniform market network. Thirdly, warfare has in fact been a much more important nation-building force than the media emphasized by Anderson. Continuous interstate competition in Europe – necessitating endless interaction between state and society in order to meet the fiscal demands of war

---

[11] B. Moore, *Social Origins of Dictatorship and Democracy*, Beacon Press, Boston, 1966.
[12] P. Evans, 'Class, State and Dependence in East Asia: Lessons for Latin Americanists', in F. C. Deyo, ed., *The Political Economy of the New Asian Industrialism*, Cornell University Press, Ithaca, 1987.
[13] A. Przeworski, *Democracy and the Market*, Cambridge University Press, Cambridge, 1991, pp. 155–5.
[14] B. Anderson, *Imagined Communities*, New Left Books, London, 1983.

– created shared identity.[15] After 1945, in contrast, the extraordinary obeisance shown to the norm of non-intervention, in large part because of the fear of nuclear war, has meant the elimination for late-developing countries of this historically important nation-building mechanism. Many late-developing countries need not seek support from their societies since the relative absence of interstate conflict diminishes the need for social rationalization.[16] Many states, especially those in sub-Saharan Africa, have armed forces – often paid for with aid given by the advanced world – of use only for domestic repression.

4 The character of the political system The character of the political system, whether democratic, authoritarian or populist/corporatist, affects its capacity to organize society. Authoritarianism enhances the autonomy of state elites: a policy can accordingly be pursued or shifted easily, since the elite is insulated from pressures deriving from civil society. In contrast, democracy – especially when that regime is established well before industrialization[17] – has often curtailed genuine late development. Such early democracy failed to break the power of the landed upper class, tending rather to encourage an alliance between the state and that class; that alliance, at least in Latin America, encouraged populism whose excessive demands helped create a pattern of oscillation between precarious democracy and dictatorship. Democracy before industrialization makes for states too weak to insulate themselves from social pressures, and therefore incapable of pursuing a steady developmental goal.[18]

An important gloss needs to be placed on all this. If authoritarianism has the capacity to force development, that is not to say that the capacity is always utilized. Further, the difficulties posed by democracy should not be allowed to obscure its benefits even at low levels of economic development. Bluntly, democracy has the ability to provide

[15] A. D. Smith, *Theories of Nationalism*, Duckworth, London, 1981; M. Mann, 'The Emergence of Modern European Nationalism', in J. A. Hall and I. C. Jarvie, eds, *Transition to Modernity*, Cambridge University Press, Cambridge, 1992.
[16] R. Jackson and K. Rosberg, 'Why Africa's Weak States Persist', *World Politics*, vol. 35, 1982; S. Krasner, *Structural Conflict*, University of California Press, Berkeley, 1985.
[17] N. Mouzelis, *Politics in the Semi-periphery*, Macmillan, London, 1976.
[18] S. Huntington has demonstrated–in *Political Order in Changing Societies*, Yale University Press, New Haven, 1968, p. 423 – that two-party and multi-party systems in Latin America have a greater tendency to coups than one-party states.

information to those in power as well as the capacity to control them; it can limit the amount of sheer disaster occasioned by authoritarianism.

5 **Cultural factors** While the importance of cultural factors to economic development has often been overstated[19], none the less some cultural legacies have played important roles in shaping state-society relations. Countries that have traditionally been ruled by a unified agrarian empire, or experienced repeated state-organized production and redistribution projects, or emphasized education, tend to have a population that is more prepared to be governed and manipulated by the state than do countries bereft of such experience.

These five factors free states from societal pressures, and thereby give them the possibility of pushing through developmental policies. History tells us, however, that such freedom can very easily be misused: authoritarian states may either not choose to pursue development at all, preferring to crush civil society and to implement policies for their private benefits, or may opt for a strategy of retreat from the market which has no long-term prospect of success: if Zaire is a classic example of the former pattern, both Argentina and the Soviet Union serve as illustrations of the latter. States possessed of autonomy from society do not orient themselves to the market unless they face the following sorts of constraints.

1 **Geopolitics** Geopolitics can force a state to take the market seriously. Whatever the general record of the United States, it has shown concern with the economic development of several important countries on its defence perimeter. Moreover, such states have benefited from warfare in a direct way: the economic development of Korea was aided by American involvement in Vietnam. The military pressures felt by Korea, and by Taiwan, was real, and a decided factor in their desire to survive through speedy economic development.

2 **Nationalism** We have suggested that a strong mass-based nationalism will increase the autonomy of a state. But nationalism has, here as elsewhere, another side. Strong nationalism can act as a check to a

---

[19] Examples include D. McLelland, *The Achieving Society*, Van Nostrand, Toronto, 1961; W. Davis, 'Religion and Development: Weber and East Asian Experience', in M. Weiner and S. Huntington, eds, *Understanding Political Development*, Little Brown, Boston, 1987; P. L. Berger and H. L. Hsiao, eds, *In Search of an East Asian Developmental Model*, Transaction, Brunswick, 1988.

state: because of it an incompetent state can lose its legitimacy quickly. Reform or revolution are the outcomes. Extreme nationalism played some part in the disastrous behaviour of Germany and Japan in the twentieth century, and it may cause xenophobia at any time. But if we consider the history of economic development, the positive impact of nationalism remains enormous. Mistakes in policy tend to be corrected since economic failure hurts national esteem.

3 **Level of legitimacy** The legitimacy of an authoritarian regime changes over time. An authoritarian state can dominate its society effectively only during the honeymoon period of its inception or whilst its charismatic leader is still in power. In the long run such a state faces legitimation problems, especially, as is often the case, when catastrophes of one sort or another have taken place. If an authoritarian regime survives revolutionary discontent, empirical evidence suggests that it may seek to cooperate with society whilst hoping to retain much of its autonomy. When this results in pragmatic and soft authoritarian rule economic development will be facilitated.

4 **Dominant ideologies** If we compare differences in economic performance between West and East Germany, between South and North Korea and, to a lesser extent, between Taiwan and China, then the importance of the character of the developmental ideology adopted becomes apparent. What matters is the eventual participation within the world market. There are clear elective affinities between ideology and state behaviour. Empirical evidence suggests that states characterized by pragmatic nationalism tend towards orienting themselves to the world market. In contrast, communist states tend to withdraw from the market. Democratic states tend to link themselves to the world market, but this is by no means a universal rule.

One point about this analysis of bounded autonomy deserve emphasis, namely that it is open – or, to put the matter more negatively, vague. This cannot be avoided. No universal weighting of the factors identified is feasible. But greater precision can now be shown when examining particular societal patterns: detailed comparison between the regions make it possible to determine which factors have played crucial roles in the creation of particular developmental patterns.

Beyond 'the Third World'

The argument implicity made so far, that late developers will have different chances depending on the character of their states, needs now to be made *explicit*. In this section, state-centred analysis is used to compare the recent economic performances of five main geographical regions: East Asia, China, India, Latin America and sub-Saharan Africa. We are fully aware that huge differences exist within these areas, and some comments will be made accentuating this. Nevertheless, the rationale of comparison is simply that the regions identified do have recognizable political economies of their own. Another way of characterizing the analysis is to say that its aim is ideal-typical in nature, with some guesses as to more conjunctural future development being left to the conclusion.[20]

(1) **Governing the Market in East Asia** East Asian states have been the centre of the economic dynamism of the late developing world since the 1960s. GNP in South Korea increased 452 per cent or an average 8.5 per cent every year between 1962 and 1980[21]; similar rates were achieved only by Taiwan, Singapore and Hong Kong. Leaving aside the two city states, it is easy to see that South Korea and Taiwan experienced similar phases of economic development: from import substitution industrialization in the 1950s to export expansion in the 1960s, followed in turn by heavy but technologically intensive industries after the 1970s – which these states now hope to use for further progress up the product cycle. Each of these shifts in policy was engineered by the state through monetary and non-monetary means, such as subsidies, foreign exchange controls, export tax incentives, and tariff barriers.[22] The extent of state intervention in East Asia contrasts very strongly with neoclassical accounts of East Asian economic development.[23] What is striking about the East Asian pattern is less the

---

[20] No claim is being made that the patterns of late development identified here constitute a complete and exhaustive list of available options. The classical heartland of Islam, the political economy of a large sub-set of which is massively influenced by the possession of petroleum, is the most striking omission.

[21] C. Johnson, 'Political Institutions and Economic Performance: The Government–Business Relationship in Japan, South Korea, and Taiwan', in Deyo, *The Political Economy of the New Asian Industrialism*.

[22] R. Wade, *Governing the Market*, Princeton University Press, Princeton, 1990; A. Amsden, *Asia's Next Giant*, Oxford University Press, New York, 1989.

[23] E. K. Y. Chen, *Hyper-growth in Asian Economies: a Comparative Study of Hong Kong, Japan, Korea, Singapore and Taiwan*, Macmillan, London, 1979.

tools, many of which have been tried elsewhere, than the general political ethic that lies behind their use: the essence of strategy is not protection but rather a policy of 'direct and escort', that is a determination to nourish industrial sectors perceived as important only until they acquire competitive advantage in the world market. In both countries, subsidies were used to distort the prices of new products so as to overcome competitive disadvantage, thereby raising the natural investment rate. It is important to note that these subsidies were not mere hand-outs, as has been the case in both Latin America and India, nor was the capital used, as it has been in Africa, to buy political power. Furthermore, both South Korea and Taiwan imposed performance standards on private firms: private companies are thus directed in the path desired by the state.

Such state-led developmentalism has been made possible by several factors. Historically, both states were ruled for a long time by unified agrarian empires. Before the arrival of Western powers, each of these societies already had a unified written language, a dominant religion, and ethnic homogeneity, while they all more or less shared a common market. The two states possessed high levels of literacy as early as the 1950s, when they were still very poor; this was a direct result of Japanese colonial rule and an indirect result of general East Asian Confucian culture.[24] This advanced political and cultural development encouraged the development of strong nationalist feelings directed against Japanese colonizers. All in all, South Korea and Taiwan deserve to be considered late developers only in the economic sense. Compared with Latin America, India and sub-Saharan Africa, these countries had a historical head start in nation-building: they had cohesive development-minded elites and populations prepared to be led by their states towards economic development.

In both states, old regime structures were destroyed as the consequence of geopolitical events. The 1948–1950 land reform in South Korea had only a limited success because the Rhee Government was so entwined with the landed upper class. But invasion and occupation destroyed the old class structure.[25] The facts that Taiwan's government was imported from mainland China and that it was

---

[24]   B. Cumings, 'The Origins and Development of the Northeast Asian Political Economy: Industrial Sectors, Product Cycles, and Political Consequences', *International Organisation*, vol. 38, 1984.
[25]   H. Koo, 'The Interplay of State, Social Class, and World System in East Asian Development: the Cases of South Korea and Taiwan', in Deyo, *The Political Economy of the New Asian Industrialism*.

backed up by pervasive military force meant that the interests of local elites could be completely ignored. Both countries, in a nutshell, had a complete land reform. The rather poor but egalitarian society that resulted proved to be good developmental material: the state had sufficient room to organize a society that had high levels of consumption and abundant, highly disciplined, cheap labour.

The extent of American help can scarcely be exaggerated. Aid monies other than those directly for military purposes financed forty and seventy per cent of gross domestic capital formation between 1952 and 1960 in Taiwan and South Korea respectively.[26] Furthermore, the strategic importance of the region forced the United States to tolerate both early import substitution policies and the high trade deficit that came when the two states adopted export-led strategies. Moreover, American pressure gave rise to the emergence of ever softer authoritarianism, firmly oriented towards the world market. Finally, the United States also provided many direct economic opportunities to the region, notably when at war with Vietnam.[27]

A final factor of great importance is that of real military pressures together with a legitimacy much diminished by battlefield defeat by communists. This is especially true of the nationalist party in Taiwan. Defeat on the mainland encouraged the nationalists, once in Taiwan, to admit their mistakes and to work out and pursue proper state policies, particularly land reform, in order to ensure their very survival.

(2) **Self-reliance in China** The People's Republic of China shares much with South Korea and Taiwan. Four thousand years of continuous civilization and rule by a meritocratic bureaucracy since 7 AD ensured that the country has high homogeneity in terms of language, culture, religious belief, ethnicity and market relations – especially, as we shall see, when compared with India. Further, national feeling, derived from both internal homogeneity and frequent fighting with nomads, was strong even before the era of European expansion; this accounts for the mass resistance shown to Europeans in the Boxer Rebellion.[28] China's nation-building process was advanced in other ways before the arrival of European imperialists. Traditional Chinese political thinking called for a strong state, able to penetrate

[26] S. Haggard, *Pathways from the Periphery*, Cornell University Press, Ithaca, 1990, p. 196.
[27] Cumings, 'The Origins and Development of the Northeast Asian Political Economy'.
[28] I. C. Y. Hsu, *The Rise of Modern China*, Oxford University Press, New York, 1970.

the society and to gather social energy so as to repel foreign invasions: such sentiments lay behind the overthrow of both the Qing dynasty in 1911 and the nationalist Government in 1949. An additional reason for loss of faith in the nationalist Government was that the extent of its ties to the traditional landed elites made it unable to institute land and tax reform.[29] These tasks were completed by the communist revolution, together with nationalization and the collectivization of industry. The old regime structure was, in a nutshell, completely destroyed.

However, China's economic performance under communism compares badly with that of its East Asian counterparts. After forty years China has established a systematic industrial system, but not an economy efficient enough to bring affluence. Crucially, communist rule brought political instability. A combination of state-led political movements and a radical strategy of economic development brought the country to the verge of economic collapse. And if the state has achieved agricultural self-sufficiency, basic literacy and higher life expectancy, its policy failures have brought stunning death tolls, notably in the great famine of 1959–61 when between twenty and thirty million died.[30]

The poor economic performance of China, at least when compared with that of the East Asian states, was the result of three factors. First, China suffered geopolitically until at least the mid-1970s. The Cold War strategy of the United States totally isolated China from the first world; equally, open Sino–Soviet conflict shortly after the death of Stalin meant that China lost all hope of aid and technical assistance from the second world. This situation pushed China towards import substitution, that is the strategy of self-reliance, rather than towards the American sphere, for the simplest of reasons: China was sufficiently large and confident to shrug off pressures from the outside. If Taiwan and Korea's world-market strategy amounted to, in Wallerstein's felicific formula, 'development by invitation'[31], China's inward-looking economic policy was occasioned by geopolitical isolation. This long isolation from the world market, together with the character of the planned economy, made Chinese industry run at a low level of efficiency: even when the growth rate was high, industrial development did not bring economic dynamism

[29]   Moore, *Social Origins of Dictatorship and Democracy*; T. Skocpol, *States and Social Revolution*, Cambridge University Press, Cambridge, 1979.
[30]   W. Lavely, J. Lee, and F. Wang, 'Chinese Demography. The State of the Field', *Journal of Asian Studies*, vol. 49, 1990.
[31]   Cumings, 'The Origins and Development of the Northeast Asian Political Economy', p. 68.

as products were either of low quality or disproportionate to demand.[32]

Secondly, in contrast to an anarchic past dominated by war and invasion, the early communist success in economic recovery, land reform, the extension of social welfare and success in the Korean war brought the communists great legitimacy. The majority of Chinese put a blind faith in Mao and his party, and gave them the power to carry out gigantic social engineering programmes such as the Great Leap Forward and the Cultural Revolution.

Finally, ideological factors also played an important role in poor Chinese performance. Utopianism encouraged the communist party to adopt radical economic development policies that brought disasters. Furthermore, ideological rigidity led the Chinese leaders to challenge changes in Eastern Europe that followed the death of Stalin: they rejected 'revisionism' and thereby caused political movements aimed at *deepening* the revolution. The state-led movement that peaked during the Cultural Revolution ended with political turmoil, near economic bankruptcy and a high cost in human life.

Our general argument gains more support if we compare Chinese economic performance before and after 1978, the year in which the state elite was forced by the disasters noted to adopt a hugely modified developmental strategy. China has allowed restructuring with minimal political liberalization, perestroika with limited glasnost. The marked successes of this strategy are very striking.[33] In the 1980s, China's GNP has increased at an annual rate of 9.5 per cent. Huge trade surpluses since 1989 have made the currency almost completely convertible and have enabled the state both to lift tariffs and to remove

---

[32] V. Nee and D. Stark, eds, *Remaking the Economic Institutions of Socialism: China and Eastern Europe*, Stanford University Press, Stanford, 1989.

[33] The contrasting failure of reform in the Soviet Union tends to be ascribed to the destruction of the peasantry and the presence of a more entrenched and centralized party apparatus. Examples of this argument are A. Aslund, *Gorbachov's Struggle for Economic Reform*, Cornell University Press, Ithaca, 1989, pp. 181–3 and N. R. Lardy, 'Is China different?', in D. Chirot, ed., *The Crisis of Leninism and the Decline of the Left: the Revolutions of 1989*, University of Washington Press, Seattle, 1991, pp. 148–53. In a nutshell, the success of contemporary Chinese strategy does not make it any the less doubtful that economic reform could have been achieved in the Soviet Union without full democratization. Note too that it would have been difficult to introduce free economic zones in the USSR. Such zones have caused severe regional imbalances in China 'which would be much more dangerous in the Soviet Union with its nationality problems; the vast majority of foreign capital in [China's] free economic zones is invested by Chinese abroad, and the USSR would not benefit from such an effect' (Aslund, *Gorbachov's Struggle for Economic Reform*, p. 183).

licences for industries no longer judged to be 'infant', so as to force them to compete internationally.[34] Ten years ago, almost 100 per cent of industrial prices were controlled by the state; the fact that this has shrunk to only 44 per cent makes it senseless to think of this social formation as a command economy.[35]

(3) **Democracy and development in India** India's remarkable history of virtually non-interrupted democracy since independence has been combined with slow but steady economic development. By the end of the 1980s, India had established a fully-fledged industrial system, capable of producing both basic necessities and high technology goods; in addition, the 'green revolution' has allowed agricultural self-sufficiency. Since independence India has never had large-scale famine, despite population pressure. In all these ways India has belied the most pessimistic predictions made about its future.[36] None the less, it is still one of the poorest nations in the world. Agricultural output still constitutes the largest part of India's GNP, whilst a third of the world's 'absolute poor' – at least according to the calculations of the World Bank[37] – still lives in India.

India may usefully be compared with China, not least because they both have huge populations. At present India enjoys more political freedom but suffers high internal economic inequality, slower economic development, lower status of women and lower levels of literacy and life expectancy. If India has never had a famine equivalent to that of 1959–61 in China, Drèze and Sen insist none the less that every eight years there are an equivalent number of fatalities in India due to low life expectancy.[38] More significantly, if India's growth rate averaged 5 per cent during the 1980s, China's was 9.5 per cent in the same period. Furthermore, India's growth was largely due, in contrast to that of China, to the rapid expansion of the service sector rather than to improvements in agricultural and industrial sectors.[39] Maybe the pessimists had something of a case after all.

[34]   *The People's Daily*, Overseas Edition, 28 January, 1992 and 16 March, 1992.
[35]   *People's Daily*, Overseas Edition, 21 January, 1992.
[36]   For example Moore, *Social Origins of Dictatorship and Democracy*.
[37]   *The Economist's Intelligence Unit*, Country Report: India, Nepal, 1991.
[38]   J. Drèze and A. Sen, *Hunger and Public Action*, Oxford University Press, Oxford, 1989.
[39]   *The Economist's Intelligence Unit*, Country Report: India, 1991.

In contrast to China and the East Asian states, India lacked strong mass nationalism. The British conquered India even before the industrial revolution, and did so with great ease–certainly in comparison with China, where foreigners, at the moment of their greatest power, were restricted to access to treaty ports. Independence in India was also gained by peaceful means, and this too indicates feeble nationalism. There are long historical patterns at work here. In ancient China, Confucius and the system of civil examinations encouraged territorial cohesion. In contrast, the important Indian institutions, the caste system and the jati division of labour, divided society. In consequence, political unity was basically alien to Indian civilization before independence; its politics have rather been dominated by the caste-based village council.[40] India remains an extremely fragmented society in terms of language, culture, religious belief, ethnicity and market relations: it still needs to undertake basic nation-building processes.

The peaceful transition to independence together with early democracy meant such old regime structures as caste, the landed elite and village control of local affairs were not destroyed. Furthermore, the strength of the business class at the time of independence limited the state's strategy for late development: in comparison with East Asia, the state is powerless to discipline industry. Rather, the state's subsidies are given away to those with good political connections, the consequence of which has been continual support for uneconomic 'lame ducks'. The state has been no more able to carry out fundamental land reform: rural areas are still controlled by local elites. Such local organization as there has been has often been against the state; at times this has been so effective as to deny the state basic revenues.[41]

It is worth noting finally that India has not been favoured in geopolitical terms. It has a population seventeen times that of South Korea, but between 1946 and 1978 it received only 50 per cent more aid from the United States. If military aid were to be included, India's total aid from the United States did not equal that sent to South Korea.[42]

---

[40] Moore, *Social Origins of Dictatorship and Democracy*; K. W. Kapp and D. Kapp, *Hindu Culture, Economic Development, and Economic Planning in India*, Asian Publishing House, New Delhi, 1963.

[41] P. Bardham, *The Political Economy of Development in India*, Oxford University Press, New Delhi, 1984.

[42] Cumings, 'The Origins and Development of the Northeast Asian Political Economy'.

(4) **Dependent development in Latin America** Latin American states gained independence in the early nineteenth century and experienced political democracy before industrialization. Their early economic development was based on direct foreign investment, which allowed the export of a few primary products. This pattern made Latin America the hinterland of the core of advanced capitalism, thus creating a rather unbalanced economic profile. Indigenous industrialization only really began in the 1930s, and the diminution of international trade at that time ensured that such development was import-substituting in character. This policy had initial successes, but it never gained sufficient salience to bring fundamental structural change to society. Large latifundia and native village communities remain the dominant form of landholding in most countries.[43] No fundamental land reform has been undertaken, and Latin America accordingly suffers from extraordinarily marked inequalities.[44] This distributional fact limited both the size and level of integration of the domestic market, and ensured such low levels of literacy and skill that industrial products could find no market niche – despite low labour costs. For many reasons, Latin American states were unable to make a successful policy shift from import substitution to export-led growth.[45] Most obviously, they had no autonomy from the established landed upper class. Accordingly, the stagnation that afflicted their economies after the 1960s brought in its tail a series of military coups. The resulting repressive governments did not change the economic situation – except, perhaps, for exacerbating it by borrowing huge amounts of petrodollars in the wake of the second oil shock. When, in the 1980s, democracy once again became the dominant ideology in world politics, politics in Latin American changed their tenor once again. But this

[43] J. Lambert, *Latin America*, University of California Press, Berkeley, 1967; W. Taylor, 'Landed Society in New Spain: a View from the South', *Hispanic American Historical Review*, vol. 54, 1974.

[44] The presence of petroleum, whose revenues could be used to buy off the upper classes, made Venezuela an exception to this rule. In this connection, see T. Karl, 'Dilemmas of Democratisation in Latin America', *Comparative Politics*, vol. 22, 1990.

[45] Neoclassical accounts – for example I. Little, F. Scitovsky and M. Scott, *Industry and Trade in Some Developing Countries: a Comparative Study*, Oxford University Press, Oxford, 1970 – ascribe the failures of Latin American development to the adoption of import substitution. This is misleading for several reasons. Most obviously, development did occur by means of this strategy – as it did still more so in East Asia. What matters is the ability to transfer from this strategy to a new one based on export. This step, taken successfully by East Asia, has historically proved beyond the capacities of Latin American states.

has made little real difference to the economic situation, and democratization remains precarious.

A series of factors explain the relative failure of late development in Latin America. Nationalism there was even weaker than in India; without Napoleon's occupation of Spain, Latin American might have remained tied to Spain for as long as was Cuba.[46] After independence, ethnic, linguistic and cultural diversities, in combination with the marked inequalities already noted, curtailed successful nation building. Furthermore, Latin American elites identified themselves with Europe, doubting whether their tropical and racially diverse countries could ever achieve a distinctive civilization, as had the United States.[47] It is scarcely surprising that these elites adopted liberal free-trade policies, and that their opponents invented dependency theory.[48]

One piece of evidence demonstrating that Latin America is still at an early stage of nation and state building is the fact that ideological cycles – from democracy to fascism to the rediscovery of democracy – always went in tandem with those of Europe. Importing a foreign ideology is not without cost. Firstly, liberalism encouraged Latin American states immediately after their independence to involve themselves uncritically in the world market. In comparison with East Asia, Latin America had no period of withdrawal from the international market in which to establish infant industries. Foreign multinationals could thus completely dominate the economies of Latin American societies, whereas in East Asia they were forced to become, as the result of the establishment of national industrial structures, mere junior partners.[49] Secondly, early democracy brought populism and political instability to the region. Since then Latin America has suffered from a continuing cyclical movement, with democracy leading to populist demands that ensure the installation

---

[46] T. S. Skidmore and P. H. Smith, *Modern Latin America*, Oxford University Press, New York, 1984.
[47] Argentina enjoyed a lower level of ethnic diversity than most other Latin American states, principally because most of its population was European in origin. However, Argentina still suffered from a low sense of nationalism, in large part because immigrants came, within a very short time-span, from a variety of European countries – a pattern which is the opposite of that of Australia and New Zealand. In this connection, see C. Waisman, *Reversal of Development in Argentina*, Princeton University Press, Princeton, 1987, pp. 51–8.
[48] For example, R. Prebisch, *The Economic Development of Latin America and Its Principal Problems*, United Nations, New York, 1950; A. G. Frank, *Capitalism and Underdevelopment in Latin America*, Monthly Review Press, New York, 1967.
[49] Evans, 'Class, State and Dependence in East Asia'.

of authoritarianism – whose mistakes then allow the whole cycle to begin again.[50] Democracy may have constrained structural change in India, but it did bring stability: in Latin America democracy has often brought only chaos.

It would be false to ascribe the character of the political economy of Latin America entirely to internal factors. From the beginning the core of capitalism found Latin America to be an ideal hinterland – especially after the disease brought by the invaders so destroyed the native people as to ensure a very low population density.[51] This stands in great contrast to Asia and even to parts of Africa, whose high population density, strong culture, local organization, sense of nationalism and tropical diseases (e.g. sleeping sickness in Africa) all served as barriers to prevent deep European penetration of their societies. Of course, North America also had very low native population density at that time, but these people were saved from peripheralization, at least in part, because Europeans were initially more interested in tropical products than in temperate crops they could produce themselves.

But geopolitical conditions have been extremely important, and these did not favour Latin America during the peak of the *Pax Americana*. Latin American states were disciplined by the United States, which considered the region its own backyard. However, the United States' political control seldom brought with it any economic benefit. After the Second World War, the United States was interested first in the reconstruction of Europe and Japan and then in that of South Korea and Taiwan, in both cases so as to ensure its own national security. Latin America was not threatened and was accordingly taken for granted.

(5) **Predatory states in sub-Saharan Africa** The economic development of post-independence sub-Saharan Africa has been disastrous.[52] After a few seemingly beneficent years, development was arrested in the 1970s and declined in the 1980s. Together with economic crisis went population explosion, large-scale famine, deforestation and indebtedness. In recent years serious drought, probably itself the result of deforestation, has hit twenty-four countries: unless quick action is taken, ten million people could die of famine.[53]

[50]   Huntington, *Political Order in Changing Societies*.
[51]   W. H. McNeill, *Plagues and People*, Anchor Books, New York, 1976.
[52]   D. Bigo, 'Is There Hope for Sub-Saharan Africa?', *Contention*, vol. 1, 1992.
[53]   *Food Crops and Special Shortages*, FAO, Rome, 1985.

The politics of the region are in an equally catastrophic situation. State elites tend to be so internally divided that military coups became the common mode of transferring power. In addition, the political systems suffered from a weak sense of nationalism, the persistence of old social structures, a low general level of state and nation building and a poor location within the world political system. All this prevented the emergence of states sufficiently autonomous to pioneer successful late development.

We may ascribe the low level of state and nation building to the fact that, before it was colonized, the region was tribal – which is to say that it was marked by a very high level of ethnic, cultural and linguistic diversity.[54] Only a few areas with settled and intensive agriculture experienced rule by states: such states were exceedingly weak, gaining revenue less from taxation of their own people than from long-distance trade in war captives and luxury goods.[55] European power changed far less in Africa than it had in Latin America. Tribes were organized into administrative units less with reference to existing ethnic or market boundaries than to facilitate the extraction of resources. This was normally achieved by establishing a coastline trading post and then declaring its direct hinterland a legitimate sphere of influence.[56] As a result, tribes were arbitrarily divided between different colonies.

Such an easy partition of sub-Saharan Africa was itself a very strong indication of weak nationalism, but the fact that it happened massively curtailed state and nation building thereafter. Furthermore, independence was led by native elites trained in Europe.[57] Whilst this was an expression of nationalism, it was clearly of a lesser order than that of, say, China: where the former could only unite urban dwellers in fighting for independence, the latter reached all social strata – and thereafter drew on their energy for developmental purposes.

The precarious nature of rule made the elites of sub-Saharan Africa less interested in development than in grabbing power. Lordship, clientelism and corruption were the hallmarks of these predatory

[54] Many of the languages in question were, of course, oral rather than written.
[55] E. Terray, 'Long-distance Exchange and the Formation of the State: the Case of the Abron Kingdom of Gyaman', *Economy and Society*, vol. 3, 1974; C. Coquery-Vidrovitch, 'Research on an African Mode of Production', in M. A. Klein and W. G. Johnson, eds, *Perspectives on the African Past*, Little Brown, New York, 1972.
[56] I. L. Griffiths, *An Atlas of African Affairs*, Methuen, London, 1984, pp. 56–7.
[57] D. K. Fieldhouse, *Black Africa, 1945–80: Economic Decolonization and Arrested Development*, Allen & Unwin, London, 1986.

states. This Hobbesian world, marked by continual coups, was not able to generate sensible developmental policy. Industrial development was emphasized at the expense of agrarian reform. Although this policy led to famine, in *political* terms it was perfectly rational: it provided the resources for gaining political support, and bought off business and the urban proletariat – both of which, unlike the poorly organized rural sectors, posed political threats to the regimes.[58] It is worth emphasizing, finally, that these states might not have been able to reorganize agriculture even had they wished to: their power is merely despotic, without any real capacity to reach into and so to reorganize social relations.

Geopolitical conditions in sub-Saharan Africa were also very unfavourable for late development. The continuing catastrophic legacy of colonialism has already been noted. Equally importantly, the fact that these states were never on the rim of Cold War defences meant that the United States had little interest in their destiny.

Conclusion: Change in World Order, Change in Late Development?

This chapter began by remarking upon the collapse of the state socialist project, and we can now conclude more generally by asking whether the change in the nature of the ordering of the world polity that follows from this will affect the patterning of late development. Obviously our comments cannot really rise much above speculation; nevertheless, they are useful because they entail some highlighting of the argument.

The change in the ordering of the world polity is not total, but it is fundamental. Most important is the simple fact that capitalism has no major competitor, no genuinely credible alternative; a consequence of this is that the bipolar division of the world has lost its bite. This accounts for one of the three elements that may be said to comprise the contemporary world order, namely that it is at times a concert of the great powers. This element of concert was occasioned, as had been the case after 1815, by the established powers when they sought to control a revolutionary regime they disliked, that of Saddam Hussein; given the likelihood that other developing states would acquire chemical

---

[58]   R. Bates, *Markets and States in Tropical Africa*, University of California Press, Berkeley, 1981; Fieldhouse, *Black Africa, 1945–80*, p. 94.

and nuclear weapons, it seems very likely that this element in the contemporary world order will not be evanescent.

A second and much touted element of the contemporary situation is the re-emergence of multipolar politics. Meetings of the G7, the fact that the links established between Germany and Russia are not subject to American control and the continuing strengthening of the Pacific economies all suggest that world order within capitalist society is maintained by the traditional mechanism of the balance of power. There is something to that notion, but it must not be exaggerated. The United States retains its military lead; and its hegemony, now exercised in a predatory rather than a benign style, can be seen both in the military rent it extracted from its economically powerful but militarily weak rivals in the Gulf War and in its ability to draw to itself most of the world's excess capital – the consequence, of course, of having a standard of living for which it expects others to pay. This is a unique world order: a system combining elements of concert and balance, yet to a considerable degree dominated by a single power that compensates for its less than remarkable economic performance by extracting resources from its allies.

The classic *Pax Americana* was far better for the advanced nations within capitalist society than for the late-developing world. Cold War ideology led to nationalism being mistaken for communism, whilst international financial institutions showed little sensitivity to developmental needs.[59] Given the continuing power of the United States, it is more than likely that this lack of sympathy will continue. Indeed it may be exacerbated. For a few late-developing countries did well from the Cold War. Current world political conditions make it unlikely that perimeter countries will receive geopolitical aid. The developing world may instead expect to be ignored. If this disadvantages perimeter countries and those that had made gains by turning from one superpower to the other, it may lead to advantage for larger but geopolitically self-contained countries. If India and Brazil look set to benefit, the biggest advantage may well accrue to China, given her regional importance, military capacity and possession of veto power at the United Nations.

If the geopolitical dimension within our notion of bounded autonomy has been affected by the end of the Cold War, so have two other factors. One of the most extraordinary facts about world politics since 1945 has

[59]   J. G. Ruggie, 'International Regimes, Transactions and Change: Embedded Liberalism in the Postwar Economic Order', *International Organisation*, vol. 36, 1982.

been the minuscule number of changes in the boundaries of states. The agreement on the norms of sovereignty and non-intervention that this has represented was based fundamentally on Cold War politics. Boundaries now look set to change, most spectacularly because the collapse of the Soviet Union has released a wave of separatist nationalism. Traditional marcher states with marked ethnic diversities caused by frequent changes in regime and historical experience of human migration will be so preoccupied internally that successful late-development is unlikely.[60] This is really a gloss upon, rather than a denial of, our basic point about nationalism. Strong mass nationalism within settled states retains its importance for developmental purposes; such nationalism gives the confidence to learn from the West and the capacity to avoid being overwhelmed by it. Equally striking is the extent to which the contemporary late-developing world is adopting strategies stressing the need for openness to the forces of the international market.

Whilst this sudden endorsement of an open world economy is likely to lead to general gain in the short run, it is easy to foresee a problem that will arise at the moment when the world economy falters: a very considerable number of states at a similar level of development now share the same developmental strategy, and this will lead to cut-throat competition in times of stress. Some countries will make it, but many will not.[61] Our analysis suggests that the survivors are likely to be those whose states have the capacity to enlarge their domestic markets, to upgrade their industries, and to escort and direct them onto the world market. Whilst a deterministic set of predictions is impossible, some hunches are worth spelling out. Please note immediately that no discussion is offered of the East Asian model of late development, on the grounds that its success is now made completely assured both by the presence of a sustainable industrial structure and by measures of political liberalization; sub-Saharan Africa receives no further discussion for

---

[60] R. Collins, *Weberian Sociological Theory*, Cambridge University Press, Cambridge, 1986.

[61] It is worth remembering in this connection that the growth rates of East Asia, Latin America and Eastern Europe were not very different in the 1970s, as A. Fishlow, 'Latin American Failure against the Backdrop of Asian Success', *Annals of the American Academy*, vol. 505, 1989 makes particularly clear. Our argument is that future crises are likely to be surmounted by structurally sound societies, as was the case in response to the second oil shock – when the economies of Latin America and Eastern Europe shrank, and those of East Asia moved towards sustainable expansion.

the opposite reason, namely that there is no likelihood of improvement within that region in the near future.[62]

China is best placed for rapid development. As noted, it is favoured geopolitically. Further, her large population and relative social equality offer a huge internal market, which will stand as a buffer against international market fluctuation. Finally, China is likely to benefit from being close to the current centre of economic dynamism – to which it is, of course, culturally linked. Hong Kong and Taiwan are likely to play especially important roles in this context,[63] probably becoming huge, special economic zones of China; the marriage of cheap but relatively high-quality labour to excess capital, market experience and leading technologies has the potential to transform not just the economy of China but that of the whole world.

But China faces problems, recognizable from the classic treatment of Huntington,[64] of creating political stability – especially after the crackdown at Tiananmen Square in 1989. Political sociology has demonstrated that working classes become genuinely militant when they face a recalcitrant state determined to refuse them access to the political process.[65] The insight at work here, that social movements gain their character as the result of their relation to the state, can be applied to the Chinese situation. The brutal suppression of the student movement will almost certainly radicalize collective action in the future, and thereby

[62] The collapse of the Soviet Union means that a set of hugely distorted economies – often blessed, however, with notable labour skills – have joined the periphery of capitalist society. The logic of our argument would suggest diverse outcomes within this world. The crimes of Hitler and Stalin have freed Hungary and Poland from the pressures of nationalist separatism and accordingly given them an advantage lacked by other Eastern European states. Geopolitics may yet play the crucial role in the region, particularly if the alliance of Poles, Czechs, Slovaks and Hungarians results in a single entry into the European Community.

[63] In 1990 44 per cent of Hong Kong's exports came originally from the mainland, whilst in 1991 70 per cent of foreign investment in China was from Hong Kong and from foreign enterprises based in Hong Kong – according to *The People's Daily*, Overseas Edition, 26 March 1992. Taiwan has the option of copying this pattern.

[64] Huntington, *Political Order in Changing Societies*.

[65] M. Mann, 'Citizenship and Ruling Class Strategies', *Sociology*, vol. 21, 1987; T. McDaniel, *Autocracy, Capitalism and Revolution in Russia*, University of California Press, Berkeley, 1988; R. McKibbin, *The Ideologies of Class*, Oxford University Press, Oxford, 1990: C. Waisman, *Modernisation and the Working Class*, University of Texas Press, Austin, 1982; I. Katznelson and A. Zolberg, eds, *Working Class Formation*, Princeton University Press, Princeton, 1986.

make a smooth state retreat difficult to achieve. Positive developments in China probably depend upon intellectuals being able to firmly check the power of the state *without* allowing themselves to become naively utopian. China's future, in a word, depends on the willingness and ability of the state to make a gradual transition to a less ideological system.

The logic of our argument suggests that other countries have more and greater problems. For many countries, with Brazil and India as possible exceptions, the collapse of the Socialist bloc has diminished the possibility of geopolitical advantage. Furthermore, the states of India and Latin America need to put a lot more effort, at least compared with China, into nation-building processes. Late development in these regions needs state-led infrastructural projects to do with education and transport, an assault on old regime structures and large-scale social inequalities, as well as a sense of realism sufficient to resist all neoclassical absolutist calls for *total* state retreat. These are formidable tasks, as is the eventual co-ordination of state and market so that state action can aid market formation whilst lessening the negative impact of world market forces on relatively weak economies.

5

CONSOLIDATIONS OF DEMOCRACY

The extraordinary events of recent years have encouraged optimism about the prospects for democracy. Sometimes such optimism can be naive and excessive. That spirit led Francis Fukuyama famously to declare that we are witnessing an 'end of history' in which liberalism, capitalism and democracy – the exact relations between which were not explained – have finally triumphed over all rivals.[1] This dangerously equates the mere breakdown of authoritarian regimes with the successful consolidation of democracies. This will not do. After all, there have been great waves of democracy in the past that have been followed by renewed bursts of authoritarian rule: thus the age of democratic revolutions was followed by Metternich's system of order, the birth of new national democracies after the Treaty of Versailles by the spread of fascism, and the confident belief of the first two decades of the *Pax Americana* that economic growth would ensure democracy by an insistence, at the time most convincing, that growth in developing countries depended upon 'bureaucratic-authoritarian' rule.[2] It would, however, be a mistake to

---

[1] F. Fukuyama, 'The End of History', *The National Interest*, vol. 16, 1989.
[2] Classic works on these oscillating moments include: R. R. Palmer, *The Age of the Democratic Revolution*, Princeton University Press, Princeton, 1959 and 1964; H. A. Kissinger, *A World Restored*, Houghton Mifflin, Boston, 1957; C. Maier, *Recasting Bourgeois Europe*, Princeton University Press, Princeton, 1975; J. J. Linz and A. Stepan, eds, *The Breakdown of Authoritarian Regimes*, Johns Hopkins University Press, Baltimore, 1978; S. M. Lipset, *Political Man*,

replace an optimistic evolutionary view with a cynical and pessimistic cyclical alternative. For the last two centuries *have* witnessed an increase, often interrupted and certainly slow, in the number of stable democracies.[3] So, this essay entertains a careful and limited optimism about the chances of consolidating some democratic openings, basing itself less on vague generalities than on historical specificities.

Some light can best be cast on what is a huge subject by beginning with three of the initial attempts, two successful and one failed, at consolidating democracy: this both allows clarification of what we characteristically mean by democracy and encourages an understanding of the support given to it by different social classes. This is followed by the listing of a set of abstract factors that enable democratic rule to be consolidated; it is important to note immediately that such factors (and the social configurations formed between them) so vary in salience over historical time as to rule out any simple model for consolidations of democracy. We shall offer instead a set of feasible possibilities for selected areas of the contemporary world.

A 'Loyal Opposition' and its Impact on Social Class

That we characteristically take democracy to mean more than rule by the people is easily demonstrated. No one can doubt but that the French Revolution placed democracy on the agenda of modern history. None the less, the bitter, no-holds-barred struggle for power among the revolutionaries points to the fact that democracy is normally held to depend upon the workings of settled institutions. What matters most of all is the creation of a loyal opposition, that is an opposition that refuses to entertain plans to change the political system and to exterminate its rivals – thus of course ensuring its own safety in the longer term.[4] Let

Doubleday, New York, 1960; G. O'Donnell, *Modernisation and Bureaucratic-Authoritarianism*, Institute of International Studies, Berkeley, 1973. For the most recent wave of democracy, see G. O'Donnell, P. Schmitter and L. Whitehead, eds, *Transitions from Authoritarian Rule*, Johns Hopkins University Press, Baltimore, 1986; D. Ethier, ed., *Democratic Transition and Consolidation in Southern Europe, Latin America and Southeast Asia*, Macmillan, London, 1990; S. P. Huntington, *The Third Wave*, University of Oklahoma Press, Norman, 1991.

[3] Figures on the matter are contained in R. Dahl, *Democracy and Its Critics*, Yale University Press, New Haven, 1989, ch. 17 and in Huntington, *The Third Wave*, ch. 1.

[4] I am influenced here by Barrington Moore, not least by an unpublished paper 'Notes and Queries on the Theory and Practice of Legitimate Opposition'.

me first describe the creation of this institution in Britain between 1675 and 1725 and in the United States between 1780 and 1840. Once that has been done, it will then be possible to see why this institution matters so very much.

During the reign of Charles II, most Englishmen had memories of civil war, regicide, treason, the political division of families, foreign interference and religious persecution. It is therefore remarkable that within half a century a form of political stability had been achieved within which opposing views and parties were tolerated. Most striking of all was the creation of the concept of a loyal opposition – a concept which in time led to state salaries for those who opposed what the party in power was trying to achieve![5] How was this transformation possible?[6]

Broadly speaking, the growth of a legitimate opposition went hand in hand with a loss of popular control: peace broke out within the elite because contestation was limited and tamed by the diminution of democracy. A myriad of policies and institutional changes support this claim. 'The rage of party' was severely curtailed both by raising the costs of elections and by the passing of the Septennial Act, making elections far less frequent than before; equally, the growth of a landed oligarchy meant that election expenses became bearable only by the very rich. Remarkably, participation in elections and levels of literacy fell in the century after the Restoration.[7]

The political elite also became more united and unified socially. The extreme Jacobites were excluded by use of treason acts. More importantly, a common identity of economic, political and social power was established by a marriage of interest: the land tax that hurt the Tories was diminished (not least because the Whigs became less belligerent), and they in turn accepted the entry of the City into the British power structure – with frequent nuptials acting as a cement to the union. What is noticeable is that every section of the political elite gained, especially since these were years of social development and economic growth in which politics was by no means the sole avenue to fame and fortune. Further, the effectiveness of the political system was enhanced by an increase in the power of the executive over the legislature, not least by the use of placemen, whose numbers rose dramatically in this period. Britain in this period, for all the

[5] A. S. Foord, *His Majesty's Opposition 1714–1830*, Oxford University Press, Oxford, 1964; G. Ionescu and I. de Madariaga, *Opposition*, Penguin, London, 1968.
[6] I rely heavily in the following paragraphs on J. H. Plumb, *The Growth of Political Stability in England 1675–1725*, Penguin, London, 1969.
[7] L. Stone, 'Literacy and Education in England, 1640–1900', *Past and Present*, no. 42, 1969.

acceptance of (non-Jacobite) opposition, came to be ruled by a single party – making it resemble, say, post 1945 – Japan rather than contemporary Britain.

Consideration of the creation of a party system in the early years of the United States, depended quite as much upon an extraordinarily favourable set of circumstances.[8] The early American leaders had sought, not least in *The Federalist Papers*, to create a world in which social harmony would reign: parties were seen as mere irresponsible factions. However, between 1794 and 1801 a peaceful transfer of power from Federalists to Jeffersonians took place, and it was not long before fully developed justifications for political parties were being produced. Again several factors stand at the back of this moderate course of political development. First, property was widely diffused, and levels of literacy were extremely high. One important corollary of this was again that politics was not all important: there were other avenues of social mobility, and anyone deprived of office was still able to prosper. Secondly, the elite had considerable training in politics. They had drawn up two constitutions, and was accordingly deeply versed in the languages of law and of rights. These were conservative men, not prone to sudden moves that would put the commonweal at risk; in effect, they felt themselves to be members of a single family.

Thirdly, the revolutionary process had not seen violence of the sort that characterized the French Revolution, and the resort to violence thereafter was not deemed natural. Moreover, the fact that the revolution had been made against the state meant that no standing army was available to suppress political rivals; and anyway this course of action was ruled out for the Federalists given that their opponents had a geographically cohesive power base in Virginia. The implicit self-denying ordinance here was much reinforced by the behaviour of the Founding Fathers. Most obviously, Washington chose to model himself after Cincinnatus – that is, he did not seek to capitalize on his military reputation, even though Hamilton had made him distrust Jefferson. But it was Hamilton who understood Jefferson's character. Jefferson was no radical: in power he effectively abandoned his own programme and adopted Hamilton's, taking care not to persecute any of his political rivals. In a nutshell, the founding moment of the new regime was one that set a powerful and beneficent precedent for subsequent politics. Finally, one should note that

---

[8]　M. Wallace, 'Changing Concepts of Party in the United States: New York, 1815–1828', *American Historical Review*, vol. 74, 1968; R. Hofstader, *The Idea of a Party System: the Rise of Legitimate Opposition in the United States, 1780–1840*, University of California Press, Berkeley, 1969.

in the crucial years in which power was transferred the United States was faced with no issues of any great import. Most obviously, no geopolitical pressures affected the United States, given that Europe was embroiled in the Napoleonic Wars.

What has been described to this point is the creation of political trust inside the elite. Contest was to be within bounds, and nothing was to be done what would disrupt a settled set of expectations. Opposition was allowed largely because those in power felt that it would not threaten their interests. It is important to emphasize again that the confidence of the powerful in this matter was enhanced by the fact that popular pressures did not present them with many problems – indeed, the British case sees a growth in political stability in part because of the exclusion of the people. The liberalization of politics had been achieved. This seems to me a historical achievement in its own right. What matters more generally, however, is the impact that institutionalizing a loyal opposition had on later democratization; of special importance in this connection is the manner in which early liberalism affects the character of social classes.

The United States tells us little about this because democratization followed so closely upon the acceptance of opposition. The fact that the people had fought for independence doomed oligarchy. Jackson placed popular politics firmly at the centre of the stage, and by the end of his presidency virtually all adult white males had the vote. In Britain, in contrast, the entry of the people onto the political stage was slow and tortured. The spread of civil society that accompanied the creation of a unique commercial society in eighteenth-century Britain served as a backdrop to the re-emergence of popular politics.[9] Popular pressures combined with divisions within the political elite to allow economical reform within the state in the wake of the loss of the first empire. Those pressures were sufficiently strong and autonomous to rule out any permanent move to reaction in response to the French Revolution. Instead a long process of franchise reform was instituted – through the process in Britain in 1914 left it less democratic in formal terms than Germany, its main geopolitical and economic rival. But this consideration should not hide the fact that German votes were of limited value: whereas Britain had full parliamentary control of expenditure, Germany most certainly did not, remaining at once politically authoritarian and socially mobilized. Much hangs upon this contrast.

[9]   G. Rude, *Wilkes and Liberty*, Oxford University Press, Oxford, 1964; J. Brewer, *Party Ideology and Popular Politics at the Accession of George III*, Cambridge University Press, Cambridge, 1976; E. A. Wrigley, *Continuity, Chance and Change*, Cambridge University Press, Cambridge, 1988.

The difference between the two cases can be understood in terms of the sequence of political development.[10] Where liberalism precedes democracy, democratization is likely to present no threat; in contrast, the entry of the people onto the political stage before the establishment of basic liberalism is likely to undermine chances for the successful consolidation of democratic regimes. The straightforward reason for this can be seen by considering the rise of labour, although the same principle applies quite generally to popular movements. Where a working-class was faced by a liberal state it tended to organize economically rather than politically; in contrast, illiberal states with anti-socialist and anti-union laws forced workers to become politically conscious. This principle helps us understand why there was no socialism in the United States and why Tsarist Russia produced a working-class that was not just politically conscious, like that of Imperial Germany, but genuinely revolutionary: in the former case citizenship had been achieved prior to industrialization, while in the latter the despotic and erratic policies of autocracy ruled out reformism.[11] The nature of the political regime affects the character of social movements in such a way as to produce vicious and beneficent cycles of political development. In Britain, a liberal state bred a moderate and reformist working-class movement – and in any case, the British middle classes never felt very threatened precisely because the franchise was not widespread. In Germany, an illiberal state produced a labour movement that sounded very threatening – a fact that was of great consequence given that there were few restrictions to male suffrage. Accordingly, the German middle classes endorsed reaction, first in the Wilhelmine period and then in Weimar, not, as with crucial sections of their British equivalents, lending their support to political reform.

These observations about the sequence of political developments are of such importance that they deserve emphasis. This can best be given by

[10]   R. Dahl, *Polyarchy*, Yale University Press, New Haven, 1971; Dahl first noted that early liberalization helped later democratization, and I am indebted to his work. None the less, the particular manner in which a liberal state determines the character of working class movements is not something that features in his account.

[11]   There is now a large literature on this point. See, *inter alia*: D. Geary, *European Labour Protest 1848–1945*, Methuen, London, 1984; R. McKibbin, *The Ideologies of Class*, Oxford University Press, Oxford, 1990; M. Mann, 'Ruling Class Strategies and Citizenship', *Sociology*, vol. 21, 1986; I. Katznelson and A. Zolberg, eds. *Working Class Formation*, Princeton University Press, Princeton, 1987; T. McDaniel, *Autocracy, Capitalism and Revolution in Russia*, University of California Press, Berkeley, 1988. For a more detailed argument of this general case, see ch. 2 of this book.

offering three reflections upon Barrington Moore's famous statement that there can be no democracy without a bourgeoisie.[12]

In so far as the bourgeoisie was opposed to the state, Moore's equation is very plausible: for democracy rests ultimately upon pluralism, that is upon a broad spread of negative resisting power. Certainly the popular pressures that helped make Britain liberal evolved naturally from commercial society. In this context, it is worth noting that it makes little sense to speak of a unitary bourgeoisie. The popular pressures that came to a head in the campaign for 'Wilkes and Liberty' were derived from the petty bourgeoisie, a class fragment that deserves a better press, certainly in contrast to large capitalists, than it has habitually received.[13] It is also important to be exact about the character of British liberalism. John Stuart Mill, to whose views about the 'rules of the game' we return later, typified liberal ideology: workers were to be given the vote provided they became literate and sober and accepted the laws of political economy. Further, if a liberal state offered workers the carrot of the right to organize, it also wielded a considerable stick against those who challenged the system radically: many of the leading Chartists were deported.[14] Nevertheless, the fact remains that this liberalism had a tremendous social impact. Workers who could organize struggled against their bosses rather than against the state; differently put, liberal society proved to be essentially stable since conflicts were diffused through civil society rather than concentrated against the regime.

But the critics of Moore's position are of course quite correct to say that the bourgeoisie has not always been the friend of liberty, as the behaviour of the German bourgeoisie in both Wilhelmine and Weimar Germany very clearly illustrates.[15] This bourgeoisie owed much of its existence to the state: the state had created the nation and aided industrialization and it thereafter served as the bulwark against genuinely radical pressures from below. This class was perfectly happy to live in an authoritarian *Rechtstaat*, in which nation and order had greater

---

[12] B. Moore, *Social Origins of Dictatorship and Democracy*, Beacon Press, Boston, 1966, ch. 7 and throughout.

[13] R. Hamilton, *Restraining Myths*, Sage, Beverley Hills, 1975; L. Weiss, *Creating Capitalism*, Basil Blackwell, Oxford, 1988.

[14] M. Mann, *Sources of Social Power*, vol. 2: *The Rise of Modern Nations and Classes, 1760–1914*, Cambridge University Press, Cambridge, 1993, ch. 15.

[15] The most sustained criticism has been offered by D. Rueschmeyer, E. Stephens and J. Stephens in *Capitalist Development and Democracy*, Polity Press, Cambridge, 1992. For a particularly striking study on Germany, see D. Blackbourn and G. Eley, *The Peculiarities of German History*, Oxford University Press, Oxford, 1984.

importance than political liberty. It would be mistaken, however, to argue that the German middle-class was inevitably illiberal. The regime played an active role in destroying liberalism through an active policy of 'divide and rule'. The state's creation of distrust between Catholic and Protestant middle-class parties weakened liberalism not just in the Wilhelmine period but in Weimar as well. In summary, the absence of liberalism owes much to interest but at least something to the strategy of the ruling elite.

Finally, critics of Moore are right to point out that the consolidation of democracy owes a good deal to a class that plays no significant role in his great *Social Origins of Dictatorship and Democracy*.[16] A priori considerations suggest that the working-class stands to benefit from democracy; comparative historical evidence demonstrates that working-class parties sought both to extend the franchise and to institutionalize social rights. None the less, this positive thesis cannot be accepted without qualification. If classes have interests, they also have, as we have seen, characteristic styles. When working-class parties adopted revolutionary rhetoric, they played some part in hindering the consolidation of democracy. Inasmuch as such rhetoric was, so to speak, thrust upon them by the way ruling elites treated them, it is almost unfair to blame working-class parties for this. But there were degrees of freedom at work in this whole area, and some blame can be attached to popular parties. Certainly the worst possible combination was the presence of a rhetoric that was not at all real, that is the striking of revolutionary attitudes by a party that was essentially reformist. The German Social Democrats exemplified this position, with catastrophic consequences in the Weimar years.

Enabling Factors, Past and Present

To turn from historical examples to a listing of analytic points is not as great a change as it might seem: just as analytic points were sought from history, so too must the analytic points be historically contextualized. This whole strategy of inquiry is, of course, heavily indebted to the pioneering work of Robert Dahl.[17] For one thing, these enabling factors are interlinked and mutually supporting, while not every case of successful consolidation has satisfied all of the enabling conditions. For another,

---

[16] Rueschmeyer, Stephens and Stephens, *Capitalist Development and Democracy*, throughout.
[17] Dahl, *Polyarchy*. His views are slightly revised and much extended in *Democracy and Its Critics*.

the openness of this set of factors leaves a great deal of room for the exercise of political skill and judgement. However, not all the factors taken to be important here are mentioned by Dahl; equally the logic of justification is often not the same for those factors he did consider.

(1) **Sequence** This factor has already been elucidated at length, and in more detailed terms than those used by Dahl himself. The main virtue of having liberalism before democratization is that it encourages moderation on behalf of those entering the political stage. This ensures that the traditional elite are not so threatened that they choose to resist democratization. Reassurance for those in power is absolutely necessary if political modernization is to take place at all: Latin American experience suggests that liberalizations from below tend to fail – in contrast to those initiated from above in which guarantees are secured for the members of the old regime.[18]

There are cases in the contemporary world that have benefited from this sequence. Hungary allowed a considerable measure of opposition before the introduction of open political competition, something that was facilitated by the political elite having realized early on that money making was a better avenue to social mobility than the mere possession of power.[19] Brazil's whole pattern of development distinguishes it from Argentina at this point.[20] One notes, further, the relatively controlled process of decompression in South Korea and Taiwan. None the less, so much attention was given to this factor for a negative reason: this beneficent sequence is not now generally available. Plans to curtail the franchise are now politically incorrect, which is not to deny that manipulation of electoral rules and vote-rigging still takes place. Still, there is great pressure to move towards democracy rather than to settle with mere liberalization. This means that contemporary consolidations of democracy are different from those in the past. They are likely to be more difficult. It is hard to establish rules to regulate conflict and at the same moment to open political space to actors likely to have been radicalized by political exclusion. The pessimism generated by this consideration is, however, offset by other factors that happily gain in power in contemporary circumstances.

[18] T. Karl, 'Dilemmas of Democratisation in Latin America', *Comparative Politics*, vol. 22, 1990.

[19] E. Hankiss, *East European Alternatives*, Oxford University Press, Oxford, 1990.

[20] J. Merquior, 'Patterns of State-building in Brazil and Argentina', in J. A. Hall, ed., *States in History*, Basil Blackwell, Oxford, 1986.

(2) **Property** The greater the concentration of property, the less likely it is that democratic rule will be consolidated. Fundamental land reform and attacks on excessive concentration of industry are necessary conditions for democracy.

In agrarian circumstances, free farmers – in New Zealand, Australia and the west of the nineteenth-century United States – have formed the underpinnings of democratic regimes. Much the same is true of the Swedish peasantry, habitually a fourth estate and possessed of considerable independence. In contrast, concentration of landholding, whether in pre-socialist Eastern Europe or in Latin America, is, with one exception, inimical to democracy. The single exception in question refers to the commercially minded landed aristocracy of eighteenth-century Britain. Where most landed elites needed the state to repress labour, the British elite, partly because of an initial concentration on agricultural products not requiring large inputs of labour, was content to survive in the market place, relatively free from and occasionally resistant to the state.[21]

In industrial circumstances, a broad spread of property holding is likely to provide support for democracy, while concentration in property is likely to be hostile to it. We have seen that, whereas popular pressures for reform in eighteenth-century England arose naturally from a civil society strengthened by the spread of commerce, forced and state-led economic development in Wilhelmine Germany created an important segment of large capitalists suspicious of democracy. In the contemporary world, the extraordinary inequalities of Latin America still remain a fundamental obstacle to successful democratization. Further, one fears that the increasing concentration of industrial power in South Korea may limit the chances for democratization: the leaders of the *chaebol* seem prone not to accept new union rights, not surprisingly given that they prospered so strikingly when labour was controlled by the state. In contrast, the diversification of economic activities within Taiwan is a positive factor that may allow further democratization.[22]

---

[21]   The importance of commercial agriculture is at the centre of Moore, *Social Origins of Dictatorship and Democracy*; the points about small farmers are taken from Dahl, *Polyarchy* and Rueschmeyer, Stephens and Stephens, *Capitalist Development and Democracy*.

[22]   A. Amsden, *Asia's Next Giant*, Oxford University Press, New York, 1990; R. Wade, *Governing the Market*, Princeton University Press, Princeton, 1991. J. J. Choi, 'Transitions of Democracy in East Asia: South Korea and Taiwan in Comparison', unpublished paper, 1992, presents an alternative view. A measure of division within the traditional elite in South Korea, with industrialists

We cannot leave this factor at this point. For what is property? During much of history property is indeed something material and physical. But this may no longer be so. Late-industrial society seems ever more to depend upon the skills of educated labour. This class fragment often depends upon freedom of information and movement, and tends to place technicism above integrating ideologies.[23] It is thus a resource for democratization, as social movements from Rio to Seoul and from Peking to Prague so clearly show. The pressures applied by educated labour are likely to be greatest, it should be noted, where it feels that its way of life is limited or blocked by the regime it faces, as was true for many socialist societies in Eastern European, most notably in the former Czechoslovakia. But even the economic success of South Korea is not such as to control anger on the part of educated labour, particularly about civil rights, education and housing conditions. But pressure from below is only one side of the equation: elites at times seek to placate educated labour in the hope that ensuing economic growth will help them in the struggle for power. In summary, a third stage in the industrial era is identifiable that is less favourable to state planning and the concentration of property than the second stage, whether conducted under capitalist or socialist aegis. So the logic of late-industrial society may favour democracy, so that there may again be something to Adam Smith's equation of 'commerce and liberty'.[24]

(3) **State** Dahl is percipient on this factor, and two comments merely echo his. Most obviously, a transition from authoritarian rule will be extremely difficult if a state has at its command powerful forces for repression capable of destroying dissent – as seems to be the case with Saddam Hussein since the Gulf War. Very few regimes have fallen when backed up by a bureaucratized army, something that sultan-like rulers akin to Somoza and Ceausescu learn to their cost.[25] As

---

becoming bitterly opposed to the economic policies of military/statist leaders, may eventually, in Choi's opinion, help consolidate democracy; in contrast, the very diversification of Taiwanese economic life may mean that the state has no single opponent able to force it far down the democratic road.

[23] E. A. Gellner, 'Plaidoyer pour une libéralisation manquée', *Government and Opposition*, vol. 14, 1979.

[24] Cf. S. Rytina, 'Under What Circumstances did a Plutocratic Elite Support Civil Liberties?', paper given at McGill University, 1991.

[25] J. Goodwin, 'States and Revolution in the Third World', PhD dissertation, Harvard University, 1988.

important, however, is the situation of the armed forces within a political elite. When their position is central, democratization can only proceed if sufficient guarantees are given to ensure that they will stay in their barracks. Latin Americans know that when the tiger is in the cage it remains important to remember that he has his own key. Further, where repressive atrocities have been committed by the armed forces, democratization is less likely because the requisite social patience is very unlikely to be present in sufficient quantities.

More generally, it should be remembered that a democratic regime is one in which state and society cooperate. It may well be necessary to break with venal and unwieldy state apparatuses, at once large and lacking in any real capacity to organize society. In the long run, however, the health of a country depends upon the presence of a relatively lean state, able to penetrate society because its citizens trust it – essentially because they know they have the capacity to correct its abuses. All this can be put in different terms. Those who have suffered from despotic regimes, especially those who experienced communism, occasionally dream of abolishing the state. But anarchy is as permanent a danger as despotism. What is required is the creation of a new type of state, simultaneously organic and constitutional rather than predatory and despotic.

(4) **International** The impact of international forces has not received sufficient attention from those concerned with problems of transition.[26] This is strange given the conspicuous importance of this factor. Germany and Japan became secure democracies in very large part at the hands of the Allies, while the defeat of the Axis powers allowed for the restoration of democracies throughout Europe. As manifestly obvious, surely, is the fact that the withdrawal of the Russian card made political change possible in Eastern Europe. Czechoslovakia was probably as ready to make a transition to democracy in 1948 as it is today: its fate has depended entirely upon the wishes of its neighbour.

Several facets of the contemporary international order favour consolidations of democracy. Perhaps most important is the historic defeat of the two great revolutions of the twentieth century: communism and fascism are no longer transnational movements capable of serving as

---

[26]   L. Whitehead, 'International Aspects of Democratisation', in G. O'Donnell, P. Schmitter and L. Whitehead, eds, *Transitions from Authoritarian Rule*, Johns Hopkins University Press, Baltimore, 1986. A forthcoming book by Diane Ethier will concentrate on the international factor.

models of development. Both were beaten in war, one dramatically, the other in a protracted but finally decisive conflict. An important point about these models is that they no longer offer much in times of peace: their emphasis on autarchy and protectionism, so characteristic of the second industrial era, reduces the living standards of their citizens. It is important to note too that there has been something of a historic change on the part of international lending agencies. Such institutions were once prone to believe that authoritarianism was a necessary price to be paid for economic growth. The evidence of many decades, demonstrating quite clearly that authoritarian regimes are often utterly feckless, has been absorbed: dictatorships are no longer automatically supported, while far greater understanding is now being shown to nascent democracies.[27]

If much of this says there is no obvious alternative, it remains important to point to factors that make contemporary consolidations of democracy extremely difficult. Most obviously, economic liberalization – the removal of subsidies, increasing privatization, ending protectionism – imposes pain and social strain. The earliest consolidations of democracy benefited from a vibrant economy capable of offering avenues of social mobility alternative to the political; if in the long run democratization does not bring at least some measure of economic success, it may well be doomed. Furthermore, it is worth remembering that the international economic order is still dominated by the United States. That predatory hegemon tends, largely for internal reasons, not to place the well-being of its greedy consumers above even its own geopolitical interests, let alone the welfare of other states. Latin American democratization depends upon the continent's ability to pay its debts, and this in turn depends upon access to open markets. Similarly, the fate of East and Central Europe may depend upon access to capital. Unfortunately, it is possible that the United States will continue to absorb, largely as a form of military rent, the world's excess capital.[28] As important for Eastern Europe is the protectionism of the European Community.

(5) **Attitudes** The necessary attitudes for a successful transition to democracy have already been identified, above all the determination not to take conflict too far and to live within a set of rules of the game.

---

27 K. Remmer, 'Democracy and Economic Crisis', *World Politics*, vol. 13, 1990.
28 For fuller justification of this point, see ch. 7.

Pacts that guarantee in advance that critical interests will not be over-thrown by political reform are accordingly of great importance.

This is a good moment to digress, so as to give an example of the openness inherent in democratization. In democratization there is everything to be said for the maxim that one should not offend one's enemies when they have power, but should be ruthless to them when they are weak. Pacts have prices attached to them – they tend to alienate the people, who are well aware that agreements are being made among the political elite behind their backs – and are best avoided when possible. If marked social inequalities necessitate pact making in Latin America, the absolute defeat of communist parties in socialist states makes it possible and wise to cleanse the bureaucratic and state apparatus of potential enemies, although care must be taken not to harm newly founded legality by arbitrary and personalized vendettas.

There are two reasons for believing that contemporary attitudes favour consolidations of democracy, both unfortunately of a rather negative character. First, no alternative models of political economy are available to help mobilize those who suffer either from expro-priation or from structural economic change. Secondly, the decisive failure of statist economic models, whether capitalist or socialist in character, together with the obvious wealth of liberal democracies, has encouraged a general belief that democracy will allow and encourage economic growth. Obviously some economic growth is necessary within a measurable time frame if such attitudes are to be maintained.

(6) **Civil Society** There is no more important topic in contemporary social and political life than the character and chances of civil society. But the concept itself is rather vague, however negatively easy it is to recognize societies that do not have it, so it is necessary to add to the classic definition of civil society – that is the notion that civil society is the presence of strong and autonomous social groups, able to balance excessive concentrations of power.[29]

A moment's thought makes it clear that this cannot be quite right. A social order in which organized groups refuse to cooperate in a common enterprise is unlikely to consolidate democracy and may indeed be doomed to failure.[30] Civil society properly understood

---

[29]   For a complete analysis, see J. A. Hall, ed., *Civil Society: Theory, History, Comparison*, Polity Press, Cambridge, forthcoming 1994.

[30]   E. A. Gellner, 'The Importance of Being Modular', in Hall, *Civil Society*.

should, accordingly, include notions of cooperation, that is of groups working both together and with a responsive state. The strength of Spanish civil society was seen in the ability of the leaders of popular movements to organize and to control their forces, thus ensuring both orderly decompression and the consolidation of democracy. In contrast, the utter destruction of civil society by state socialism made liberalization impossible; it further entails a dreadful vacuum in post-communism, which remains a threat to the consolidation of democracy. The Latin American situation stands interestingly between these two types. Civil society is present, but it is still weak: the independent unions of north-west Europe stand in marked contrast with the clientelist unions of the Southern Cone of Latin America,[31] while the creation of strong political parties is very much a task for the future.[32] On some occasions popular leaders have been strong enough to make pacts and fill political space; their inability to control their own forces on other occasions has led to the abrupt ending of attempts to open the political system.

It is also important to stress that the notion of civil society does and should retain connotations of civility. One way of expressing the matter firmly is to insist that there is no link between civic virtue and civil society, despite the popularity of both notions in a single audience. The former tradition surfaced in Rousseau and fed through to the French Revolution: it distrusted secondary organizations and sought to make human beings unitary. Civil society represents the exact opposite: it endorses social diversity, together with a different view of the self.[33] It is well worth noting that the culture of civil society – in essence, that is, the requisite attitudes already discussed – is often less the cause than the consequence of political openings. So civil society can be seen as the result of groups choosing to live together when their attempts at domination have failed. The idea of toleration developed from the power stand-off in Europe at the end of the era of religious wars; stalemates in the contemporary world may similarly lead to further increases in civility.

(7) **Single Culture** This factor is so obvious that it needs little commentary.[34] We have already seen that the absence of a single culture in

---

[31] N. Mouzelis, *Politics in the Semi-periphery*, Macmillan, London, 1986.
[32] F. Hagopian, 'Post-authoritarian Latin America: State Retreat and Political Reorganisation', paper given at McGill University, 1991.
[33] J. A. Hall, 'Sincerity and Politics', *Sociological Review*, vol. 25, 1977.
[34] A full consideration of this factor is, however, given in ch. 6.

Wilhelmine Germany made it possible for Bismarck so successfully to prevent the emergence of liberal democracy. Beyond that, one is tempted to say: *remember* Yugoslavia! More particularly, one can predict that newly independent Slovenia, blessed with an homogeneous population, is more likely to consolidate its democracy than newly independent Croatia. This principle is all too easy to apply to other cases, perhaps especially to many of the former republics of the Soviet Union.

(8) **Memory** The importance of this factor is especially obvious in contemporary Eastern Europe. Existentialists have argued convincingly that it is impossible to live in a void, bereft of identity, with everything always open to question. The collapse of socialist ideas and institutions means that memories of the past are of the greatest importance. Where some are blessed, others are cursed. The Czech Republic has clear memories of industry and of the beginnings of a functioning liberal democracy; in addition, the situation of Bohemia within Austria-Hungary represents a long tradition of constitutional politics. Romanians, Bulgarians and Albanians have nothing like this to remember; the absence of a model may well prove to be of the greatest importance.

Other memories can be as important, not least because they help create attitudes that favour consolidations of democracy. Memories of disasters – a Revolt of the Asturias, an invasion by Russian tanks in 1956 or 1968, a Kwangju Incident or a Tiananmen Square – can both fundamentally de-legitimize a regime and so discipline the people as to make them able to find a different way. Founding moments are equally important. When 'history is on the move' one has the sensation of events speeding up, and of crucial decisions coming to the fore. The decisions taken in such open moments become codified and pattern later events. One example of this, the beneficial consequences of Washington's decision not to make use of his military reputation, has already been noted.

The Chances for Consolidating Democracy

The pay off for the discussion so far is simple and to the point. What are the different chances for consolidating democracy within the main areas in which it is now being attempted? It would be idle to pretend that this author knows every region – let alone all countries within them – equally well; but some points do seem clear, and an attempt at general explanation may concentrate attention more generally.

A genuinely consolidated democracy is perhaps best judged to be one in which the alternation of parties in power is regular and accepted.[35] By this standard, the consolidation of democracy in Southern Europe is complete. Let me concentrate on the Spanish case.[36] Here there was a mass of favourable factors: the desire to enter the European Community, self-discipline going back to memories of the Revolt of the Asturias, the slow withdrawal of the military from political life, superlative political skill during the founding moments and the presence of popular leaders committed to dialogue and able to control their forces – especially, perhaps, socialist and communist leaders chary of any social experiments that would create resistance. Spain benefited, moreover, from having a notably courageous monarch, who played an important role in helping to crush one attempted *coup d'état*. But not everything in the Spanish situation was favourable: the presence of regional nationalisms highly resistant to the centre presented considerable problems. The difficulties of dealing with the Basques and, to a lesser degree, the Catalans were severe – even including the assassination of one prime minister at a crucial point in the transition to democracy. That these difficulties were overcome is testimony to the force of the positive enabling factors.

The situation of most Latin American countries is by no means so rosy. Let me begin by noting that classic patterns of social formation, well illustrated in Argentina and Brazil, have always seemed likely to lead to different chances for consolidation of democracy within the region. Early democracy in Argentina made it much harder for any process of liberalization to be controlled in such a way that the powerful would not be so threatened as to strike back; populism equally encouraged economic policies which were so catastrophic that they took Argentina out of the list of the top economic powers.[37] Additional negative factors include the presence of the military, an international situation hurting the economy through debt repayment, and the lack of genuine autonomy in the organization of the main civil society groups. Brazilian liberalization is, in contrast, a more top–down affair, and to that extent has

[35] R. Dahrendorf, *Reflections on the Revolution in Europe*, Times Books, New York, 1990.
[36] J. Maravall, *The Transition to Democracy in Spain*, St Martin's Press, New York, 1982.
[37] C. Waisman, *Reversal of Development in Argentina*, Princeton University Press, Princeton, 1987.

slightly greater hopes for success.[38] Against that must be set, however, the fact that Brazilian civil society is even less developed than that of Argentina, being largely confined to the coastal strip that is tied to the world economy.

We can gain some understanding of the most recent developments in Latin America by turning to Mexico, whose turn away from protected import-substitution-industrialization is of great moment.[39] The state's retreat from the complete control and management of its economy seems, however, not to have been followed by political reorganization. On the contrary, between 1988 and 1991 the governing party improved its position in regional elections; Mexico looks set, in other words, to remain a single-party state. Furthermore, the opening to the world market and the selling of state industries was made possible only by the use of pork-barrel politics routed through traditional clientelist networks. Traditional levers of power seem as present in contemporary Argentina and Brazil, both of which seek to imitate Mexico's new developmental model. Such developmental changes as there have been in those countries, notably the emergence of regional caudillos in Brazil, do not augur well for democracy. What continues to be sadly lacking throughout Latin America is a strong civil society, armed with its own developed political parties, that is truly independent of and so made capable of influencing the state. All three countries touched on here currently suffer from falling living standards, very great and continuing inequality and the absence of fundamental land reform. One can hope that a swing back to authoritarian rule will not again take place in Latin America; but this hope is not at all well grounded in beneficent social trends.

Development in East Asia is now well enough known for it to be contrasted graphically with that attempted in Latin America.[40] The political economy of this region has benefited from fundamental land reform,

---

[38]   This point has been challenged by F. Hagopian, 'Democracy by Undemocratic Means?', *Comparative Political Studies*, vol. 23, 1990. Some pacts have been so cosy and exclusionary, in Hagopian's view, that they have diminished trust, thereby hindering the consolidation of democracy. I take her argument as a criticism of the abuse of pacts, rather than a dismissal of them. Pacts may make sense, in other words, only when there are several parties to them.

[39]   F. Hagopian, 'Post-authoritarian Latin America'.

[40]   P. Evans, 'Class, State and Dependence in East Asia: Lessons for Latin Americanists', in F. C. Deyo, ed., *The Political Economy of the New Asian Industrialism*, Cornell University Press, Ithaca, 1987; B. Cumings, 'The Abortive Abertura: South Korea in the Light of Latin American Experience', *New Left Review*, no. 173, 1989.

and this gave the state considerable autonomy, as did an abundance of 'geopolitical capital', to plan economic development; that autonomy was, in addition, used extremely intelligently – protection to infant industries was not long lasting, the emphasis being on export-led development rather than on mere import substitution.[41] Such development occurred in regimes that were highly repressive, and bereft of traditions of civil society. None the less, the chances that political developments in this region will be sustained seem to me better than they are in Latin America. Here liberalization can precede democratization, the latter taking place in conditions of relative economic success rather than, as in Latin America and post-communist societies, in the midst of massive unemployment caused by total structural adjustment.

Korean chances of further political development are improving rapidly. There has been long-term pressure from educated labour, but that has been markedly countered by extreme concentration of property in the *chaebol*. International politics occasioned and underwrote military repression, but the possibility of reunification is the pivotal development that may have positive consequences. In a united country it will become impossible to label a reforming party disloyal, and thereby to ignore it. What seems most likely in the short run is a move towards a Japanese-type situation in which opposition is allowed, but in which a single party always wins elections: despite the presence of elections, I consider this a grand liberalization rather than a full consolidation of democracy. For these developments to become more secure, greater inclusion of political opponents will prove necessary, as will the creation of a new system of labour relations.

In contrast, Taiwan's move towards democracy, which seemed so secure (based as it was on a much more diversified society) is beginning to face problems. The nationalist party, which seeks to break the connection with the mainland, is coming to be classified as a disloyal opposition. As democracy can only work in the absence of visceral conflict, as the disagreements it can handle must be manageable within shared understandings, the political future in Taiwan is no longer completely bright.

Consideration of former communist societies must begin by noting that their situation is, within the context of this chapter, radically idiosyncratic. The attempt to make a complete and linked transition from authoritarianism to democracy proved to be impossible. Civil society had been so destroyed in this world that a reforming elite could find

[41]   Deyo, *The Political Economy of the New Asian Industrialism*. Cf. the argument of ch.4 in this volume.

no partner with which to make pacts, so as to conduct a controlled decompression of political life.[42] In consequence, the name of the game in this part of the world is now democratization rather than liberalization. Further, these societies are attempting an extraordinary double and simultaneous transition to democracy and capitalism. Many scholars suggest that the reform plans of most elites are likely to be watered down if not actually thwarted by instant democratic pressures: it is hard to see how economic liberalization can be achieved without the defeat of some large-scale strikes in the heartlands of heavy industry due to be destroyed by the introduction of the market.[43] It is with this factor in mind that it has been suggested that the East will come to resemble the South, that it is likely to follow the Latin American pattern – which was in the interwar period, by and large, its own – of dependent capitalism in combination with polities oscillating between democracy and authoritarianism.[44] When one adds to this the realization that many former communist societies are involved in basic nation building, that they are engaged in a nothing less than a triple transition to modernity, the idea of successfully consolidating democracy comes to seem counter-intuitive.[45]

Not all the legacies of communism are so unfortunate, and to that extent the pessimism so far identified may be overdone. Most immediately, depoliticization has resulted from an absolute disenchantment with the past, leaving a good deal of steering room for elites to push through economic reforms. Further, there may be little to fear from movements from below:

> . . . it also follows that it is entirely possible to have pluralism and a wide variety of small groups competing for influence without ever pulling large numbers of people into political life . . . if states remain strictly liberal and do not grant organizational advantages to large groups, it may well be

---

[42]   This argument is made in more detail in ch. 3.

[43]   The most sustained analysis is that of A. Przeworski, *Democracy and the Market: Political and Economic Reforms in Eastern Europe and Latin America*, Cambridge University Press, Cambridge, 1991, but see too J. Elster, 'When Communism Dissolves', *London Review of Books*, 24 January, 1990 and C. Offe, 'Capitalism by Democratic Design? Democratic Theory Facing the Triple Transition in East Central Europe', *Social Research*, vol. 58, 1991.

[44]   A. Przeworski, 'The 'East' Becomes the 'South'?', *Political Science and Politics*, vol. 24, 1991 and *Democracy and the Market*. Cf. B. Misztal, 'Must Eastern Europe Follow the Latin American Way?', *European Journal of Sociology*, vol. 33, 1992.

[45]   Offe, 'Capitalism by Democratic Design?'

possible to maintain pluralism without extensive mass involvement. If, for example, workers are free not to join unions, many will simply not join.[46]

The sequence giving liberalism before democracy may be best, especially if it is part of a package that includes a successful economy, but liberalism by itself may depoliticize and so continue that weird vacuum of post-communism that leaves the state sufficient autonomy to press on with reforms. Further, post-communist societies have no equivalent of Latin America's intact and powerful landed elite. Socialist revolution destroyed the landed elite, while those *nomenklatura* which did not enter business are now very clearly defeated – except, of course, those who have retained power by changing their colours, that is by moving from communism to nationalism. All in all, the amount of resistance from within the elite to radical change is in historical terms rather low. In addition, at least at present, democracy is associated with wealth: the dislike of state intervention of any sort among leading sectors of public opinion is at times disconcerting. Most important of all, however, is something that has nothing to do with the legacy of communism, namely geography. Many East and Central European states are extremely happy to have policies directed by experts associated with the European Community. The desire to return to Europe means that there is considerable resistance to the reintroduction of authoritarianism.

If these factors lend advantage, it remains important to stress that depoliticization is not at all the same thing as the consolidation of democracy. Most obviously, the absence of faith in a regime can lead at any time to the emergence of symbolic politics, and in particular to trust in one's ethnic group. This situation is most likely to block moves to democracy in most of the former Soviet Union given the large number of ethnic Russians resident in the former peripheral republics.

More generally, a country is strong only when an orderly civil society works with its state. At present, most states in former communist societies may have autonomy but this scarcely makes up for the absence of linkages with society. This is particularly true of privatization. It is mistaken to say that the old *nomenklatura* have the choice of becoming nationalists or of entering the market. There is a third option: such actors can benefit from privatization whilst retaining links with the state. This situation of continuity with the past, of privatization without marketization, of a class dependent on the state, is extremely

---

[46] E. Comisso, 'Property Rights, Liberalism, and the Transition from 'Actually Existing Socialism'', *East European Politics and Society*, vol. 5, 1991, pp.185, 187.

dangerous.[47] Such political capitalists may not be efficient, while their skimming off of profitable sectors will subject the state to an intolerable fiscal crisis if greater subsidies are required to support the remaining industry; both processes may give capitalism a bad name and so encourage both cynicism and rage. All this deserves summary. Continued atomization means that the political deficit will not be overcome. Democracy depends upon the restoration of trust, between the state and society quite as much as within the elite itself.

Beyond these general considerations is great diversity. At worst, Tocqueville's great fear – that the legacy of despotism will be continuing atomization consequent on hatreds created by divide-and-rule politics – may prove to be prescient. If so, we may be faced with this scenario:

> The segregation of the classes, which was the crime of the late monarchy, became at a late stage a justification for it, since when the wealthy and enlightened elements of a population were no longer able to act in concert and to take part in the government, the country became, to all intents and purposes, incapable of administering itself and it was needful that a master should step in.[48]

Any reversion to authoritarianism is likely to be married to nationalism, whose future role can scarcely be exaggerated. Further, it is very likely that different forms of corporatism – 'societal' ones including workers, 'statist' ones closest to new capitalists – will emerge in the region, given that this form has the capacity to manage crisis.[49] Only a few states are likely to make a full transition to recognizably Western politics. The countries of the Vysehrad Triangle are obviously best favoured: they have some memory of oppositional politics from Austria-Hungary, suffer least from symbolic politics, broke clearly with communism, are beginning to gain stable political parties, are likely to draw most investment and may gain access to the European Community. Success is of course not guaranteed: nationalist sentiments may still cost Hungary dear, although they have probably ensured Czech success (against the background of Slovak backwardness); the European Community may seek to deepen rather than to broaden; and reversion to the inter-war

---

[47]　J. Staniszkis, *The Dynamics of the Breakthrough in Eastern Europe*, University of California Press, Berkeley, 1991, part 1.

[48]　A. de Tocqueville, *The Old Regime and the French Revolution*, trans. S. Gilbert, Anchor Books, New York, 1955, p. 107.

[49]　J. Staniszkis, 'Contribution to the Analysis of the Corporative State Emerging in Poland', *Politicus*, 1992. Cf. C. Maier, *Recasting Bourgeois Europe*, Princeton University Press, Princeton, 1990.

situation of geopolitically non-viable states threatened on both sides is a distinct possibility. Slovenia may draw close to Austria and the Baltic states to Scandinavia, thereby ensuring successful consolidations of democracy. In contrast, it is hard not to be more and more pessimistic the farther one looks towards the East. It is unlikely that the role of the state will diminish in Romania and Bulgaria, while the situation in Russia is hugely threatening.

Much has recently been made of democratization spreading in other areas of the world, and a few comments are in order. China's attempt to fuse authoritarianism with the market are unlikely to prove success-ful in the long run, although it is important to note that most business-men currently depend upon the state rather than upon autonomous civil society, not just for their existence but also for their profits.[50] General reasoning would suggest that democratization has the best chance of success after greater development and an increased softening or liberal-izing of a regime. It is worth stressing that the presence of perestroika before glasnost makes this chance more genuine than it has been in other socialist societies. But change in China is some way away, and any guess at its form is unlikely to be high-powered. Harsher views are suggested by experience elsewhere.

Indian democracy seems threatened by the revival of regional and religious sectarianism – which is not to say that a turn towards author-itarianism would in fact help its economic development. The revolt against authoritarian rule in Africa is of course profoundly to be welcomed. But there remains a world of difference between the breakdown of authoritar-ian rule and consolidations of democracy. The structural problems that most African societies still face – tribalism, underdevelopment and over-mighty armed forces – are such that one must doubt whether any of the transitions from authoritarian rule will be successfully completed.

Finally, it is vital to note that the current wave of enthusiasm for democracy has not swept over every part of the world. Islam's purita-nical style, so clearly on the ascendant in the contemporary world, does represent a societal model in its own right, and it is one that clearly opposes democracy. That an opposition must be loyal for democracy to work was powerfully apparent in the recent Algerian elections: had the Islamic party come to power, democracy would have been destroyed, just as it has been in any case.

---

[50] D. Wank, 'Entrepreneurship, Social Structure and Politics in Post-Mao China', PhD dissertation, Harvard University, 1993.

Conclusion

The starting point of this chapter was Fukuyama's claim that the triumphs of liberalism, capitalism and democracy have ended history. The arguments advanced here can usefully be seen, to begin with, as specifying (as Fukuyama did not) some of the relations between liberalism, capitalism and democracy. Liberalism is certainly part of what we customarily mean by democracy, and its early advent massively helped consolidate democracy by domesticating demands that came from below. Early liberalism was itself largely the product of the first commercial society, and to that extent capitalism played some part in the consolidation of democracy. Equally, the fact that late-industrial capitalist society bases itself less on state central planning than on information may favour consolidations of democracy, especially if political leaders understand and act upon the 'logic' of industrial development. More generally, however, it is worth noting that every contemporary democratic society is capitalist. There is something in Weber's view that capitalism, by distinguishing economic from political power, is a needed base condition for democracy.[51] All this underlies the claim made here that the acceptance of capitalism is one of the rules of the game that allow democracy to function.

But it is important to draw some distinctions about this point. During the period of transition from authoritarian rule, there is a great deal to be said for the making of pacts that so reassure the powerful that they need not oppose political development. However, in the long run democracy must involve some uncertainty about outcomes. If the rules of the game include acceptance of the market principle, they do not, in the long run, necessitate acceptance of any particular division of property. A fuller consideration of John Stuart Mill lends support to this point. Mill was entirely consistent in seeking to have conflict and change within certain accepted rules of the game. But if the laws of political economy had to be accepted, there remained much room for schemes of improvement that would raise the conditions of workers so dramatically that the distribution of property and income would be revolutionized.

What is at issue can be put in different terms. Capital should not be allowed to rest on some putative absolute rights; it needs instead constantly to justify its existence by efficient performance. As it happens, there are good reasons for believing that social democracy is both a

---

[51]   M. Weber, 'Socialism', in W.G. Runciman, ed., *Weber: Selections in Translation*, Cambridge University Press, Cambridge, 1978.

just and an efficient option for a nation state within capitalist society. To note that we have options, that others would dispute the preference noted, is of course to refute Fukuyama. Just as the ending of the Cold War has unfrozen history, so too do consolidations of democracy open up rather than close down historical possibilities.

6

NATIONALISMS, CLASSIFIED AND EXPLAINED

Understanding nationalism is so obviously an urgent necessity that there is much to be said for the provision of a clearly delineated overview of the state of play among theorists of the subject.[1] What exactly do we know about a force whose impact on this century has been, against the expectations of mainstream social theory, greater than any other?

My overview will be active rather than passive. The use of the plural in the chapter title gives away one central claim: no single, universal theory of nationalism is possible. As the historical record is diverse so too must be our concepts. This is not, it should be stressed, to suggest a move from universalism to complete particularism, from a general theory to national histories. On the contrary, middle ground can be cultivated by delineating various ideal types of nationalism: each has a characteristic logic and social underpinning highlighted by a name, an exemplar and, somewhat loosely, a characteristic theorist.[2] But I move

---

[1] An earlier version of this paper was given at a conference on 'Theories of Nationalism' organized by the Central European University in Prague. I am indebted to comments received and arguments made there, and in particular to N. Stargardt, S. Graubard, H. Meadwell, W. Wesolowski and, as always, M. Mann.

[2] The typology offered here incorporates and adds to that in P. Alter's fine but insufficiently known *Nationalism*, Edward Arnold, London, 1990. My argument as a whole resembles that of W. Mommsen, 'The Varieties of the Nation State in

beyond classification to explanation: a second claim is that the patterning underlying different types is political rather than social.

The sort of analysis required is similar to that which now characterizes the study of economic development. Most obviously, it has come to be widely recognized that there are different routes by means of which economic development can be achieved.[3] The initial path may not have been captured by Max Weber, but there is everything to be said for his insistence that it was original, in the sense that it was unconscious and unplanned. In contrast, all other forms of economic development have been imitative, seeking to copy something whose dimensions were broadly known. Such secondary imitation may, as in East Asia, benefit from qualities entirely different from those needed for invention: conformity may now matter more, for example, than rampant individualism.[4] Further, we now also appreciate that late development is far from a unitary affair. The heavy industrialization of late nineteenth-century imitators – turned, via Lenin's admiration for the German war economy, into the general model of state socialism – seems to be markedly ineffective once the age of national mercantilism is replaced by an interdependent world economy, genuinely based on an international division of labour. We shall see that nationalism faces historical stages, albeit not to quite the same extent as does economic development.

But it is important to stress a further analogy. The character of the stages of economic development are affected by history in an entirely different sense, that is in terms of idiosyncrasy or accident. More particularly, the modern world political economy has been and continues to be deeply affected by the political style of the United States.[5] Similarly, some types of nationalism have been affected by particular historical combinations of analytic factors, whose conjunction may not recur.

Modern History: Liberal, Imperialist, Fascist and Contemporary Notions of Nation and Nationality', in M. Mann, ed., *The Rise and Decline of the Nation State*, Basil Blackwell, Oxford, 1990. The looseness in question comes from citing some theorists in connection with a single type of nationalism when in fact their approach considers varied nationalisms. Injustices at this point are corrected in the course of this chapter.

[3] For a justification of this view, see ch. 4.

[4] N. Abercrombie, S. Hill and B. Turner, *Sovereign Individuals of Capitalism*, Allen & Unwin, London, 1988.

[5] This is a point made on many occasions, and with ever greater force, by S. Strange. See particularly 'The Persistent Myth of Lost Hegemony', *International Organisation*, vol. 41, 1987.

Nationalism Defined, its Modernity Emphasized

Just as differences in routes need not entail the absence of a singular sense of economic development, so too the variety of nationalisms does not rule out a unitary definition. Nationalism is considered here very convention-ally.[6] It is the belief in the primacy of a particular nation, real or con-structed; the logic of this position *tends* – beware this cautious note! – to move nationalism from cultural to political forms, and to entail popular mobilization. This is meant to be an omnibus definition, but it as well to note two further presuppositions that distinctively prejudge crucial issues.

First, the definition is often linked to the view that there have been three great ages of nationalism: the foundation of new states in Latin America in the early nineteenth century, the enlargement engineered by Wilson at Versailles and the much greater and more genuinely creative expansion of the international order as the result of decolonization.[7] There is indeed much to be said for the view that nationalism flourishes as the result of the collapse of empires; this view makes us realize that the collapse of the Russian empire means that we are faced now with a fourth great moment in the history of nationalism. Nevertheless, the omnibus definition should not be linked to the idea that nationalism is in any absolute sense linked to separatism. Very much to the contrary, the spirit of nationalism can dominate established states. If the contempor-ary United States, as is possible, becomes mobilized, as the result of either incautious elite manipulation or sentiment genuinely coming from below, around the conviction that Japan is an economic enemy, then this will deserve to be considered an example of nationalism.

Second, there is everything to be said, despite the works of John Armstrong and Anthony Smith, for the view that nationalism is modern.[8] There have, of course, always been distinctive cultures, and particular upper classes have had some sense of shared ethnic solidarity.

---

[6] Cf. E. Gellner, *Nations and Nationalism*, Basil Blackwell, Oxford, 1983, ch. 1; J. Breuilly, *Nationalism and the State*, Manchester University Press, Manchester, 1982, ch. 1; E. Hobsbawm, *Nations and Nationalism since 1780*, Cambridge University Press, Cambridge, 1990, pp. 9–13 and ch. 1.

[7] J. Mayall, *Nationalism and International Society*, Cambridge University Press, Cambridge, 1990, p. 64. The excellence of this book is marred at this point by the declaration that 'there are no more empires to collapse and therefore very limited possibilities for further state creation by this route'.

[8] J. A. Armstrong, *Nations before Nationalism*, University of North Carolina Press, Chapel Hill, 1982; A. D. Smith, *The Ethnic Origins of Nations*, Basil Blackwell, Oxford, 1986.

But the power of the nationalist idea, that people should share a culture and be ruled only by someone co-cultural with themselves, seems to me historically novel. The crude logistics of most societies in history – bereft of effective mass communication and cheap transport – meant that most human beings were stuck in very particular segments, quite unable to share a sense of destiny with people they had no chance of meeting.[9] In this connection, it is well worth noting that the actual sharing of destiny came much later than is often realized even to the core societies of north-west Europe. The much cited findings of Eugen Weber's *Peasants into Frenchmen* have recently received stunning support from Susan Cotts Watkins's demonstration that fertility patterns in Western Europe become national only in the early twentieth century.[10]

The theorist who has realized the modernity of nationalism most fully is Ernest Gellner.[11] His contribution to the study of nationalism has been fundamental, so it is sensible – not least since my argument departs from his – to consider his basic interpretation of nationalism immediately, even though this goes against the chronology that otherwise charac-terizes the argument. Nationalism is seen by Gellner in terms of the *logic of industry*. At the basis of this theory is the insistence that an industrial society depends upon a common culture. This probably depends upon sharing a language and certainly upon sharing an extended cultural code. The destruction of local cultures in Algeria meant an attack upon French and Berber and a favouring of mass educa-tion in Arabic; more serious problems, and far greater resistance,

[9]   P. Crone, *Pre-industrial Societies*, Basil Blackwell, Oxford, 1990; M. Mann, *Sources of Social Power*; vol. 1: *A History of Power from the Beginning to A.D. 1760*, Cambridge University Press, Cambridge, 1986; B. Anderson, *Imagined Communities*, London, 1983; Gellner, *Nations and Nationalism*, ch. 2.

[10]   E. Weber, *Peasants into Frenchmen*, Chatto & Windus, London, 1979; S. C. Watkins, *From Provinces into Nations*, Princeton University Press, Princeton, 1991.

[11]   E. Gellner's earliest statement is in his *Thought and Change*, Weidenfeld & Nicolson, London, 1964, ch. 7. A slightly revised version of his position appeared as 'Scale and Nation', *Philosophy of Social Sciences*, vol. 3, 1973. The most complete statement of his position is *Nations and Nationalism*. Important differ-ences between these statements are noted by A. D. Smith, 'Ethnic Persistence and National Transformation', *British Journal of Sociology*, vol. 35, 1984. Gellner's position continues to change, as can be seen from 'Nationalism and Politics in Eastern Europe', *New Left Review*, no. 189, 1991; 'Nationalism Reconsidered and E. H. Carr', *Review of International Studies*, vol. 18. 1992; 'L'avvento del nazionalismo, e la sua interpretazione. I miti della nazione e della classe', in P. Anderson, ed., *Storia d'europa*, Einaudi, Torino, 1993.

obtained in the Nigerian case. Two analytic points are being made here. On the one hand, industrial society is held to depend upon the ability to communicate in an abstract manner with people over space, with strangers whom one has not met and never will meet. On the other hand, massive social engineering is required because 'nationalism is not the awakening of nations to self-consciousness; it invents nations where they do not exist'.[12]

The ferocity of this phrase led to a magisterial rebuke from Benedict Anderson: '. . . Gellner is so anxious to show that nationalism masquerades under false pretences that he assimilates 'invention' to 'fabrication' and 'falsity', rather than to 'imagining' and 'creation'.[13] While this is right, as is the related point that a history of imagining makes nation building easier, [14] it should not be allowed to detract from the essential correctness of Gellner's point. There is no firm sociological mooring to the nation whatever, [15] not in language, not in religion, not in ethnicity, and Gellner is quite right to insist in consequence that nation is far harder to define than nationalism.[16] There is no reason to accept the sleeping beauty view propounded by nationalist ideology, that nationalism is the awakening of something extant which had merely been dormant.

Gellner needs to be defended quite as much on another point. A characteristic attack has been directed against his position, namely that it fails because it is functionalist. It is certainly true that functionalism cannot be intellectually correct; any theory of this type must be ruled out of court. Logically, functionalism takes a consequence as a cause, the expression of a societal need as a reason for the existence of institutions that seek to look after it. Life is not like that – I have plenty of needs, many of which go unmet – and neither is history. But proper specification of Gellner's theory can point to a mechanism explaining why attempts are made to meet these societal needs, and this ensures that the theory does not fail. The mechanism is simple. Many nationalist leaders in the twentieth

---

[12]   Gellner, *Thought and Change*, p. 169.
[13]   B. Anderson, *Imagined Communities*, rev. ed., Verso, London, 1991, p. 6.
[14]   Analyses of earlier imaginings are contained in Armstrong, *Nations before Nationalism* and Smith, *The Ethnic Origins of Nations*. Cf. L. Greenfeld, *Nationalism*, Harvard University Press, Cambridge, 1992. It seems to me that Gellner now accepts the spirit of this point: his most recent essays cited above make much of the difference between national awakening in Germany and Italy, already possessed of high cultures, and in the 'time zone' further to the East— where invention was, so to speak, complete.
[15]   I owe this point, that nationalism 'lacks sociological moorings and depends upon strong political projects', to N. Stargardt.
[16]   Gellner, *Nations and Nationalism*, throughout but especially ch. 5.

century have been aware of the connection established by Gellner: they are modernizers consciously aware of how to create industrial society. Such modernizers seek to break down the segments of the traditional order so as to create a common culture capable of integrating all citizens. Daniel Patrick Moynihan realized this in his famous complaint, when American Ambassador to the United Nations, that many Third World nationalists had been trained at the London School of Economics. Certainly Jomo Kenyatta, who can serve as the exemplar of this type of nationalism, was trained there, by no less a figure than Malinowski.[17] An interesting footnote in Jadwiga Staniszkis's *Dynamics of the Breakthrough in Eastern Europe* states that A. Jakovlev changed his mind about the nationalities question in the former Soviet Union because reading Gellner made him convinced that people had to recognize nationalism in order to reach capitalist development.[18] This is perhaps less empirical support for Gellner's theory than direct creation of the evidence! But that is a distraction. The general claim I am making is that Gellner's account of this type of nationalism is a great success; it goes a very long way to explain the third wave of nationalism identified. It may well be that the theory derives from the periods that Gellner spent in North Africa in the 1950s and 1960s: it is that sort of experience that is being theorized.

Classic Patterns

Gellner's theory is not truly universal partly because it fails to explain the very first emergence of nationalism in eighteenth-century Britain and France. The nature of the failure is obvious: nationalist sentiments are clearly in place before the emergence of industry. This type of nationalism can be explained in terms of the *logic of the asocial society*; this expression is Immanuel Kant's and refers to that multipolarity, unique in civilizational terms to north-west Europe, that led to endless competition between states.[19] The general character of this system has been theorized

[17] Breuilly, *Nationalism and the State* offers several interesting comments on Kenyatta. A related article, at once powerful and disturbing, is that of S. Pederson, 'National Bodies, Unspeakable Acts: the Sexual Politics of Colonial Policy Making', *Journal of Modern History*, vol. 63, 1991.

[18] J. Staniszkis, *The Dynamics of the Breakthrough in Eastern Europe*, University of California Press, Berkeley, 1991, p. 294.

[19] J. A. Hall, *Powers and Liberties*, Basil Blackwell, Oxford, 1985.

most powerfully by Otto Hintze and Charles Tilly.[20] Their finding is that wars make states quite as much as states make war. Continual competition between states leads to an arms race requiring ever greater funding. Kings are thus forced not just to sit on top of the various cultural segments within their territories, but also to interact with them ever more closely in order to extract ever greater funds.

One way in which monies were extracted was through the provision of the services of justice. Another was through the increasing territorialization of social life: if one example of this was a burgeoning ability to provide order, that is to successfully claim a monopoly of violence, another was an incipient economic nationalism that increased the customs and excise revenues on which monarchs relied. Over time, a state able to consolidate its territories into a single unit subject to bureaucratic rules fared best in warfare. Such national states often gained strength through cooperating with civil societies they could not completely control: the absence of great despotic power did a great deal to increase their infrastructural reach.[21]

A characteristically brilliant essay by Michael Mann, the theorist of this type of nationalism, begins by noting that the eighteenth century bred marked increases in the communicative capacities of civil society.[22] In England these were pioneered from below by the creation of a unique pre-industrial commercial revolution, and on the continent from above by both the military and economic demands of enlightened absolutism. The entry of the people onto the political stage accordingly became possible, rather against the expectations of such of its leading theorists as Adam Smith and David Hume. One such entry led to the creation of the United States, whose political culture remained overwhelmingly universalist despite the change from 'people' to 'nation' in the important founding documents of 1776 and 1789. The French Revolution was

---

[20]   O. Hintze, 'Military Organisation and the Organisation of the State', in F. Gilbert, ed., *The Historical Essays of Otto Hintze*, Princeton University Press, Princeton, 1975; C. Tilly, *Coercion, Capital and European States*, Basil Blackwell, Oxford, 1990. Cf. Mann, *Sources of Social Power*, vol. 1.

[21]   These dimensions of state power were identified by M. Mann, 'The Autonomous Powers of the State: Origins, Mechanisms and Results', *European Journal of Sociology*, vol. 25, 1984. For an attempt to remove confusions from these categories and to push them a little further, see J. A. Hall, 'Understanding States', in J. A. Hall, ed., *The State*, Routledge, London, 1993.

[22]   M. Mann, 'The Emergence of Modern European Nationalism', in J. A. Hall and I. C. Jarvie, eds, *Transition to Modernity*, Cambridge University Press, Cambridge, 1992. Cf. M. Mann, *Sources of Social Power*, vol. 2: *The Rise of Classes and Nation States, 1760–1914*, Cambridge University Press, Cambridge, 1993.

also universalist given that one could choose to become French, but the body to which people were to belong was on this occasion clearly that of a particular nation-state, with some Jacobins proving unwilling to trust those who had not learnt French.[23]

This concentration on the nation is best explained by the fact that civil society increased its capacities at the very time when Europe was torn apart by the long War of the Atlantic, that is the visceral struggle over the long eighteenth century between Britain and France. This meant that states were forced to extract historically unprecedented amounts from their societies.[24] One consequence of this was state reform, by the ending of 'old corruption' in Britain and by revolution in France. Another consequence was, however, the emergence of nationalism. The crux of the matter is that both processes were entwined, that the struggle for representation raised the question of identity.

A very full portrait of the processes involved for Britain , coming both from below and from above, has now been given to us by Linda Colley's *Britons*. This was a complex affair. A British nationalism certainly existed first, founded on the notion of a Protestant people under attack from Europe's Catholic monarchies.[25] But there was also an *English* nationalism, often directed against the Scots – not least because they did so well out of their connection with Britain.[26] In many ways, John Wilkes is the best exemplar of such nationalism, as he is for the struggle for representation more generally.[27] He was an apologist for the blunt ways of John Bull, for roast beef and Yorkshire pudding, and for the liberties established in 1688. It was entirely characteristic that a typical procession of Wilkes supporters in 1768 assembled at a tavern named after William of Orange before setting out to vote for their hero under banners of Magna Carta and the Bill of Rights; equally many Wilkes songs were sung to the tunes of 'Rule Britannia' and 'God Save the King'.[28] All this was of course contrasted to the mannered artificialities of the French aristocracy and, somewhat later, to the geopolitical greed of Napoleon. It is scarcely surprising that the French replied in kind by inventing the image of perfidious Albion.

---

[23] Hobsbawm, *Nations and Nationalism since 1780*, pp. 18–23.
[24] Full details are available in the tables in Mann, *Sources of Social Power*, vol. 2, ch. 11.
[25] L. Colley, *Britons*, Yale University Press, New Haven, 1992, p. 18
[26] Colley, *Britons*, pp. 117–32.
[27] J. Brewer, *Party Ideology and Popular Politics at the Accession of George III*, Cambridge University Press, Cambridge, 1972.
[28] These details are taken from Colley, *Britons*, pp. 111–12.

Whilst there can be absolutely no doubt about the impact of the ideals of social mobility represented by Napoleon, we can best approach the next type of nationalism, dubbed here *revolution from above*, by noting recent scholarship on the logistics of the French armies.[29] It is not the case, as was once believed, that the French armies spread nationalism by design. Absolutely to the contrary, the fiscal crisis of the French state meant that its armies plundered huge sums from territories it was forced to conquer, and continued to do so for years because such territories were made to pay for occupying French troops. French rule was imperial, and it accordingly led to nationalist reactions.

The concept of a revolution from above is, of course, taken from Barrington Moore's great *Social Origins of Dictatorship and Democracy*.[30] Here it highlights a type of nationalism pioneered by states with previous histories, choosing to change their social structures in order to survive. If this is to say that the logic of state competition is at work here as it was with the previous type, the social base of this type of nationalism is distinctive. This third type of nationalism has been recognized best by John Breuilly in his treatment of the Meiji reformers reacting to the incursion of Commander Perry and of their Prussian predecessors responding to the possibility that their state might disappear after its defeats at Jena and Auerstadt.[31]

I take as the exemplar of such nationalism Karl von Clausewitz, a member of the circle which included Scharnhorst and Gneisenau but better known to us than them because of his stature as the theorist of war.[32] That theory was necessitated by the appearance in 1793 of a force:

> . . . that beggared all imagination. Suddenly war again became the business of the people – a people of thirty millions, all of whom considered themselves to be citizens . . . The people became a participant in war; instead of governments and armies as heretofore, the full weight of the nation was thrown into the balance. The resources and efforts now available for use

[29]   T. C. W. Blanning, *The French Revolution in Germany: Occupation and Resistance in the Rhineland, 1792–1802*, Oxford University Press, Oxford, 1983; S. Schama, *Patriots and Liberators*, Alfred A. Knopf, New York, 1977. On this topic more generally, see D. Kaiser, *Politics and War*, Harvard University Press, Cambridge, 1990, part 3.
[30]   B. Moore, *Social Origins of Dictatorship and Democracy*, Beacon Press, Boston, 1966.
[31]   Breuilly, *Nationalism and the State*, chs 9 and 13. Cf. Alter, *Nationalism*, pp. 34–7. Both these authors prefer the term 'reform nationalism'.
[32]   This paragraph draws heavily on P. Paret's superb *Clausewitz and the State*, Princeton University Press, Princeton, 1976.

surpassed all conventional limits: nothing now impeded the vigour with which war could be waged . . .[33]

The diagnosis the reformers made after their own defeat stressed the need to change society completely if Prussia was to survive. The professional armies of Frederick the Great would never be able to compete against citizens in arms. Thus it was a necessary to abolish feudalism and to contemplate arming the people so that something like the Spanish guerrilla resistance would become possible. Frederick William III disliked this latter proposal, but the possible curtailment placed on Clausewitz's career was occasioned by a different matter. In 1812 Prussia briefly made peace with Napoleon. Clausewitz was appalled that a peace had been made against the national enemy, resigned his commission and fought in the Russian army against the French. All of this perhaps reflects the fact that Clausewitz was something of an outsider. It may well be significant that Clausewitz's family was not a member of the grand aristocracy: he himself depended upon state service quite as much as the lesser samurai of the Meiji Restoration.[34] But if on this occasion the old regime – scared of the popular mobilization that the call to the nation entailed – won, in the long run Germany was created as the result of revolution from above.

The creation of completely new states in Latin America resulted from a very different type of nationalism, that curious compound of *desire and fear blessed by opportunity* that is exemplified in Símon Bolívar himself and particularly well understood by John Lynch.[35] The desire for independence had two sources. On the one hand, the ideas of the Enlightenment, gained more from the United States (whose importance as a model cannot be overstressed) than from Spain, gave an impetus to ideas of freedom, reason and order. Much more important, on the other

---

[33] C. von Clausewitz, *On War*, trans. M. Howard and P. Paret, Princeton University Press, Princeton, 1976, p. 592.

[34] Breuilly, *Nationalism and the State*, ch. 15.

[35] I have relied most heavily here on G. Masur, *Símon Bolívar*, University of New Mexico Press, Albuquerque, 1969, J. Lynch, *The Spanish-American Revolutions: 1808–1826*, Norton, New York, 1973; and L. Bethell, ed., *The Independence of Latin America*, Cambridge University Press, Cambridge, 1987. J. Merquior's 'Politics of Transition', *Government and Opposition*, vol. 16, 1981 noted some time ago that Gellner's theory of nationalism failed to confront the first great wave of state creation; Gellner admits as much in *Nations and Nationalism*, p. 135. A first attempt to bring the Latin American experience into the centre of nationalist studies was made by B. Anderson: the revised edition of *Imagined Communities* changed the title of the fourth chapter to 'Creole Pioneers' in an attempt to underscore the importance of this historical experience.

hand, was an extreme disenchantment with a metropolis at once corrupt and underdeveloped. One element was economic. Spain wished its colonies to produce bullion and to absorb its own manufacturing products and, to that end, increasingly attacked local economic development, not least because its involvement in European war increased its own fiscal needs. For a long period, trade was monopolized by a Spanish elite, which consistently overcharged for imports and underpaid for exports.

Another element was social. Attempts to increase control by sending out officials from Europe were particularly humiliating to local Creoles, whose standards of education and attainment were habitually far greater: 'the lowest, least educated and uncultivated European', Alexander von Humboldt observed, 'believes himself superior to the white born in the New World'.[36] Added to these sentiments was fear. The Creole planters were a small minority sitting atop large Indian and slave populations upon whose continued quiescence their position depended. The revolt of Tupac Amuru showed them the dangers of an assault on their privileges in their own lands, but it was the use made by Toussaint l'Ouverture of the slogans of the French Revolution that really terrified them. Their adherence to Enlightenment ideals did not go so far as to countenance the loss of their land, let alone self-destruction. Hence their own nationalist revolutions in the early years of the nineteenth century, suddenly made possible by Nelson's breaking of the link with the Peninsula and by Napoleon's invasion, were exceptionally socially conservative. Whilst sheer logistics entailed the creation of separate states, the mobilization of the people, generally characteristic of nationalist politics, was strenuously avoided.[37]

This segmentation of social life has continued to characterize Latin America, not least because the relative absence of geopolitical conflict has not thereafter made it necessary for states to increase their infrastructural powers.[38]

In contrast, what is striking about *Risorgimento nationalism*, at least at first sight, is that it comes from below. This type of nationalism is extremely well known, not least because of Hroch's demonstration of the three-stage development from the collectors of folklore, to the ideologists of nationalism, to the final moment at which cultural revival

---

[36]   J. Lynch, 'The Origins of Spanish American Independence', in Bethell, *The Independence of Latin America*, p. 25.
[37]   This point about logistics is strikingly made by Anderson, *Imagined Communities*, ch. 4.
[38]   K. J. Holsti, 'Armed Conflicts in the Third World: Assessing Analytical Approaches and Anomalies', paper given at McGill University, 1993.

becomes political demand.[39] Two particular forces fuelled movement from below. First, there was a notable increase in the number of educated people in nineteenth-century Europe, an increase that often began before states sought to create normative integration within their territories.[40] Second, economic development moved many from the countryside to the city: the destruction of the traditional segmentary cultures of such people made them available for nationalist propaganda.[41] An important general point to be made about this type of nationalism is that it deserves to be considered liberal, that is it stressed civic loyalty within a democratic regime rather than ethnicity. Both John Stuart Mill and Mazzini were famously amongst its numbers, and the conjunction of their names makes it clear that the hope of the age was that the setting free of oppressed peoples would usher in a reign of peace.[42] There is a blissful innocence about their particular dreams, which came to be exploded once non-historic nations, most notably the Irish, insisted on their right to a state.

Hroch's marvellous phenomenology of nationalism hardly explains why there was a transition from cultural to political nationalism. But it is not hard to see what is happening. Consider the career of František Palacký, the Czech historian who followed Herder in seeing the Czechs as a peaceful people oppressed by both Magyars and Germans.[43] He had begun working for the Bohemian Museum in the 1830s, and his great history was begun in German. Increasing anti-German feeling, consequent on the state's attempt to make German the language of officialdom, led him in the 1840s to start writing in Czech. But it was the events of 1848 that pushed him into politics. The Czechs refused to join the National Assembly in Frankfurt and felt deeply threatened by plans concocted there that might have led to their cultural demise. They

---

[39]   M. Hroch, *The Social Preconditions of National Revival in Europe*, Cambridge University Press, Cambridge, 1985. Gellner's 'L'avvento del nazionalismo, e la sua interpretazione' critically evaluates Hroch's argument, albeit so as to underscore nationalism's social roots. Later in this chapter it will become clear that the weakness of both Gellner and Hroch resides in their downplaying of political determinants of nationalism.

[40]   L. O'Boyle, 'The Problem of an Excess of Educated Men in Western Europe, 1800–1850', *Journal of Modern History*, vol. 42, 1970.

[41]   Hroch's work at this point is, of course, superb.

[42]   J. S. Mill, 'Of Nationality, as Connected with Representative Government', ch. 16 of his *Representative Government* in his *Three Essays*, Oxford University Press, Oxford, 1975. Mazzini's views are amusingly described in Hobsbawm, *Nations and Nationalism since 1780*, chs 1 and 4. Cf. Alter, *Nationalism*, ch. 3.

[43]   In so doing, I am following Breuilly, *Nationalism and the State*, p. 100.

participated instead in a counter-meeting in Prague, which firmly stressed that the best hopes for the Slavs, given their geopolitical position between Russian and Germany, remained with the Habsburgs.[44]

Reflection on this episode leads to two analytic points. First, the move from cultural to political nationalism was occasioned by blocked social mobility. This should not be seen, as wise words of Ernest Gellner emphasize, in purely economistic terms, as if people became nationalists in order to get better jobs, true though that sometimes has been.[45] What matters is the prospect of humiliation and the fear that one's children's lives will suffer. In the Habsburg lands the switch to political nationalism did not, in a sense, come from below: it was rather the desire of a modernizing state to conduct official business in a single language that suddenly placed some in the position of facing blocked or perhaps downward mobility. State intervention occasioned popular response.

The second analytic point is much more general, but it can be approached by asking bluntly whether the Habsburg enterprise was doomed by nationalism to collapse. General considerations suggest a negative answer, at least for a particular sort of Habsburg enterprise. By that I have in mind the Kremsier reform proposals of 1849, the main clause of which asserted that: 'All peoples of the Empire are equal in rights. Each people has an inviolable right to preserve its nationality in general and its language in particular. The equality of rights in the school, administration and public life of every language in local usage is guaranteed by the state.'[46] Had this been enacted, different nationalities may not have sought to escape the empire. The analytic point is best described with reference to Albert Hirschman's classic distinction between exit, voice and loyalty: when it is possible to have voice inside a system, exit loses its attraction.[47] Differently put, the nature of political regime matters: historically and habitually nationalism has involved

---

[44] A. J. P. Taylor's unsurpassed *The Habsburg Monarchy 1809–1918*, Hamish Hamilton, London, 1948, chs 5–7 gives details both of the particulars and the general context of this story.
[45] Gellner, *Nations and Nationalism*, pp. 60–2.
[46] This is cited in A. Sked, *The Decline and Fall of the Habsburg Empire 1815–1918*, Edward Arnold, London, 1989, p 143. I am much indebted to this book and to the same author's 'Historians, the Nationality Question and the Downfall of the Habsburg Empire', *Transactions of the Royal Historical Society*, vol. 31, 1981.
[47] A. Hirschman, *Exit, Voice and Loyalty*, Harvard University Press, Cambridge, 1970. Hirschman has recently claimed (in 'Exit, Voice and the Fate of the German Democratic Republic: An Essay in Conceptual History', *World Politics*, vol. 45, 1991, p. 194) that exit is quintessentially a private matter. Nationalism shows that this need not necessarily be so.

separation from authoritarian polities. The general analytic point is then hopeful, given the problem of minorities: multinationalism may be possible, as Switzerland indicates, although limitations to the linguistic capacities of most human beings suggest that it is scarcely likely to become the norm.

The Habsburgs did not, of course, consistently take this liberal option.[48] The explanation for their failure has everything to do with geopolitics. First, defeat by Prussia allowed Hungary to gain its historic rights. The fact that the Hungarians felt threatened, perhaps because they were not a majority in their own lands, led to that policy of forced Magyarization which gave impetus to southern Slav nationalism:[49] the creation of Austria-Hungary effectively ruled out federal reform. Such reform was probably unlikely for a second reason. The Habsburgs were not prepared to retrench, to allow some territories to secede and to concentrate on economic development rather than geopolitical prestige. The monarchy's *raison d'être* had been and remained that of being a great power. Still, it is noticeable that after 1867 the empire did not look set to fall apart. Its elements were clearly unable to agree, but geopolitical facts remained, and the Czechs did not yet look prepared to risk going it alone. What changed everything was defeat in war.

The last classic type of nationalism is *integral nationalism*. This has sometimes been seen as a reaction to Versailles or, more generally, as a response that logically had to follow given that the drives for social integration of the new nations founded at that time were always likely to disadvantage minorities. Certainly there is a change in mood with integral nationalism: it is illiberal. There is no longer room for the belief that human beings, seen as possessing inalienable rights, need the carapace of a nation, that all nations can develop together in a positive sum game. On the contrary, universalism is held to be a feeble myth: the fact that one should think with one's blood naturally turned nationalist quarrels into Darwinian zero-sum affairs. Ethnicity has now completely taken over from civic obligation.

The theorist of integral nationalism is Ernst Nolte.[50] This form of nationalism was well in place before it received its ultimate form in German national socialism, so cannot be completely explained in terms of a reaction to Versailles. It may well be that integral nationalism is bred

---

[48] O. Jászi, *The Dissolution of the Habsburg Monarchy*, University of Chicago Press, Chicago, 1961; M. Mann, *The Sources of Social Power*, vol. 2, ch. 10.
[49] Taylor, *The Habsburg Monarchy*, p. 290.
[50] E. Nolte, *Three Faces of Fascism*, Holt, Rinehart and Winston, New York, 1965. Cf. Alter, *Nationalism*, chs 2 and 4.

more generally by the trauma of defeat: it certainly seems to help explain the life and deeds of the Action Française and its leader Maurras, who invented the name of this type of nationalism and who stands as its best exemplar.[51] But this is too partial an explanation. We can see what has been missed from the explanation of its classic turn-of-the-century form by considering carefully Max Weber's admonition in his 1895 inaugural address: 'We must grasp that the unification of Germany was a youthful spree, indulged in by the nation in its old age; it would have been better if it had never taken place, since it would have been a costly extravagance, if it was the conclusion rather than the starting-point for German power-politics on a global scale.'[52] In the context of his time, Weber's nationalism was of course liberal, although Poles familiar with Weber's wartime views about how Germans should behave in the East are not likely to accord him that epithet.[53] None the less, it is crucial to stress that the context of that time included the myth of imperialist mercantilism. A newly industrialized country like Germany had risen in part through trade, and its future could have been assured by continued adherence to that trading route: but some voices argued that secure sources of supply and sale necessitated territorial possession. In a nutshell, Germans preferred to act as 'heroes' rather than as 'traders'.[54] The fact that Bethmann Hollweg listened to such voices was one element in the pattern that led to disaster in 1914.[55]

Something needs to be said about the social base of this integral nationalism. Studies of the popular leagues pressing for expansion to the East and for a *Weltpolitik* in late Wilhelmine Germany have shown us that these views were attractive to the educated, to those whose careers were associated with a German state of which they were proud – a fact that undermines Hobsbawm's influential view that nationalism turns

[51]   Alter stresses the importance of defeat in his *Nationalism*, pp. 46–50, following E. Lemberg, *Nationalismus*, Rowohlt, Reinbek, 1964. Sources used for Maurras include Nolte, *Three Faces of Fascism*; E. Weber, *Action Française*, Stanford University Press, Stanford, 1962; Michael Curtis, *Three Against the Third Republic*, Princeton University Press, Princeton, 1959.

[52]   W. G. Runciman, ed., *Max Weber: Selections in Translation*, Cambridge University Press, Cambridge, 1978, p. 266. Cf. W. Mommsen, *Max Weber and German Politics 1890–1920*, Chicago University Press, Chicago, 1984.

[53]   For details, see Mommsen, *Max Weber and German Politics, 1890–1920*, pp. 211–27

[54]   W. Sombart, *Händler und Helden*, Duncker und Humblot, Leipzig, 1915. Cf. J. A. Hall, *International Orders*, Polity Press, Cambridge, forthcoming 1994, ch. 4.

[55]   A particularly powerful appreciation of this point is given by Kaiser, *Politics and War*, part 4.

nasty towards the end of the nineteenth century because it comes to be rooted in the lesser bourgeoisie.[56] This respectable but radical right nationalism played some part in limiting the Wilhelmine state's room to manoeuvre in the years immediately before 1914, and this helped cause the outbreak of war.[57] The rules of diplomacy depend upon the state's chief actors being part of international society: academic realism rests upon the presence of transnational identity. What radical nationalists were demanding at this time was an end to transnational identity so that national society could be favoured – in a world seen, and as much by Sidney Webb as by Maurras or Max Weber, largely in Darwinian terms.

This emphasis on the pre-1914 origins of integral nationalism is not meant to detract from its intensification after 1919. It is of course true that many of Wilson's borders are still intact, though this is in part because of the ethnic cleansings unleashed by the two great revolutions of the twentieth century. However, one cannot help but note how disastrous was the Versailles settlement in East Central Europe. Regimes were created that were geopolitically unviable, that lacked firm guarantees, that were prone to quarrel amongst themselves, and that possessed minorities whose suppression invited irredentist claims.[58] In a sense, this provided Hitler with a set of cards, the playing of which allowed for such viciousness that nationalism thereby gained a reputation from which it has not recovered.

Reprise: from Society to State and Regime

Any specification of different types of nationalism needs to be fairly close to historical reality if it is to fulfil its purpose, that of helping general thought and the understanding of particular cases. I believe that the

[56]   The two most important studies of popular nationalism are G. Eley, *Reshaping the German Right*, Yale University Press, New Haven, 1980 and R. Chickering, *We Who Feel Most German*, Allen & Unwin, Boston, 1984. The views of Hobsbawm are spelt out most fully in *Nations and Nationalism since 1780*, ch. 4, especially p. 118.

[57]   Mann, *Sources of Social Power*, vol. 2, ch. 21. I rely on Mann's argument for the rest of this paragraph. Cf. G. Eley, 'Some Thoughts on the Nationalist Pressure Groups in Imperial Germany', in P. Kennedy and A. Nicholls, eds, *Nationalist and Racialist Movements in Britain and Germany before 1914*, Macmillan, London, 1981.

[58]   K. J. Holsti, *Peace and War*, Cambridge University Press, Cambridge, 1991, chs 8 and 9; E. H. Carr, *The Twenty Years Crisis, 1919–1939*, Macmillan, London, 1939.

typology offered to this point is close to reality and stand by it and by the claim that there are many kinds of nationalism. But, I wish to look at the two obvious ways in which this typology might be criticized. A measure of disagreement with the second criticism will move my argument beyond phenomenology towards underscoring important theoretical points.

The first criticism is obvious, namely that the typology should be expanded. John Breuilly's complete treatment of nationalism makes systematic use not just of 'revolution from above' but also of the distinction between separatist and unification nationalism, and it does so for social worlds with and without nation states.[59] The most recent work of Ernest Gellner, keen to understand nationalism in post-communist societies, has made much of a brilliant essay by John Plamenatz to note differences within Risorgimento nationalism between the German and Italian cases, definitively possessed of extant high cultures, and the situation further to the east, where cultures were almost completely invented.[60] Finer analyses would also result from distinguishing more clearly between popular sentiment, the dreams of intellectuals and the manipulative practices of politicians.[61] The validity and helpfulness of these distinctions, however, seem to me to be such that they could be included within the typology presented, were greater space available to allow for its full elaboration.

The fact that there are so many types might well encourage exactly the opposite comment, somewhat in the spirit of Pirandello, to the effect that these types need an integrating general theory. This would, I suspect, be Gellner's response, so this is a good moment to return to his theory. It is not, in fact, hard to see how one can reduce the number of cases. Some mileage can be had by extending the notion of industrialism in the logic of industry to include the capitalist development that provided the human *matériel* for Risorgimento nationalism. Better still, I believe, would be to take the notion of blocked mobility, properly understood in the sense of humiliation, and say that it is an essential part of what is going on within the logic of industry.[62] That link is precisely at the heart of Gellner's real and best attempt to produce a general theory of nationalism, that is a

---

[59] Breuilly, *Nationalism and the State.*
[60] J. Plamenatz, 'Two Types of Nationalism', in E. Kamenka, ed., *Nationalism: the Nature and Evolution of an Idea*, Edward Arnold, London, 1976. The essay is discussed in Gellner, 'L'avvento del nazionalismo, e la sua interpretazione'. Gellner's arguments echo those of T. Schieder, *Der Nationalstaat in Europa als historisches Phänomem*, Westdeutscher Verlag, Cologne, 1964.
[61] I owe this point to W. Wesolowski.
[62] Humiliation is also distinctively part of Latin American nationalism, which

second and more general theory that does not fall foul of the functionalism of the industrial society school to which, as noted, he is recently
somewhat prone.[63] More particularly that connection is necessary for
him, for otherwise the logic of industry could in principle take place
within large empires, that is it has no need to take on the national
form: put differently, the actors in this category seek to modernize
apart from and even against metropolises that had discriminated against
their talents. All this is to say that Gellner theorizes his own Czech
background as much as he does North Africa and that he has accordingly been unfairly treated to this point by being considered the theorist
only of the logic of industry.

I can see the logic of this type of integrating argument and can think of
additional reasons to avoid dogmatism about my own concepts. For one
thing, we can now see that the types represent in part stages, with the
logic of asocial society, for example, being unique and therefore unavailable for later use. For another thing, it will soon be seen that integral
nationalism in the contemporary world sometimes loses bite because the
drive for ethnic homogeneity is no longer so closely connected to economic mercantilism, nor is it now easy to cage politicians so that they are
forced to ignore the realities of transnational society. However, I still
think that the logic of asocial society, revolution from above, desire
and fear blessed by opportunity, and integral nationalism escape the
integrating argument outlined.[64] I prefer my types of nationalism on
phenomenological grounds: my exemplars are very different sorts of
people and they would have been uneasy in each other's company. But
it is neither desirable nor necessary to leave matters at this point. For a
certain amount of patterning is implicit within the types presented: explanation has rested less on social than on political factors, notably on those
concerned with state and regime.

We can begin by noting that Gellner's trinitarian view of human
history is too simple: he is too much of an economic materialist, almost

---

lacks, however, a modernizing impulse. Nationalism by trade, discussed below, is
as prone to draw on such feelings, despite its overtly more instrumental approach.
[63] This general theory is most clearly present in Gellner, *Thought and Change*,
which I find generally to be more convincing than *Nations and Nationalism*.
[64] An extraordinary essay by P. Anderson, 'Science, Politics, Disenchantment',
in Hall and Jarvie, eds, *Transition to Modernity*, compares Gellner and Weber on
nationalism so as to reach the conclusion that the former's theory is generically
functionalist, failing to make the viciousness to which nationalism can be prone
part of its conceptual apparatus.

a marxist in reverse, in imagining that history is structured simply by evolution from foraging–hunting to agrarian production and then to modern industry, powerful as these forces undoubtedly were.[65] More particularly, there are two notable ways in which modernity has been seen here to predate the coming of industry. First, civil society connections expanded in the eighteenth century, most spectacularly in Britain as the result of a commercial revolution that preceded the advent of the industrial era.[66] Secondly, multipolar state competition was born in the agrarian era and flowed into the industrial era: it was never a merely superstructural affair, being often powerful enough to disrupt the histories of economy and society.[67] States certainly mattered for nationalism. Most obviously, a long process of state building in north-west Europe created national states and territorialized social relations. Still more importantly, it was the fiscal needs of states, ever engaged in war, that led to those fights for representation which encouraged the emergence of national sentiment. The forces of civil society, left to themselves, tend not to breed political action: what mattered was their interaction with the demands of states.

But the nature of regime has as important an impact as the state *per se*. We know that at the turn of the century working classes differed in their levels of militancy according to the regimes with which they interacted: the presence of a liberal regime meant that class conflict took on an industrial rather than a political character, whereas the political exclusion of autocracy and authoritarianism concentrated attention on the state both because of its arbitrariness and its refusal to allow unions to organize.[68] Early realization of this point lay behind Max Weber's call for limits to Wilhelmine authoritarianism. Neither capitalists nor the state had anything to fear from liberal measures towards the working class: on the contrary, the more class felt itself to be part of society, the less likely it

---

[65]   E. Gellner, *Plough, Sword and Book*, Collins Harvill, London, 1988.
[66]   This is made particularly clear in E. A. Wrigley's *Continuity, Chance and Change*, Cambridge University Press, Cambridge, 1988. B. Anderson's sociology of nationalism differs from Gellner on this point: what matters to him is the advent of print culture rather than industry *per se*.
[67]   For a criticism of Gellner at this point, see J. A. Hall, 'Peace, Peace at Last?', in Hall and Jarvie, eds, *Transition to Modernity*.
[68]   There is a large literature on this point. See, inter alia: D. Geary, *European Labour Protest 1848–1945*, Methuen, London, 1984; R. McKibbin, *The Ideologies of Class*, Oxford University Press, Oxford, 1990; Mann, *Sources of Social Power*, vol. 2; I. Katznelson and A. Zolberg, eds, *Working Class Formation*, Princeton University Press, Princeton, 1987; T. McDaniel, *Capitalism, Autocracy and Revolution in Russia*, University of California Press, Berkeley, 1988. For a justification of this point, see ch. 2 in this volume.

was to embrace radicalism.[69] The same paradoxical principle – that openness increases cohesion – applies to nationalism.[70] The omnibus definition given at the start carefully noted that cultural nationalism *tends* to become political. In fact, we have seen that a liberal option was available within the Habsburg domains, which, had it been adopted, would probably have satisfied the main nationalities by respecting their historic rights – which is to say that nationalism might not have become political. This option was ruled out by the Habsburgs, convinced as they were that federalism would have undermined their geopolitical dreams. My guess is that this perception may have been inaccurate, as most certainly was the case with that of those Wilhelmine politicians who failed to sense that their working class could be coopted best by reform. Might not the empire actually have been strengthened, as Masaryk thought, if it had embraced this liberal option? Obviously, this question can never be decided. But there is much to be said for endorsing the ethic of eighteenth- rather than of nineteenth-century theorists: political arbitrariness creates much more anger than does social inequality. People prefer reform to revolution, the possibility of peaceful change to the dangers of the barricades. Liberalism thus diffuses conflict through society whereas authoritarianism concentrates it.[71]

Modern Variations

The first modern variation has already been encountered as the logic of industry, but analysis of the impact of the United States within its sphere of influence in the post-war era can enhance understanding of its character. Most obviously, decolonizing nationalism owed something to American dislike (for ideological and economic reasons) for European empires. This clearly hastened the end of the Dutch empire, and it was not without influence in the British case. Nevertheless, the logic of the situation favoured decolonization. Empire became costly as soon as European troops had to be used, as was the case when faced even with relatively minor rebellions. The British, once deprived of the Indian army, understood this almost immediately and quickly handed over territories

---

[69] Weber made his views especially clear in his wartime reflections on the historical sociology of Wilhelmine Germany. These writings are available as 'Parliament and Government in a Reconstructed Germany', in his *Economy and Society*, trans. G. Roth and C. Wittich, University of California Press, Berkeley, 1978, especially p. 1391.
[70] This point lies at the heart of Mann's brilliant *Sources of Social Power*, vol. 2.
[71] A fuller justification of this point is given in ch. 2.

to groups whose claims to represent 'nations' they often knew to be farcical.

In contrast, the French fought longer and harder and even dreamt of a greater France within which modernization could take place. One of Raymond Aron's most impressive and influential exercises in logic – demonstrating that this policy would significantly lower the standard of living within France itself – effectively destroyed that illusion.[72]

All the same, the subsequent career of these new states was deeply influenced by the terms of the American system. Most importantly, the world polity for most of the post-war period has been extraordinarily conservative. A truly amazing obeisance was given to the norm of sovereignty, with the result that very few boundaries have changed; if the United States supported this norm, it was, of course, as much in the interests of the post-colonial states themselves. This is not to deny that the American system sometimes coped poorly with the post-colonial world. The rules of the international market upon which it insisted helped advanced countries far more than countries seeking to develop.[73] More importantly, it was prone to consider nationalism as if it were communism, thus letting itself get trapped in Vietnam and landing itself with the Ayatollah Khomeini rather than settling for Mossadeq. Still, in historical terms the United States favours trade rather more than heroism, and its empire is now almost completely non-territorial. By and large, the Third World is less exploited than ignored.

The fact that the United States has been the sole genuine hegemon that capitalist society has ever possessed has had a fundamental impact on the states of the advanced world.[74] Trading has quite generally replaced heroism, economic ambition now mattering more than geopolitical dreams. Some mercantilist tricks are still practised by such states as Japan and France, and far more by the European Community in this present moment of uncertainty, but these are difficulties facing the world political economy rather than disasters likely to engulf it. The situation remains the exact opposite of that of the inter-war years: the fundamental stability of the geopolitical settlement is likely to allow for compromise in the economic arena. If this decline of economic imperialism is likely to curtail any revival of integral nationalism, so too is the American system that has undoubtedly encouraged the internationalization of key elites – who are most distinctively no longer so caged by

---

[72]   R. Aron, *La tragédie algérienne*, Plon, Paris, 1957.
[73]   J. G. Ruggie, 'International Regimes, Transactions and Change', *International Organisation*, vol. 36, 1982.
[74]   Hall, *International Orders*, chs 3 and 4.

nationalist pressure groups. But concentration on established states should not be so overdone as to detract attention from an essentially novel form of nationalism, *nationalism by trade*. The boldest theorist of this type is Tom Nairn, but Hudson Meadwell's recent arguments point in the same direction.[75]

Nationalism by trade is novel in seeking separation for regions of advanced societies. Nairn stresses that such nationalism is likely to do best when the region in question has good chances for economic prosperity: just as the six counties of Northern Ireland had no desire to be impoverished through connection with poor Catholic peasants, so too Catalans and Spanish Basques, perhaps even northern Italians, wish to protect their economic interests. A representative of this sort of nationalism is the leader of the Parti Québecois, Jacques Parizeau, whose strategy is that of convincing the Québecois that they would be richer without the rest of Canada. The likely career of this sort of nationalism is hard to predict. There have been very few exits from liberal systems, and the diminished geopolitical need for centralized and unitary states makes it possible to allow for the introduction of federal and consociational deals capable of appeasing discontent.[76] If this has happened in Spain, it most certainly has not in Scotland – where the absence of a local assembly has meant that the majority have been governed for many years by leaders distinctively not co-cultural with themselves. But economic changes may increase the opportunities for this type of nationalism by reducing the costs of transition that it would involve. If Adam Smith is right, the limitation of the size of the market decreases affluence: if one can separate and stay within a larger market, as in Europe but not yet for sure in North America, nationalism by trade starts to look a good bet. But if this happens, it is important to note that it does not matter much: political democracy and an open trading system are unlikely to be impaired by this sort of nationalism.

No survey of nationalism can omit mention of two unfolding situations – one obvious but the other potentially still more important, both being as yet hard to conceptualize – which may give rise of novel types of nationalism. The first of these situations is that facing the post-communist world; the second is that confronting many post-colonial states.

In retrospect, it is obvious that the Bolsheviks continued the work of the Tsars, thereby so delaying nation building that its contemporary

[75] T. Nairn, *The Break-up of Britain*, New Left Books, London, 1977; H. Meadwell, 'The Politics of Nationalism in Québec', *World Politics*, vol. 45, 1993.
[76] I owe this point to M. Mann.

incidence is that much sharper and more determined. The peoples of the former Soviet Union itself were always likely to be attracted to nationalism for the imperial system that dominated them was led by Russians, whose depredations were not merely political and economic but quite as much ecological.[77] This suggests that there is something to Linz and Stepan's suggestion that the early calling of elections might have held together both the Soviet Union and Yugoslavia as it did Spain.[78] It is certainly true that neither Gorbachov nor Milošević accepted the need for immediate federal elections, while more generally it is important to recall that intermarriage rates in much of Yugoslavia were beginning to undermine the clearness of ethnic divisions, diminishing the historical backlog of hatred. None the less, I doubt whether this argument captures the specificity of the situation in Eastern Europe, although an obvious sympathy for the general ethic lies at the core of this chapter.

It is vital to pay more attention to one important legacy of communism, namely its destruction of civil society. It is beginning to be accepted that this made the liberalization of communist regimes virtually impossible. The slow decompression of authoritarian capitalist societies was made possible by pacts with organized forces within civil society; this strategy was simply not possible for those seeking to liberalize authoritarian socialism.[79] Put another way, it is a mistake to mechanistically apply to the exit from socialism theories derived from the exit from authoritarian capitalism. Similarly, lessons about nationalism learned from Spain may well not fit post-communist reality. The destruction of civil society together with the vacuum created by the absolute collapse of the socialist project probably meant that the force of nationalism simply could not be contained. Consider in this context the social character of nationalist leaders in post-communism. It is very noticeable that former communists unable to succeed in the market have been attracted to nationalism for the most self-interested reasons. One has the impression that Mečiar at times scarcely believed in the manipulative tricks in which he was engaged.

A very great deal in this world remains open. What is noticeable at present is that nationalism in the territories of the former Soviet Union is, at least in comparison with those of former Yugoslavia, by no means utterly violent. The initial group of successor states are based on the

[77]   A. Khazanov, 'The Collapse of the Soviet Union', *Nationalities Papers*, forthcoming 1994.
[78]   J. Linz and A. Stepan, 'Political Identities and Electoral Sequences: Spain, the Soviet Union and Yugoslavia', *Daedalus*, vol. 121, 1992.
[79]   R. Bova, 'Political Dynamics of the Post-communist Transition: a Comparative Perspective', *World Politics*, vol. 44, 1991, especially pp. 131–2. For a full account of the point in question, see ch. 3 of this book.

union republics. Of course, it is extremely easy to point to the potentialities for matrioshka nationalism.[80] That this looks most likely in the North Caucasus may well have something to do with Georgia's decidedly integralist nationalism.[81] In contrast, matrioshka nationalism is somewhat curtailed in Russia by Yeltsin's adherence to democracy: the desire to exit is again held in abeyance by the possibility of voice. This factor also explains the remarkable success of the Ukraine in holding together different religions, languages and ethnicities within a single state.[82] And it raises a final consideration. The softer, more federalist and more democratic route is made possible by the remarkable fact that geopolitical conflict has been controlled and limited in this part of the world since the end of the Cold War. Were Russia again to embrace heroism, the protection of powerful states would become vital. Such states would likely pay little heed to the demands of their own nationalities.

The considerations raised here bring us to the post-colonial situation. Anthony Smith is surely right to stress that nation-building and state building in post-colonial societies have often been very difficult.[83] We need not accept his positive thesis – that European nations depended on a single ethnic core – to endorse the view that the absence of any shared political history and the presence of tribalism present unique problems. The extraordinary stability that resulted from obeisance to the norm of non-intervention – endorsed by the Organization of African Unity even at the price of accepting Idi Amin – has a sting in its tail at this point. Acceptance of this norm has meant that there have been extraordinarily few inter-state wars in the Third World since 1945, which should not for a moment detract attention from the vast numbers of deaths in *civil* wars.[84] Consequently states have often been content to rest on top of different segments rather than to rationalize their societies.

---

[80] I. Bremmer and R. Taras, eds, *Nations and Politics in the Soviet Successor States*, Cambridge University Press, Cambridge, 1993; R. Szporluk, 'The National Question', in T. J. Colton and R. Legvold, eds, *After the Soviet Union*, W. W. Norton, New York, 1992; *National Processes in the USSR: Problems and Trends*, USSR Academy of Sciences, Nauka, Moscow, 1992; A. Khazanov, *Soviet Nationality Policy During Perestroika*, Elek, Virginia, 1991; 'A Country of Countries', *The Economist*, 27 March 1993.

[81] S. Jones, 'Georgia: a Failed Democratic Transition', in Bremmer and Taras, *Nations and Politics in the Soviet Successor States*.

[82] B. Krawchenko, 'Ukraine: the Politics of Independence', in Bremmer and Taras, *Nations and Politics in the Soviet Successor States*.

[83] A. D. Smith, 'State-making and Nation-building', in J.A. Hall, ed., *States in History*, Basil Blackwell, Oxford, 1986.

[84] Holsti, 'Armed Conflicts in the Third World' provides figures on this point.

In a horrible sense, Third World countries have not had enough war, or perhaps not enough war of the right type. They are quasi-societies, not nation states.[85] Their states desperately need to be strengthened so that they can provide that basic order we have come to take for granted.

This consideration suggests a worrying conclusion. It looks as if the ordering of world politics may be about to change. The norms of sovereignty and non-intervention are now at something of a discount, and it may well be that rules for intervention, made possible by a concert of the great powers, will now come to the fore. In one way this is profoundly to be welcomed: it may make liberalism real.

But perhaps in another way this new development may not be such good news. There are many, many minorities whose cause could call for intervention: not just Bosnian Muslims, nor just Palestinians and Kurds, but, according to one recent survey, at least 250 other minorities currently at risk.[86] To give statehood to all such minorities would more than double the number of states in the world. Further, let it be remembered that there are perhaps 8,000 languages in the world, most of which could be used to put forward nationalist claims.[87] Given that not every language can have a state, one wonders about the wisdom of interventionist policies that may weaken states which need to be strengthened. Thankfully we are not completely without intellectual resource at this point: if the breakup of Yugoslavia teaches us one thing for sure, it is that international recognition should be withheld from a state until it puts in place internationally acceptable protection for minority rights. Genscher failed to do this with Croatia. But this is a single point. The dilemma as a whole – between universal liberalism and the building of states, whose creation may still be humanity's best hope – is far too complex, at least for me, to solve.

[85] R. H. Jackson, *Quasi-states: Sovereignty, International Relations, and the Third World*, Cambridge University Press, Cambridge, 1990.
[86] T. R. Gurr and J. R. Scarritt, 'Minority Rights at Risk: A Global Survey', *Human Rights Quarterly*, vol. 11, 1989. This survey is cited by Holsti, 'Armed Conflicts in the Third World'.
[87] Gellner, *Nations and Nationalism*, pp. 43–50.

7

WILL THE UNITED STATES DECLINE AS DID BRITAIN?

Determining whether the United States is going to decline as did Britain has clearly become one of the questions of the age, with the presumption in the United States distinctively being that the answer will be yes. Thus Paul Kennedy's *The Rise and Fall of the Great Powers* lends itself to this interpretation, despite the author's many cautionary words.[1] Similarly, the first 1988 issue of the trade journal of American international political economists, *International Organisation*, has several articles whose analyses take for granted that American hegemonic decline has already occurred.[2] If this is believed, it is likely to affect policy in a dramatic manner.

One broad thrust of this chapter is sceptical of the claim that the United States will decline as did Britain. Two points are made against the Cassandras of decline. First, the extent of American decline tends to be exaggerated. A few others have seen this,[3] but it is noticeable that their

---

[1] P. Kennedy, *The Rise and Fall of the Great Powers*, Random House, New York, 1987.
[2] This assumption has not lost its power since this chapter was written in 1988. Little revision has been made here. This is deliberate: both the likely failure of Thatcherism and the weakness of the Soviet bloc were evident before their actual demise. Redrafting now would significantly strengthen the main contentions of the argument.
[3] B. Russett, 'The Mysterious Case of Vanishing Hegemony; or, Is Mark Twain Really Dead?', *International Organisation*, vol. 39, 1985; S. Strange, *Casino Capitalism*, Basil Blackwell, Oxford, 1986; S. Strange, 'The Persistent Myth of Lost Hegemony', *International Organisation*, vol. 41, 1987.

arguments have failed to dent the self-confidence (no lesser word will do) of what the *New York Times* refers to as 'the school of decline'.[4] If evidence of American power is adduced, the characteristic reply tends to be that this does not really weigh much against what is considered to be a long-term secular trend: the United States may merely be at the stage of Britain in, say, 1880 rather than 1931 – what is held to matter is that worse is sure to come. My second point may help to resolve this stand-off in debate. Extremely forceful, if banal, considerations suggest that the world polity facing the United States now is nothing like that which faced Britain at the end of the nineteenth century. The differences, moreover, are systematically to the advantage of the United States; in consequence, it is extremely unlikely that it will lose pre-eminence as completely as Britain did. These points can be encapsulated by saying that the analogy, whether implicit or explicit, between the undoubted decline of Britain and the contemporary situation of the United States is of limited usefulness.

But there is another side to my general argument. To stress fundamental differences is not to dispute that there has been *some* decline in the position of the United States, nor would it be sensible to deny that it might go further. Different processes of decline are identified, with special focus being given to the situation of 'hegemonic leaders'. More particular and detailed attention still is devoted to the ways in which adherence to certain aspects of liberalism accounts for decline. An implication of this last point deserves highlighting. It may well be that hegemonic leadership in capitalist society needs to adhere to liberalism's insistence on the virtues of free trade, but there is no reason to believe that the Anglo-Saxon preference for well-developed equity markets and for limiting state power should be seen as dictated by, or necessary to, hegemonic rule. In general, it will be maintained that the causes of the decline of the contemporary United States do resemble those recognizable from the British case. But the processes identified are not those considered important by the most significant theory asserting 'hegemonic decline'; some credence is lent instead to the view that the particular nature of Anglo-Saxon liberalism is important in explaining decline.

Drawing up a balance sheet of the extent of American decline is a difficult task, but it is undertaken in the conclusion; this is a necessary preliminary for the final answer to the question posed. But first we must consider different theories of decline, and certain implications they raise; we can then analyse the British and American cases in turn.

---

[4]   P. Schmeisser, 'Is America in Decline?', *New York Times*, 17 April 1988.

Theories of Decline, Modern and Classical

We can start to gain some grasp on the nature of decline as an analytic category by noting and then commenting on three general causes of decline usefully identified by Mann.[5] First, economically powerful nation states that swim inside the sea of capitalist society are prone to suffer decline as the practices accounting for their ascendancy diffuse throughout the larger society. Secondly, leading states tend to decline as the result of geopolitics, either because of over-extension or because of participation in war. Finally, societies tend to institutionalize the moments of their success, so making it difficult to be as endlessly flexible as the demands of capitalist society necessitate: distributional coalitions are created that make social adaptation difficult.[6]

Obviously decline is seen as having two sources, either internal or external. The diffusion of practices throughout capitalist society is thus a more or less inevitable external cause of decline given that comparative advantage in general and the advantages of backwardness in particular have always allowed developing states faster growth paths than those of mature economies; in the same spirit, it must be said very clearly that some decline in the position of the United States in the last half-century was made inevitable by the recovery of its chief economic competitors from a situation of considerable internal destruction, a recovery that the United States actively sought, largely for geopolitical reasons. Geopolitics can be as much a force affecting states from the outside, as when heavy expenditure for defence is made necessary by the presence of a ruthless, aggressive and powerful competitor; equally, however, it can be ascribed to internal factors, as when a rash elite foolishly and unnecessarily over-extends commitments. Social blockages, of course, are by definition to be considered entirely an internal matter. A more subtle point follows from this. Decline has two connotations that need to be clearly distinguished. On the one hand, decline is normal and inevitable, the result, as noted, of factors beyond the power of any single nation state. On the other hand, decline is seen as being linked to degeneracy and corruption; here the implication is of failure to do as well as possible. In consequence, we can say that the main feature of recent British history is not relative decline *per se*, but the fact that this relative decline was so steep, in fact becoming absolute between 1979 and 1984.

[5] M. Mann, *States, War and Capitalism*, Basil Blackwell, Oxford, 1988, ch. 8.
[6] Cf. M. Olson, *The Rise and Decline of Nations*, Yale University Press, New Haven, 1982.

All that has been said so far refers to the decline of nation states in general. Let us now turn to an important recent theory in order to advance an argument rather than to add, at least at this stage, to the history of ideas , though it adds a further element to the picture. The theory in question has usefully been dubbed 'hegemonic stability theory', and it has gained general intellectual ascendancy in explaining the fateful careers of Britain and the United States.[7] The most obvious tenet of the theory is that the stability of capitalist society as a whole depends upon the presence of a leading power prepared to exercise hegemony – a term with rather different connotations – so that certain public goods can be assured. For Kindleberger the most important such goods are a stable medium of exchange, an insistence on free trade, the export of capital for development and the ability to absorb world surplus capacity.[8] The cogency of this claim seems much reinforced by considering the other side of the coin. The absence of a single hegemon – before 1914 when Imperial Germany challenged Britain, and in the inter-war vacuum when the latter was too weak and the United States unwilling to provide leadership – is held to have contributed to chaos, and then to war. All this is striking, if somewhat tautologous, and much of it has been accepted even by critics of hegemonic stability theory. Thus Keohane, whose somewhat implausible argument (derived, it should be noted, far more from theory than from evidence) is that cooperation between leading capitalist powers is made possible when a hegemon declines owing to the continuing presence of the liberal institutions it had built, also fears the wars that can result from the way changes in relative national economic power affect the conduct of states; it is simply his prescription for world order that differs.[9] In passing, however, it is worth noting that a genuinely radical critique, that of George Liska, is available.[10] He argues that war tends to result when a balance of power is disrupted by a single state, notably Britain in the nineteenth century, which gains too much power and so calls forth no-holds-barred rivalries. Interestingly, David Calleo, a follower of Liska, has been led by the logic of this theory to resist frequent cries to prop up failing hegemonic power; it would instead

[7]   R. Gilpin, 'Economic Interdependence and National Security in Historical Perspective', in K. Knorr and F. Trager, eds, *Economic Issues and National Security*, Regents Press, Lawrence, 1977; R. Gilpin, *War and Change in World Politics*, Cambridge University Press, Cambridge, 1981; R. Gilpin, *The Political Economy of International Relations*, Princeton University Press, Princeton, 1987.
[8]   C. Kindleberger, *The World in Depression*, University of California Press, Berkeley, 1973.
[9]   R. Keohane, *After Hegemony*, Princeton University Press, Princeton, 1984.
[10]   G. Liska, *International Equilibrium*, Harvard University Press, Cambridge, 1957.

be better to knock the hegemon off its perch as quickly as possible so that we can return to the normal balance of power politics.[11]

This chapter is not centrally concerned with these main elements of hegemonic stability theory. Concentration is instead on the claim, not always spelt out clearly in the literature but distinctively a part of current political debate, that hegemonic power is necessarily self-liquidating, that the exercise of leadership is such as to sap the strength of the great power that provides it. Two prime examples of this process are often given.

First, hegemonic powers often allow industrializing states to protect their infant industries while continuing to offer access to their own rich and well-developed markets.[12] In the long run, this lack of genuine multi-lateralism undermines the hegemon's domestic industry, a claim made most strikingly by Representative Richard Gephardt in the US presidential campaign of 1988.

A second service the hegemon is seen as providing is that of defence against common enemies. Here too the hegemon is held to suffer as the result of carrying a disproportionate share of the burden; Olson and Zeckhauser are typical here in using the language of collective goods theory in claiming that it is in the interest of smaller states to free ride on their leader[13]. The economic consequences of this are held to be catastrophic. William Grieder is a characteristic voice in claiming that the United States spends a much larger part of its GNP on defence than its main trading partners, the presumption being that this plays an important part in explaining different growth rates within capitalist society.[14] The most discussed example of this is NATO – perhaps curiously, given that the situation of Japan makes the case much better. But in either case, the analysis results in calls for a renewed round of burden-sharing negotiations.

All these theories consider that there are economic and geopolitical dimensions of both the rise to and the decline from pre-eminence, as well as of the complex interrelations between them; I shall follow their lead. What is less obvious and so more in need of stress is the implicit moral claim of the thesis that hegemonic power is necessarily self-liqui-dating. Jean-Paul Sartre famously declared that 'hell is other people'. Hegemonic stability theory implies that 'decline is other people'. The

---

[11] D. Calleo, *Beyond Hegemony*, Basic Books, New York, 1987.
[12] S. Krasner, *Asymmetries in Japanese–American Trade*, Institute of International Studies, University of California, Berkeley, 1987.
[13] M. Olson and R. Zeckhauser, 'An Economic Theory of Alliances', *Review of Economics and Statistics*, vol. 46, 1968.
[14] W. Grieder, 'Why Can't Our Allies Defend Themselves?', *Rolling Stone*, 16 June 1988.

hegemon slaves away in the long-term general interest, but other states, selfishly thinking only of their own short-term goals, slowly undermine what is in fact the very source of their own prosperity. Thank goodness virtue is its own reward! Sustained scepticism about this claim will return us to alternative theories of decline made forcefully aware of their very different moral flavour. Whilst it is very important indeed to recognize that important elite members, as well as large sections of the public, of hegemonic powers do sometimes see themselves in Durkheimian terms as providers of norms and services for the larger society, it is crucial to remember the view from below. Let us recall the comment of the British general Calgacus, which Tacitus records in *The Agricola*: 'To plunder, steal, rape, these things they falsely call imperial rule; they make desolation and call it peace.'[15] Words quite as strong have been directed against the British and the American desire for open markets. Although openness is, according to liberal theory, designed to benefit all, the worm's eye view, especially as formulated by Alexander Hamilton and his German disciple Friedrich List, naturally leads to charges of hypocrisy; for some are more equal than others, and economically advanced nations in capitalist society naturally favour openness when they have the capacity to make the most of it.[16]

This general point gains further salience once we remember the way leading states tend to behave when they consider their powers to be diminishing. Thus the United States has chosen to run a budget deficit nearly every year in the last quarter-century, that is it has broken the norm that its agency, the IMF, has so rigorously imposed on other states. This raises the analytic possibility that the hegemon might choose to free ride on the system, that is to use its undoubted muscle to extract systematic advantage from smaller and weaker powers. Still more important is the fact that those tasks judged to be common by the United States are often seen in an entirely different light by its allies, as evidenced by European members of NATO refusing to accept 'out of area' tasks, to the evident anger of the United States.

This sceptical note amounts to saying that a hegemon is not necessarily a neutral norm-giver akin to the Latin Christian church in the early

[15] My attention was drawn to this reference by David Spiro.
[16] R. Szporluk, *Communism and Nationalism*, Oxford University Press, Oxford, 1988; W. M. Earle, 'Adam Smith, Alexander Hamilton, Friedrich List: The Economic Foundations of Military Power', in W. M. Earle, ed., *Masters of Modern Strategy: Military Thought from Machiavelli to Hitler*, Princeton University Press, Princeton, 1943.

European middle ages.[17] On the contrary, a hegemon is a great power. Putting things like that makes it possible to contrast theories of decline which blame others with theories blame the great powers themselves. We have seen that one such theory, present in the works of Polybius, Machiavelli, Gibbon and Montesquieu, concentrates on the way arrogance can lead to disastrous geopolitical over-extension. The rise of a great power is held to result from its having occupied a marcher position, a factor often linked to military prowess; decline results from over-extension, which brings with it the costs of two-front wars and of the repression of nationalities.[18] Decline is the result of a great power mistakenly over-extending itself in a way that entails ruin, both geopolitically and economically.

The other theory of this type, as noted, stresses the diffusion of practices throughout capitalist society. Adam Smith insisted, against his friend David Hume, that there was no inevitable reason why a rich country should not continue to stay rich; rather by moving up the technological ladder it would serve the general interest in allowing new states to take over old industries.[19] But this would only be possible, Smith asserted, as long as there were no 'errors of police', no governmental policies that allowed the institutional arrangements of one moment to gel and petrify. If Smith's theory had much to be said in its favour, it proved none the less to be a poor guide to practice. The very notion of society involves the cohesion of expectations and institutions, as Polanyi famously stressed,[20] and no nation state within capitalist society has as yet been able to perpetuate the moment of its success. It is worth noting how very difficult it is to imagine this happening. The rise to power is often associated with the possession of a particular manufacture. However, it is possible, as Gershenkron (following Veblen) noted some time ago, for an industrializing state either to copy the technology without accepting various institutional limitations and social achievements, or to pioneer a new technology that is closed off to the leading power because of that institutional mix; both factors contribute to making the growth path of late industrializing countries faster than

[17] M. Mann, *Sources of Social Power*, vol. 1: *A History of Power from the Beginning to 1760 AD*, Cambridge University Press, Cambridge, 1986, ch. 10.
[18] R. Collins, *Weberian Sociological Theory*, Cambridge University Press, Cambridge, 1986.
[19] I. Hont, 'The 'Rich Country – Poor Country' Debate in Classical Scottish Political Economy', in I. Hont and M. Ignatieff, eds, *Wealth and Virtue*, Cambridge University Press, Cambridge, 1983.
[20] K. Polanyi, *The Great Transformation*, Beacon Press, Boston, 1944.

that of the leading power.[21] In addition, the leading power tends, in its senescence, to export the capital its prior industrial success had created. This necessitates export-led industrialization on the part of developing societies; however, such exports to repay loans are likely to undermine the domestic industry of the leading power.

To summarize, hegemonic stability theory tends to assume that their primacy in the world would have been assured except for the burdens that the hegemon was forced to bear. We should not accept this too easily. The leading edge of capitalist society has never remained in the same place for long, and there is no *a priori* reason to believe that it would have remained in the United States for ever had that country *not* entered the world scene.

A diminution in power of a leading state inside capitalist society might be explicable in traditional terms, as the result of over-extension or of internal social rigidities, rather than as the result of the cost of services that it provides for capitalism as a whole. We should in particular be suspicious of ideologists claiming that hegemonic services are somehow neutral; we should remember de Gaulle's complaint that the foreign policy of the United States represented a traditional drive for ascendancy cloaked in idealism, a complaint that was raised quite as much against Britain in the nineteenth century. However, it would be a mistake not to underline a crucial difference between the traditional policy of great powers and that sought by Britain and the United States. Where traditional rule often favoured conquest, Britain and the United States preferred when possible to maintain an empire of free trade; a contrast needs to be made, in other words, between formal and non-territorial empire. The success or failure of ruling powers within capitalist society is likely to depend upon the extent to which they can avoid formal territorial possession.[22] If liberalism's aims here might in principle stave off decline, the same may well not be true of adherence, to other aspects of that protean doctrine.

One final set of theoretical observations is necessary before turning to a comparison of the British and American cases. If real purchase is to be gained in this comparison, something needs to be said about the sources

---

[21]   A. Gershenkron, Economic Backwardness in Historical Perspective, in B. Hoselitz, ed., *The Progress of Underdeveloped Areas*, Chicago University Press, Chicago, 1952.

[22]   R. Robinson and J. Gallagher, 'The Imperialism of Free Trade', *Economic History Review*, vol. 6, 1953. Cf. B. Porter, *Britain, Europe and the World, 1850–1982*, Allen & Unwin, London, 1983; M. Doyle, *Empires*, Cornell University Press, Ithaca, 1986.

of state economic and geopolitical policy. Bluntly, to speak without question of 'the state' in the international arena is to prejudge important matters, to fail to examine whether state leaders act at the behest of societal forces. It is not at all easy to separate the leading social actors from each other. Was American post-war policy designed to secure a free world or a world open to a free economy? To what extent were such policies those of an elite genuinely autonomous from the main capitalist actors? Occasionally such separation is analytically impossible: Cobden and Bright really believed that the progress of trade would serve the politics of peace. But it is *often* possible to locate moments of autonomy for particular social actors; it is worth while saying something about the particular actors that will appear in this chapter.

The external actions of states tend to be seen in two ways. Realism in all its forms stresses that state leaders seek security for their societies in an asocial world; in the modern world, this search has necessarily had to involve economics quite as much as traditional geopolitics. This is a rich theoretical tradition, but it is capable of being brutalized; Morgenthau did precisely this when he argued that the goal of every state was to enhance its power.[23] In fact, the goals of states can and do vary, the desire for peace or wealth being quite as real as the desire for power.[24] Another way of making this point is to insist that perceptions of security vary; such variations may result from national experience as a whole but they may, of course, reflect the perceptions of particular groups within a nation.

The force of realism in the contemporary world seems amply justified by the behaviour of states in South-east Asia since the withdrawal of the United States. Great powers like to have weaker ones on their borders, and it is not at all surprising to discover China's hostility to Vietnam, particularly as seen in the former's adherence, in its support for Pol Pot, to the old geopolitical maxim that 'the enemy of my enemy is my friend'.[25] I mention this because the dominant version of the second way in which foreign policy has been conceptualized, namely that stressing its domestic roots, argues that the control of the state by capitalists causes war. This theory was first adumbrated by Hobson, and it is the way mainstream marxism, which ought to be more troubled than it is by the plain fact that capitalism is divided by states, has sought to explain state behaviour. As this approach is both powerful and well known, let

[23] H. Morgenthau, *Politics Among Nations*, Alfred Knopf, New York, 1973.
[24] R. Aron, *Peace and War*, Weidenfeld & Nicolson, London, 1966.
[25] D. Smith, 'Domination and Containment', *Comparative Studies in Society and History*, vol. 19, 1977.

me pay more attention to another domestic factor in the making of foreign policy, not least because its improperly understood implications are intellectually exciting and morally disturbing.

In so far as liberalism divorced itself from capitalist theory, it produced a distinctive theory arguing for popular control over state policy, a theory that reached an idiosyncratic apogee in the American founding fathers' desire to continue the spirit of their revolt against the state by controlling power completely by splitting responsibility between Congress and the Executive.[26] This tradition raises very complex issues, but two basic approaches can be distinguished, the more negative of which has tended to dominate debate. Tocqueville was among the first to stress the negative side of the equation in the American case.[27] He argued that the people would be slow to anger, but remorseless in the execution of war. In either case, it would be difficult to conduct foreign policy according to realist principles: state leaders would be constrained from threatening when threats were needed, and incapable, because of popular passion, of calling a halt once war had ceased to fulfil its Clausewitzian role as a 'continuation of policy by other means'.

This negative view, especially in connection with the United States, has been further stressed by George Kennan,[28] the author in the late 1930s of a manuscript seeking to curtail democracy, and by Henry Kissinger.[29] One reason for caution in accepting this view is plentiful evidence of consensus between the people and foreign policy makers; Kissinger's habit of blaming foreign policy failures on the domestic political system occasionally masked his own misjudgments. Of course, this is to voice scepticism about the extent to which popular will constrains the makers of foreign policy.

But there is a positive view of the way popular will does constrain foreign policy elites. One element of this viewpoint received its most vigorous statement in 1795, in Kant's *Perpetual Peace*.[30] Kant argued that liberal states should establish a league, based on constitutionalism and economic interdependence, and that this would guarantee peace. In a brilliant article, Michael Doyle, in common with Margaret Thatcher, has pointed out that liberal states have a remarkable record of not going to war with each other, although he adds the cautionary note that the

---

[26]   J. A. Hall, *Liberalism*, Paladin, London, 1988.
[27]   A. de Tocqueville, *Democracy in America*, trans. G. Lawrence, Anchor Books, New York, 1969, pp. 659–664
[28]   G. Kennan, *American Diplomacy*, Chicago University Press, Chicago, 1951.
[29]   H. Kissinger, *White House Years*, Little, Brown and Company, Boston, 1982.
[30]   Immanuel Kant, *Perpetual Peace*, in C. J. Friedrich, ed., *The Philosophy of Kant*, Modern Library, New York, 1949.

ideological nature of liberal states may make them particularly warlike to those they judge to be not just geopolitical but ideological rivals as well.[31] A second element of a positive appreciation of liberalism is that an appeal to the people may enable the foreign policy elite to escape from sectoral pressure: the state may become *free from* particular groups if it can insist on a right to be *free to* represent a more general will. None the less, the ultimate validation of liberalism remains the capacity to prevent state elites making chaotic mistakes.

As it happens, I believe that a liberal political system has opportunities and costs for the conduct of foreign policy. In order to see the ways in which this is so and to cast light on the other issues raised, it is necessary, given that they cannot be resolved by fiat, to turn to the historical record. Let us first examine, in broad contours, the reasons for the decline and fall of Britain, and then turn to the more complex case of the United States in the modern world political economy.

Britain's Decline and Fall

Most British academics have their own theories about Britain's decline, and the version presented here amounts in large part to a gloss upon them.[32] Before considering decline, however, it is as well to remember the nature of initial British pre-eminence and, still more important, to recount how this pre-eminence came to be challenged.

Britain entered the world stage at the end of the eighteenth century. John Brewer has recently demonstrated the sheer extent of the armed forces which made geopolitical triumph possible.[33] A crucial enabling factor in this connection was the financial revolution of the late seventeenth century, that is the founding of the Bank of England and the related rise to pre-eminence of the City of London. This in turn is explicable only by the absence of absolutism; as Tocqueville realized, the upper classes cooperated with the state, particularly in matters of taxation, precisely because they felt able to control it – itself a consequence both of the centralized nature of English feudalism and of limited state competition consequent on isolation from the European land mass.

---

[31] M. Doyle, 'Kant, Liberal Legacies and Foreign Affairs', *Philosophy and Public Affairs*, vol. 12, 1983.
[32] Cf. G. Ingham, *Capitalism Divided*, Macmillan, London, 1984; A. Gamble, *Britain in Decline*, 2nd edn, Macmillan, London, 1985; P. Anderson, 'The Figures of Descent', *New Left Review*, no. 161, 1987; Mann, *States, War and Capitalism*; K. Middlemas, *Politics in Industrial Society*, André Deutsch, London, 1979.
[33] J. Brewer, *The Sinews of Power*, Hutchinson, London, 1989.

Because of this Britain was the most highly taxed country in the world by the end of the eighteenth century, with extraction, as a proportion of national product, being perhaps twice that of France.[34] It is noticeable that this entry onto the world stage predates the Industrial Revolution;[35] equally striking is the fact that it was the result of well-developed militaristic skills. However, after the industrial revolution Britain not unnaturally adopted a rather full-blooded version of liberalism: commercial specialization and free trade were emphasized, even though this meant removing the protected status of home agricultural producers. Trading with the world was initially conducted without the benefit of much formal empire:

> The middle class did not require diplomats to tout for trade for them, which would have been distasteful, or to go for war for trade, except in situations where such wars could be justified on higher and purer grounds. A young, vigorous, dynamic economy like theirs, almost without serious competitors in the markets of the world, could get along very well on its own, without help.[36]

This is to say that Victorian ideology, according to which the rule of the market had replaced the traditional conflict of states, was highly self-serving. Other states were well aware of this. They pointed out in particular that the supposed loss of geopolitical security consequent on the repeal of the Corn Laws was in reality no such thing as long as Britain maintained a navy powerful enough to secure its sources of supply. Furthermore, Britain was perfectly capable of continuing to play at traditional balance of power politics when it proved necessary, as it did in the case of Egypt, even though middle-class, non-interventionist liberals might be unhappy with this.

It seemed for some considerable time as if the British liberal dream of peace through interdependence, of the spread of trade and eventually of the parliamentary system, might be realizable. Throughout the 1850s and 1860s tariff walls in Europe fell, and it could be claimed that this aided the general economic advance of the time. But there was always a worm

---

[34]   Brewer, *The Sinews of Power, p. 89.* Cf. P. O'Brien and P. Mathias, 'Taxation in Britain and France, 1715–1815: a Comparison of the Social and Economic Incidence of Taxes Collected for the Central Governments', *Journal of European Economic History*, vol. 5, 1976; P. O'Brien, 'The Political Economy of British Taxation, 1688–1815', *Economic History Review*, vol. 41, 1988.
[35]   E. A. Wrigley, *Continuity, Chance and Change*, Cambridge University Press, Cambridge, 1988.
[36]   Porter, *Britain, Europe and the World*, p. 15.

in the bud of this liberal dream. States interfered with the market in the most obvious way. Each state desired to have a set of productive industries that would ensure strategic security. These military origins to industrialization led to the creation of surplus capacity in the world economy, something that became obvious in the recession of the 1870s.[37] At this moment, two possible strategies, neatly encapsulated in the title of Werner Sombart's *Händler und Helden*, came to the fore.[38] The trading policy was to adapt one's national society to the logic of the world market, to allow productive activities to die out as they became unprofitable; the heroic alternative was to maintain such activities, not least because they played a vital part in securing national security.[39]

The close similarity of the interests of capitalists and those of foreign policy makers in Britain meant that its trading strategy, albeit with the protection of the Royal Navy, was bound to be maintained. In contrast, Imperial Germany moved towards the alternative pole.[40] The state elite was responsible for this change. It drew upon its own militarist traditions, themselves based on Germany's insecure geopolitical position in central Europe, insisting that to allow the entry of cheap grain would make Germany dependent on the world market as long as access to that market was controlled by the British navy. Closely related to this was the fact that tariffs were a specially good source of revenue.[41] In the longer run, the *junkers*, as producers of grain historically in favour of free trade, came to support this policy, as it protected them against cheap grain from North America; their views were much magnified by the over-representation they gained in the Prussian Estates. Similarly, protectionism became attractive to heavy industrialists, though much less so to the traders of Hamburg. None the less, the prime move towards protectionism was made by Bismarck, largely in order to be able to finance the army whose victories had cemented German unity.

---

[37] G. Sen, *The Military Origins of Industrialisation and International Trade Rivalry*, Frances Pinter, London, 1984.

[38] W. Sombart, *Händler und Helden*, Duncker and Humblot, Leipzig, 1915.

[39] Polanyi, *The Great Transformation*; P. Gourevitch, *Politics in Hard Times*, Cornell University Press, Ithaca, 1986.

[40] P. Kennedy, *The Rise of the Anglo-German Antagonism, 1860–1914*, Allen & Unwin, London, 1980; H. U. Wehler, *The German Empire 1871–1918*, Berg, Leamington Spa, 1986.

[41] J. M. Hobson, 'The Tax-seeking State: Protectionism, Taxation and State Structures in Germany, Russia, Britain and America, 1870–1914', PhD dissertation, London University, 1991.

The initial German move towards protectionism did not by itself lead to a visceral, no-holds-barred conflict between Britain and Germany. As long as Germany's expansionist aims were limited to mainland Europe, Britain would accede to them. In the last analysis Bismarck understood this. Perhaps too he understood the logic of the market. Germany's first bid for colonies was very clearly an exercise in geopolitics rather than in foreign economic policy, and Bismarck had no trouble at all withdrawing from this first bid, not least perhaps because his banker Bleichröder had very quickly realized that the rates of return from colonial possessions were miserably low.[42] However, German policy came to demand a place in the sun, even in the Congo, and a consequence of this was the decision in 1897 to build a navy, the real origin of the Anglo–German antagonism. Such a policy was in the interest of particular capitalists. In addition, domestic reformist pressure, most notably that of the Social Democratic Party, supported an expansion of the navy rather than of the army, for fear that the latter could be used for internal repression. But the decision depended most of all on the chief state actors, most notably Tirpitz, whose brilliant propaganda campaign captured the ear of the Kaiser. In one sense perhaps, the decision needs no real explanation. It is normal for rising powers to exert their strength, and almost inevitable that challenges to Britain would be mounted once she had disrupted the balance of power by taking on a world role.

Perhaps the fact that complex interpretations have been offered is the result of our knowledge that the First World War was a catastrophe. Nevertheless, it is worth emphasizing that what matters about economics is often less economic reality *per se* than what is *believed* to be the facts of the matter. The German economy was booming and colonies were neither needed nor immediately profitable; but, the rationale that imperial possessions were necessary for long-term prosperity was widely accepted, not least by Max Weber. It is noticeable in this context that capitalists tend not to produce their own geopolitical visions. In Imperial Germany, however, many capitalists who did not stand to benefit from empire acceded to the geoeconomic vision produced by others. Those who are supposed to be hard-headed counters of profit and loss are often no more immune to romantic appeals than other social actors.

It would be unsatisfactory to leave matters at this point. Britain wished to appease Germany and would have done so had that been possible. The

---

[42]   F. Stern, *Gold and Iron*, Vintage Books, New York, 1986. Cf. L. Davis and R. Huttenback, *Mammon and the Pursuit of Empire*, Cambridge University Press, Cambridge, 1987.

problem was that no specific and negotiable demands were made by Imperial Germany, and this ruled out the sort of colonial settlements that had been achieved with France and Russia. The reason for this was simple. The German state was not truly modern; it was rather a court at which policy resulted from favouritism. The absence of a bureaucratic and rational state meant that Germany ended up without a properly worked-out grand strategy. For a short period, under Caprivi, a genuine attempt was made to embrace a trading strategy. Therafter, there tended to be *two* heroic strategies. *Weltpolitik* did not mean that the traditional drive to the East was abandoned – thus avoiding, through reconciliation with Russia, a war on two fronts. Every social group received the policy it demanded, in an endless process of log-rolling; no rigorous attempt was made to establish a clear set of priorities.[43] Even after the famous 'war meeting' of 1912, little thought was given to matters of general strategy:

> . . . to most members of Wilhelm's entourage, economic expansion and even world power were first and foremost means to maintain the domestic status quo. Their intrinsic advantages were secondary. They were meant to provide somehow enough prosperity and/or nationalist prestige to quell the pressure for reform at home. How they managed this did not matter. MittelAfrika, MittelEuropa, it was all the same so long as the victory was large enough to sustain the power of the Junkers and their Kaiser. The means thus stood only in oblique relationship to the end, making it all the harder to fashion a consistent policy. The usual ways to measure success, economic growth, acquisition of territory, increase in influence, could not be used under such a system because the question was not 'have we expanded' but 'have we expanded enough' (to reach the greater goal)?[44]

The result of failing to master one's own fate was a drift to war. A system of alliances against Imperial Germany was formed because so many states were threatened. Self-fulfilling fears of encirclement, together with increasing middle-class nationalist and militarist pressure'[45] meant that state leaders felt increasingly trapped; in the end they resorted to war in part from despair. The lack of a modern state apparatus was quite as much to blame for Germany's drift to war as

[43] This is brilliantly argued by J. Snyder, *Myths of Empire*, Cornell University Press, Ithaca, 1991, ch. 3.

[44] I. Hull, *The Entourage of Kaiser Wilhelm II, 1888–1918*, Cambridge University Press, Cambridge, 1982, p. 253.

[45] G. Eley, *Reshaping the German Right*, Yale University Press, New Haven, 1980.

authoritarianism: put differently, there is much to be said for the Kant/ Doyle position but the crucial mechanism at work concerns the ability to calculate rationally rather than popular pressure *per se*.

Some time has been spent understanding the German challenge because it is a very important step in explaining British decline. Later on it will, by process of analogy, help us to understand American foreign policy.

There is little evidence to suggest that British hegemony determined the shape of nineteenth-century economic life at any point. Britain was not especially aggressive in seeking to break down tariff barriers, not least because it had no real muscle by means of which to impose its will on continental powers that possessed considerable armed might.[46] That such barriers did come down in Europe between the 1850s and 1870s was essentially because the states concerned found it in their own immediate interests. Britain had found in the 1840s that a rationaliza-tion of tariff barriers increased state revenue; before 1846 over 1,200 items had been subject to various levels of tariff, even though by far the greatest part of its revenue derived from a mere nine. The taking of hundreds of items off the books hurt smugglers badly and made it possible to police the remaining items in such a way that enhanced revenues were assured, even at lower tariff rates, while the costs of collection were dramatically slashed. Not surprisingly other countries followed suit.[47]

If British hegemony is a myth, what then assured the smooth working of capitalism for much of the nineteenth century? Mercantilist policies had been massively encouraged between 1713 and 1815 by the conflict between France and England. With the ending of the War of the Atlantic, together with the entry of Germany and Russia onto the scene, basic European order could be maintained by the traditional means of a bal-ance of power between the leading states. Germany's behaviour destroyed this balance.

With this in mind we are in a position to deal with the claim that British decline was caused by the provision of hegemonic services for capitalism as a whole. There is little truth in this. Most obviously, Britain never provided general defence for capitalism as a whole, although the Royal Navy did provide the particular service of policing

[46]   T. McKeown, ' "Hegemonic Stability" Theory and Nineteenth Century Tariff Levels in Europe', *International Organisation*, vol. 37, 1983.
[47]   I am drawing here on P. O'Brien and G. Pigman, 'Free Trade, British Hegemony and the International Economic Order in the Nineteenth Century', paper presented at the ESRC conference on 'States and International Markets', 1991.

the sea lanes. Bluntly, Britain's short-lived primacy in the market was never matched by pre-eminence in state-to-state relations. Further, its decline cannot be ascribed to excessive defence expenditures for capitalist society as a whole because its main rivals had at least comparable costs by the beginning of the twentieth century.[48]

In a similar vein, it is probably mistaken to see the late nineteenth-century monetary system as genuinely hegemonic. The Germans and the French had their own monetary blocs, and the French were able to invest in Russia in francs rather than in sterling. The crucial evidence for a monetary hegemony comparable to that of the United States in the 1960s – when one power alone could increase money in circulation, thereby extracting seigniorage – would have been persistently large deficits of Britain with Paris, Berlin and New York, that is evidence to show that Britain financed its deficit by making others hold sterling. But most scholars believe this not to have been the case: 'Britain is said to have had sufficient income from trade, investment, and services, plus the Indian milk cow, to remain in balance with the other major centres', while such sterling balances as were held resulted from economic calculation rather than from hegemonic coercion.[49] An assessment needing examination is that British industry was hurt by allowing continued access to its own markets while its own products were banned from much of the continent and from the United States, a claim that led Arthur Balfour to argue for what one theorist has termed 'specific reciprocity' – that Britain should force open protected markets by threatening to close off its own.[50] It is hard to know how to weigh this factor; against it can be set, in a moment, a different economic model.

The more traditional, neutral factors of previous theories of decline seem to explain the British case with greater conviction. The single most important factor is simply the exhaustion brought on by fighting Germany in two world wars. The financing of those wars led to the liquidation of most claims against the rest of the world. Much of this was, of course, hidden by the fact that Britain emerged on the winning side; but fundamental weakness was absolutely apparent within months

[48] Systematic evidence for this contention is given in ch. 8.

[49] D. Calleo, 'The Historiography of the Interwar Period: Reconsideration', in B. Rowland, ed., *Balance of Power or Hegemony: The Inter-War Monetary System*, New York University Press, New York, 1975, p. 241. Cf. P. Lindert, *Key Currencies and Gold, 1900–1913*, Princeton University Press, Princeton, 1969.

[50] A. Friedberg, *The Weary Titan: Britain and the Experience of Relative Decline, 1895–1905*, Princeton University Press, Princeton, 1988, ch. 2; R. Keohane, 'Reciprocity in International Relations', *International Organisation*, vol. 40, 1986.

of the end of the Second World War.[51] Furthermore, Britain had become exhausted as the result of state competition more generally. It was the challenge from other states, and particularly the fear that imperial rule by other powers might close off markets, that led to the acquisition of formal empire towards the end of the nineteenth century. This was a sign of weakness rather than of strength. It was always likely that a territorial empire would cost the country more than it was worth, and modern economic historians have lent much support to this view;[52] the popularity of the empire and the need, given Britain's dependence on imported food, to protect trade routes none the less make the acquisition of territory comprehensible. As it was, resources and commitments were brought fairly closely into line before 1914, and it was this that enabled the first German challenge to be surmounted. In the inter-war years, however, the increasing strength of nationalism made it more difficult to concentrate attention on the challenges posed by Hitler.[53]

Economic decline is probably best explained in similarly neutral terms. British industry had been based on a very limited set of important technologies, and these had conquered the world market without the benefit of having been sharpened by competitive rivals. It was scarcely surprising that an institutional package consolidated on the basis of its historical success. Even when Imperial Germany was moving towards a second industrial revolution, based on technical education and chemicals, it remained possible for Britain's older industries to remain in profit. But the British economy did not under-perform particularly badly before 1914, as its development of service and leisure industries clearly demonstrated.[54] Britain's initial economic decline was in largest part relative and inevitable.

If one reviews British policy as a whole, what is most striking is how normal decline is; it does not require, as would a miracle of rejuvenation, much commentary. The uneven nature of capitalist development was bound to lead to a loss of economic pre-eminence. When this was allied to geopolitical challenges and so to increasing imperial costs, British power was always going to be unsustainable. But if Britain had very poor cards to play, could it have played them better? The answer to this, for the most part, must be negative. The challenge from Germany

---

[51]   R. Gardner, *Sterling–Dollar Diplomacy*, Macmillan, London, 1969.

[52]   Davis and Huttenback, *Mammon and Empire*; P. O'Brien, 'The Costs and Benefits of British Imperialism', *Past and Present*, no. 120, 1988.

[53]   Kennedy, *The Rise and Fall*, ch. 6.

[54]   S. Pollard, *Britain's Prime and Britain's Decline*, Edward Arnold, London, 1989.

was real, and there were genuine limits to how far Britain could go in appeasement, even though allowing the rising power a major role was the only route to safety. I am no longer even sure that the British decision to continue fighting in 1917 was so irrational, even given the destruction of war: if Germany had then held on to the territory it had conquered, as it demanded, a further dose of *Weltpolitik* might have proved even more fatal. More importantly, it is extremely unlikely that the radical modernizing strategy of Chamberlain, much favoured by some later critics, would have reversed decline if it had been instituted. The fundamental weakness of the policy was less working-class hatred of expensive food than the reluctance of Canada and Australia to be forced to remain primary producers; these states wanted genuine rather than dependent development.[55] Furthermore, imperial preference would certainly have intensified imperialist pressures elsewhere – pressures that historically were partly mollified by Britain, allowing others to trade in her empire until the 1930s. All this can be summarized by saying that most British policy was determined by factors beyond national control, that placing foreign policy-making in different hands would have made very little difference.

However, it would be grossly mistaken to argue that every avenue of change was closed for a full a century. It became particularly clear after 1945, for example, that British decline was no longer simply the effect of other states catching up as the transfer of people from agriculture to industry enhanced their growth rates: that did help account for the strengthening of the positions of both France and Germany, but it failed to account for the continued low rates of British economic growth. It is certainly true that British decline was exacerbated by the character of market forces created by British history, that trade tended to be in low-technology goods with the Commonwealth, largely to repay wartime loans, but in the more competitive and dynamic European markets of the years immediately after 1945 the inability of the state to alter such structures and to modernize becomes ever more surprising.[56] It thus becomes necessary to establish which actors were responsible either for policies that exacerbated decline or for the blocking of others that might have led to renewal.

Some responsibility can be laid at the door of the people. In foreign policy, domestic pressure played some role in preventing Sir Edward Grey

---

[55] B. Semmel, *Imperialism and Social Reform*, Routledge & Kegan Paul, London, 1960.
[56] A. Milward, *The Reconstruction of Western Europe, 1945–51*, Methuen, London, 1984; P. Hall, *Governing the Economy*, Polity Press, Cambridge, 1986.

giving Imperial Germany the unambiguous warning that might have changed its perceptions.[57] In general, however, the makers of foreign policy were relatively insulated from popular pressure, and their successes and failures were largely their own. A much more celebrated argument about the way popular pressure caused economic decline is seen in the claim that a militant working class prevented economic restructuring. This view has dominated recent British politics and much academic debate. It is largely wrong. The British working class has only rarely been politically militant, and such economic views as it has had – whether original or in favour of keeping the status quo – were largely the result rather than the cause of economic decline. This point can be put differently by saying simply that the British elite was considerably cushioned from working-class pressures; the failure to create an economically dynamic economy is accordingly to be laid at its door.

Some shading needs to be given to the boldness of this picture. Union power was from the beginning deeply entrenched in the Labour Party, and sustained attempts at economic renewal from that quarter might have met with resistance. Furthermore, the British working class was always likely to prove a poor corporatist partner because its long history prior to industrialization meant that (in contrast, say, to its Swedish counterpart) it lacked centralized institutions and a vital interest in national economic affairs. But it is unclear how much of an obstacle this would have proved to a determined, modernizing elite. No such elite was present in the crucial period ending with the 1960s, by which time union militancy had increased in such a way as to block plans for reform.

If attention is to be given to internal social blockages, to distributional coalitions standing in the way of societal flexibility, it makes much more sense, as many scholars now realize, to ask whether the policies of the British state were determined by the interests of the financial sector of capital.[58] There can be no doubt of the increasingly deleterious impact of the unholy trinity of City–Treasury–Bank of England upon British industry. First, the great sophistication of the equity market has meant that profits have been made through trading in money, rather than through

[57]   C. Nicolson, 'Edwardian England and the Coming of the First World War', in A. O'Day, ed., *The Edwardian Age: Conflict and Stability, 1900–14*, Macmillan, London, 1979.

[58]   Ingham, *Capitalism Divided*; Anderson, 'The Figures of Descent'; S. Newton and D. Porter, *Modernization Frustrated*, Unwin Hyman, London, 1988; Mann, *States, War and Capitalism*.

investing in domestic industry. In consequence, British industry has suffered from low levels of capital formation, a factor that goes much further in explaining the low rates of workers' productivity than *de haut en bas* comments about the laziness of British workers;[59] in addition, industrialists have constantly had to concern themselves with the provision of short-term profits so as to pay out dividends to shareholders, inattention to whose interests can easily lead to takeover bids. Secondly, the City has consistently argued in favour of high exchange rates. This lay behind the catastrophic return to gold in 1925 and the stop-go policies of the period from 1945 to 1971; the growth of the eurodollar market in London in more recent times has, if anything, enhanced the City's power. The judgement to be made about this is simple: the single biggest obstacle to British economic recovery for most of the post-war period has probably been the excessive strength of the pound and the volatility of the interest rates necessary to ensure that strength.[60] Thirdly, the City, Bank and Treasury have together consistently argued against the adoption of industrial policies, a factor which reflects the idiosyncratic, 'budgetary' nature of British state capacity. This package of policies breathes the spirit of economic liberalism, and it is this complete trust in market forces that characterizes Anglo-Saxon liberalism as a whole. Such policies were a source of strength when Britain had a strong industrial lead, but they led to less than optimal industrial performance when other nation states developed strong banking–industrial links and to genuine catastrophe when, between 1925 and 1931 and for most of the period since 1945, they caused Britain's exports to be priced out of the world market.

The importance of the financial sector can be appreciated by reference to the work of Rubinstein.[61] His finding – that the very rich in Britain have been landowners and financiers rather than, at any time, industrialists – allows considerable scepticism to be cast on the thesis of British decline proposed by Martin Wiener.[62] Wiener suggested that the aristocratic embrace undermined bourgeois virtue, sending the sons of businessmen to semi-rural retreat in the spirit of William Morris and Laura Ashley. In fact, the British elite had no aversion to money-making; on the

[59] T. Nichols, *The British Worker Question: a New Look at Workers and Productivity in Manufacturing Industry*, Routledge & Kegan Paul, London, 1986.
[60] S. Strange, *Sterling and British Policy*, Oxford University Press, Oxford, 1971.
[61] W. D. Rubinstein, *Men of Wealth*, Croom Helm, London, 1981
[62] M. Wiener, *English Culture and the Decline of the Industrial Spirit*, Cambridge University Press, Cambridge, 1981.

contrary, it discovered the best avenue to riches that was available. Nevertheless, we do need a theory that stresses the sleepiness of the British elite. There remains much to be said for the contention that the financial sector constrained rather than controlled the political elite.[63] An autonomous elite sought to restore sterling's international role because it was obsessed by the politics of prestige; thus we should not accept the view of Harold Wilson in the early 1960s as a determined opponent brought to heel by finance capital – it makes no sense to say that he was defeated when he and his party had no real alternative strategy of their own.

This conclusion can be generalized, and for the most banal of reasons. Since 1945 the reinvigoration of most advanced nation states within capitalist society was the result of their elites being shocked by catastrophe, most notably by defeat in war. A British victory was taken as an imprimatur of the success of British institutions, something symbolized by the success of history and the scorn shown to sociology within that country. There was recognition that times had changed, but the strategy adopted was to keep things as close to normal as possible. This was most clearly expressed in Macmillan's words to Crossman while attached to Eisenhower's headquarters in Algiers in 1942: '[We] are the Greeks in this American empire. You will find the Americans much as the Greeks found the Romans – great big, vulgar, bustling people, more vigorous than we are and also more idle, with more unspoiled virtues but also more corrupt. We must run [this HQ] as the Greek slaves ran the operations of the Emperor Claudius.'[64] Of course, this Polybian strategy of playing Greece to America's Rome was then generalized[65] – curiously given that the fate of the Greeks inside the Roman Empire was by no means entirely pleasant. This policy has proved to be disastrous.

If continual loyalty to finance rather than to industry is one side of the coin, the other is continued adherence to the tradition of national militarism. A full 50 per cent of Britain's research and development funding now goes towards weapons, an absolute madness given the short production runs involved.[66]

[63]   S. Blank, 'Britain: the Politics of Foreign Economic Policy, the Domestic Economy, and the Problem of Pluralistic Stagnation', in P. Katzenstein, ed., *Between Power and Plenty*, University of Wisconsin Press, Madison, 1978.

[64]   A. Horne, *Harold Macmillan*, vol. 1: *1894–1956*, Viking, New York, 1988, p. 160.

[65]   H. B. Ryan, *The Vision of Anglo-America*, Cambridge University Press, Cambridge, 1987; C. Maier, *In Search of Stability*, Cambridge University Press, Cambridge, 1988.

[66]   J. Kingman, 'Science and the Public Purse', *Government and Opposition*, vol. 21, 1986.

In this connection, it is worth saying something about the 'Thatcherite Revolution'. Margaret Thatcher sought to treat economic decline as the equivalent of defeat in war, and there is no doubt but that she has fundamentally changed British political discourse by making generally obvious what has been true for some time – that Britain is a small state whose future depends on her ability to survive in the international market. But the desire for reform has not been met by any comparable overhaul of institutions or policy. If the chief institutions that gave Britain initial success were those of the City and of the military, they have by no means been dismantled: on the contrary, what is most striking is the extraordinary degree of basic continuity. This is more generally true. Adherence to economic liberalism has not been limited to the recognition that Adam Smith still rules externally; rather, disastrous attempts have been made to impose his marketist views internally. Such total loyalty to *laissez-faire* has meant that little attempt has been made to create comparative advantage through the creation of a skilled work-force and by means of industrial policy. Britain has survived the Thatcherite years by means of North Sea oil, whose revenues have masked the huge increase in expenditure on unemployment that otherwise would probably have caused electoral revolt. But the failure of the 'Thatcherite Revolution', and the likelihood that Britain will continue to do far less well than it might have done constitute a different story. All in all the best summary judgement on British decline in general remains that of A. J. P. Taylor: 'the English people of the twentieth century were a fine people and deserved better leaders than on the whole they got'.[67]

The United States: Down, but not Out

Two tasks confront us when considering the position of the United States in the contemporary world. On the one hand, the inappropriateness of the analogy with British decline can be demonstrated by showing both that American decline has not gone very far and that the structure of the world polity is likely to limit the extent of that decline. But, on the other hand, we need to see if the processes explaining such decline as there has been are similar to those that affected Britain. In particular, is American decline, such as it has been, the result of traditional factors, or does it

[67] A. J. P. Taylor, 'Accident Prone, or, What Happened Next', *Journal of Modern History*, vol. 49, 1977, p. 18.

rather result from the provision of services for capitalist society as a whole?

One doubt is worth mentioning immediately. Theorists of decline occasionally give the impression that the United States could once do as it wished but now is but more or less impotent. This image of a golden age is much exaggerated. Difficulties with allies have plagued the United States throughout the post-war period, and it is not the case that American views always prevailed or that various allied contributions did not affect important outcomes. The United States sought, for example, to establish genuine multilateral, liberal economic norms and it hoped too to avoid a continental commitment to Europe: in fact it ended up with what Ruggie has felicitously called 'embedded liberalism' and with NATO, while its allies, from the start, refused to share its perceptions of the Soviet Union and so to place security above trade.[68] None the less, the United States did and still does gain what it wants on crucial occasions, even if much sound and fury hides this basic fact. This is not to deny that there has been some change, most dramatically with the closure of the gold window in 1971, but we are coming to realize that what has changed is the manner in which power is exercized – now far less benign, indeed predatory on the part of the hegemon[69] – rather than any absolute loss of power. Let us consider in turn the military, economic and monetary bases of continuing American strength.

The military power of the United States is scarcely in question. It alone stands in rivalry to the Soviet Union, even though its lead in nearly all the main military technologies makes it very much first amongst equals. But only these two states are real superpowers, possessed of first- and second-strike nuclear capabilities. In itself, however, this does not convince the theorists of decline for the perfectly sensible reason that defence procurement in the end rests upon the capacity of an economy to support it. Can the American role be sustained now that the United States has moved from being $141 billion in credit to the rest of the world in 1980 to something like $500 billion in debt by 1988, with the clear likelihood that that debt will massively increase? It is necessary, however, to be rather sceptical of the various indices used

---

[68] J. G. Ruggie, 'International Regimes, Transactions and Change: Embedded Liberalism in the Postwar Economic Order', *International Organisation*, vol. 36, 1982; Maier, *In Search of Stability*; M. Mastanduno, 'Trade as a Strategic Weapon: American and Alliance Export Control Policy in the Early Postwar Period', *International Organisation*, vol. 42, 1988; Gardner, *Sterling–Dollar Diplomacy*; A. Van Doermal, *Bretton Woods*, Macmillan, London, 1978.

[69] Cf. J. Conybeare, *Trade Wars*, Basic Books, New York, 1987.

to mark American decline. The figures of indebtedness to the rest of the world, for example, are exaggerated by the fact that the book value of American interests overseas is given at purchase price rather than current worth; such debt is, of course, much more the result of the policies of Ronald Reagan than the result of any long-term processes of secular decline. In addition, it should not be forgotten that for much of the 1980s surpluses in important states like California should be set against the federal budget deficit; once that has been done the total deficit stands at something like 2 per cent of GNP – not a strikingly high figure, and historically normal for this particular nation state. Further, one should not forget that debt is denominated in dollars; it is thus subject to diminution should the United States print money, and thereby inflate the dollar and the world's economy.

Equal care should be taken when dealing with protectionism. Hegemonic stability theory suggests that a decline in economic strength will lead to a demand for protectionism, and the very considerable upsurge in informal quotas of various sorts seems to suggest that this is now true of the United States. But protectionism is only half-hearted. It is important to note that the 1988 Trade Bill demanded, as have American negotiators over recent years, increasing *openness* in services, agriculture and shipping.

It is equally important to be suspicious of what trade figures reveal given the huge increase in intra-firm trade – by now perhaps a third of world trade. A more accurate index of American economic power is the share of total world product controlled by American companies; let it be remembered that much American investment has been of the multinational kind rather than the portfolio variety favoured by the British and that this shows continued strength. More specifically, the loss of pre-eminence as debilitated economies recovered seems to have bottomed out in the early 1970s, with the United States holding more or less the same share over recent years.[70] This index is itself open to question, and Robert Reich has suggested that American companies' share of world product means little if the international division of labour in such companies has the United States responsible only for invention and assembly, with complex profit-creating skills moving ever more towards East Asia.[71] This picture might seem to be supported by the discovery that an increasing number of patents for manufacturing processes are taken out in Japan, but this in turn is questioned by those who argue that real

---

[70] Strange, 'The Persistent Myth'; R. Gilpin, *US Power and the Multinational Corporation*, Basic Books, New York, 1975.
[71] R. Reich, *Tales of a New America*, Vintage Books, New York, 1988.

industrial strength is best measured by software patents, vital for most advanced contemporary industrial products: these are still the preserve of the United States. It seems possible, moreover, that America is regaining a competitive edge in middle-sized companies,[72] while the most recent study suggests that the United States continues to dominate in the newest areas of high-technology goods.[73] In general, there is little agreement as to the nature of economic power today; so it is scarcely surprising that no index is accepted as its measure.

A similarly mixed story can be told about the position of the United States within the world monetary system. At first sight the seigniorial privilege of the dollar standard, that is the unilateral right to expand the money supply, has been removed with the floating exchange rate 'system' inaugurated in 1973. But the dollar remains the world's main currency, and the United States seems to have retained enormous power within the contemporary world monetary system.[74] Under the floating system, Germany ceased to be the chief supporter of the dollar, but its place was taken first by Saudi Arabia and then by Japan. One of the services that a hegemonic power was supposed to provide, at least in Kindleberger's eyes, was that of exporting capital to the rest of the world. In fact, world capital has flown *to* the United States, largely as the result of Reaganomics. There is certainly no denying that it was the policy of the United States that created a strong dollar in the early 1980s, and it is the policy of the United States since the Plaza Accords that have made for a weaker dollar: in both cases, the largest player determined the rules of the game, and it has proved impossible for smaller players to design alternative rules without the cooperation of that player. The impact of these policies on Latin America is such that its export of capital to Western banks is now running at something between 4 and 5 per cent of GNP. This is the brutal exercise of great power – so great, indeed, as to make the Third World's success in controlling its minerals and commodities pale into insignificance.[75] So this is an appropriate point at which to recall that a leading power can free ride on the system: strength can be used to extract advantage.

[72]   'A Portrait of America's New Competitiveness', *The Economist*, 4 June 1988.
[73]   R. McCulloch, *The Challenge to US Leadership in High Technology Industries (Can the US Maintain Its Lead? Should it Try?)*, National Bureau of Economic Research, Working Paper 2513, Cambridge, 1988.
[74]   S. Strange, 'Still an Extraordinary Power: America's Role in a Global Monetary System', in E. E. Lombra and W. E. Witte, eds, *Political Economy of International and Domestic Monetary Relations*, University of Iowa Press, Ames, 1982; Strange, *Casino Capitalism*.
[75]   S. Krasner, *Structural Conflict*, University of California Press, Berkeley, 1984.

The present power of the United States can be summarized by saying that it stands at the top or close to the top on all 'power indicators'. But the question of decline is not likely to be resolved by noting this since what some see as a glass half full will seem half empty to others. Let us turn instead to those features of the world polity that make the position of the contemporary United States unlike that of Britain at the end of the nineteenth century. An initial point worth emphasizing is that the United States has not suffered a massive defeat in war. This is not to deny the importance of Vietnam, but the United States was able to pass on part of the costs of the war to its allies by sending its inflation throughout capitalist society. Perhaps, however, this consideration will not much sway the school of decline: might not Vietnam be the Boer War of the United States, with worse to come?

There are good reasons for believing this to be most unlikely. There is no equivalent of Imperial Germany facing the United States. Its geopolitical rival stands outside capitalist society, while its capitalist economic rivals are geopolitically dependent upon it. There is, in other words, none of that super-imposition of conflicts that tends to so increase the intensity of conflict.[76] Very importantly, both these sets of relations are essentially stable.

Recent evidence does give the clear impression that the difficulties facing the Soviet Union – above all, slowing growth at a time when the dynamism of capitalist society is ever more apparent – are far more serious than those facing the United States, a situation exactly opposite to that in which Britain found herself from the 1870s. The behaviour of socialist China since 1957 now makes it impossible to deny that *the* communist menace is a myth; the Soviet Union faces a war on two fronts, with a correspondingly enormous strengthening of the geopolitical position of the United States. The reform policies of both China and the Soviet Union seem set to make communism infinitely less threatening in any case. Moreover, there are well-understood rules concerning spheres of influence between the United States and these major powers; the two superpowers, in particular, are ever more, to use Raymond Aron's expression, 'enemy partners', perhaps most obviously in wishing to prevent the proliferation of nuclear weapons.[77]

The situation that faces the United States within capitalist society is quite as favourable, and it is so in a manner that is historically novel. Japan and Germany were reconstructed as the result of American

---

[76]   R. Dahrendorf, *Class and Class Conflict in Industrial Society*, Stanford University Press, Stanford, 1959.
[77]   Aron, *Peace and War*, part 4.

geopolitical victory: both are secure democracies wedded to trading rather than to heroic strategies. It is extremely unlikely that either Germany or Japan will mount a challenge to the American system. In addition to the particular characters of these states, there are good general reasons for believing that the world economy will not return completely to a no-holds-barred conflict between trading blocs, although there may well be some increase of this type.[78] The fundamental justification for this belief is simply that the speed of technological change makes it ever more catastrophic for a state to withdraw from the world market, something realized by most state leaders and enshrined by them and their leading industries in the sudden spread of joint ventures of very varied sorts.[79] Also, there is now some awareness that traditional protectionist policies are no longer likely to work: how can one protect one's industries against, say, Japan, if that country chooses to assemble in Thailand parts made in South Korea so as to import them into the United States via Mexico? In the case of the United States, the impact of free trade institutions and mentalities, both internally and externally, is likely to make it particularly difficult to adopt any pure protectionist stance.[80] In addition, new political groupings demanding a retention of liberal multilateralism are springing up to counter others seeking protectionism.[81] Finally, it is very clear that many states find the post-war settlement popular and that they will go to considerable lengths to preserve it: that settlement solved the 'German problem' and the 'Japanese problem', while there is widespread awareness that bipolarity in a nuclear age has a great deal to recommend it.

This general situation gives the United States certain clear advantages. The weakness of its geopolitical rival and the absence of challenges from within capitalist society mean that it does not have to acquire formal territorial empires. Of course, Vietnam represented precisely such a formal commitment. But what may prove to be important about that debacle is that it will not be repeated; certainly the United States has

---

[78]   Gilpin, *Political Economy of International Relations.*
[79]   Cf. R. Rosecrance, *The Rise of the Trading State*, Basic Books, New York, 1986.
[80]   J. Goldstein, 'Ideas, Institutions and Trade Policy', *International Organisation*, vol. 42, 1988.
[81]   I. M. Destler and J. Odell, *Anti Protection: Changing Forces in United States Politics*, Institute for International Economics, Washington, 1987; H. Milner, 'Resisting the Protectionist Impulse: Industry and the Making of Trade Policy in France and the United States during the 1970s', *International Organisation*, vol. 41, 1987.

an alternative grand strategy available, as argued in detail below. But its situation as a whole is made completely different by the fact that the economic challenge of Germany and Japan is that of allied states. Such states are not likely to replace their trading strategy with a new autarchic and heroic alternative. Further, Britain's move to territorial empire was made virtually inevitable by the extent to which it traded with the world, and it was scarcely surprising that this led other states to fear they might in the long run be excluded. In contrast, the United States trades far less, that is trade is a smaller proportion of its national product, and it therefore has less need to secure markets through territorial possession – something which may mean that the development of capitalist society is not again so dramatically interrupted by the logic of geopolitics.

Crucially, however, the United States has very considerable leverage over its allied economic rivals, both because it provides their defence and because their economic success is partly dependent on the sheer size of the American market – which the United States could, unlike most other states, close given the huge resource base its continental status affords it. At times seigniorage has been obvious, notably in passing inflation on under the Bretton Woods system; but it is as present today, from the necessity of supporting the dollar to Japan's enforced abandonment of its plans to build fighter planes – a geopolitical form of industrial subsidy.

The situation of the United States differs from that of Britain in a further and absolutely fundamental way. Paul Kennedy is right to argue that Britain's decline had to be great because it had so massively overreached its natural power ranking, that is the portfolio of demographic, geopolitical and natural resources.[82] But there certainly *has* been relative decline, and it is time to turn to assessing its causes. Should we accept the claims of hegemonic stability theory in this case? Has the United States become exhausted because of the burden of defence it has provided for capitalist society as a whole and by its obeisance to liberal multilateralism in the face of formal and informal protectionism elsewhere?

There is some truth to both these claims, but each has recently been subject to much exaggeration. Figures indicating that the United States' economy is being undermined by high defence expenditure, both absolutely and in comparison with her allies, need to be treated with the utmost care. Most obviously, defence expenditure is not now particularly high by historical standards, and it is hard to credit it with causing economic decline given the economic successes of South Korea and

[82] Kennedy, *The Rise and Fall*, ch. 8.

Sweden, both of which pay as large a share of GNP for defence as the United States.[83] Equally, it should not be too easily believed that defence spending is bad for the American economy. The trade-off between defence spending and economic performance is extremely complex,[84] but it is clear that the United States, with long production runs and research at the frontiers of technology, has gained something; certainly the Japanese regard American defence spending, especially when overseen by the Defence Advanced Research Projects Agency, as more or less equivalent to an industrial policy.[85] Recent studies suggest that concentration on defence has not had deleterious effects on domestic industrial capital formation;[86] the National Research Council has added to this the discovery that there is sufficient engineering talent left after concentration on defence for the health of domestic productive industry.[87] Figures for allied defence expenditures tend to be highly distorted;[88] they do not include 'offset payments' nor do they allow for hidden allied costs such as those of conscription and the provision of physical assets.[89] A proper accounting would suggest that the major members of NATO and France pay nearly as large a share of GNP for defence as does the United States for *its worldwide interests*; Japan, of course, pays very significantly less.

In the European case, some of the difference is explicable by the fact that Europeans prefer a defensive strategy that happens to be cheaper, in contrast to the expensive offensive strategy not unnaturally favoured by the United States. Importantly, all figures exclude the informal economic privileges that accrue, as argued, to the United States as military rent and as bribes to ensure that its markets remain open. It is this that

---

[83]   Cf. J. Nye, 'America's Decline: a Myth', *New York Times*, 10 April 1988.

[84]   S. Chan, 'The Impact of Defense Spending on Economic Performance: a Survey of Evidence and Problems', *Orbis*, vol. 29, 1985.

[85]   Reich, *Tales of a New America*.

[86]   D. Greenwood, 'Note on the Impact of Military Expenditure on Economic Growth and Performance', in C. Schmidt, ed., *The Economics of Military Expenditures*, St Martin's Press, New York, 1987; K. Rasler and W. R. Thompson, 'Defense Burdens, Capital Formation and Economic Growth', *Journal of Conflict Resolution*, vol. 32, 1988.

[87]   National Research Council, *The Impact of Defense Spending on Nondefence Engineering Labor Markets*, National Academy Press, Washington, 1986.

[88]   K. Knorr, 'Burden Sharing in NATO', *Orbis*, vol. 29, 1985; D. Wightman, 'United States Balance of Payments Policies in the 1960s: Financing American Forces in Germany and the Trilateral Negotiations of 1966–79, unpublished paper; K. Dunn, 'NATO's Enduring Value', *Foreign Policy*, vol. 71, 1988.

[89]   G. Treverton, *The 'Dollar Drain' and US Forces in Germany*, Ohio University Press, Columbus, 1978; Knorr, 'Burden Sharing'.

leads the advanced states to prop up the dollar and, in Japan's case, to increase its aid budget massively rather than to establish its own aerospace industry; in these ways, the allies informally pay for the cost of defence.

Equally sceptical points must be made about the claim that decline results from the protectionism of others. German economic success at the end of the nineteenth century may have been helped by tariff walls, but it was not fundamentally ascribable to that; the same seems true of Japan today. Bergsten and Cline argue that if Japan had no import barriers at all, America's near fifty billion dollars trade deficit with Japan in 1985 would only have been reduced by five to eight billion dollars, and that five billion dollars would have been added to the deficit if the United States had removed its own considerable barriers to Japanese imports.[90]

Although they are hard to prove in any decisive manner, traditional theories of decline seem to offer a more plausible account of what is happening to the United States. Just as Britain institutionalized its moment of economic success, so too America allowed a set of institutions to consolidate around those Fordist politics of productivity that came to the fore under Roosevelt.[91] Such industrial giantism seems less adapted to the flexible trading system of the contemporary world economy, partly because of the failure of the United States to provide the sort of social infrastructure that underlies it.[92]

American failure to adapt partly reflects its sheer size; it has often chosen to use its power to change international norms rather than to make its society flexible enough to compete, an option that now seems to have ever diminishing returns. Equally important, however, may well be the importance of finance capital within American society; if this sector has not yet reached the historic importance it gained in British history, the ways in which finance is currently favoured over industry, as in the fact that 'junk bonds' are tax deductible, offer obvious resonances.

The whole point at issue can be summarized by saying that one reason for distrusting the 'decline by service provision' thesis of hegemonic stability theory is that it fails to pay proper attention to the

---

[90] F. Bergsten and W. Cline, *The United States – Japan Economic Problem*, Institute for International Economics, Washington, 1987.
[91] Maier, *In Search of Stability*.
[92] M. Piore and C. Sabel, *The Second Industrial Divide*, Basic Books, New York, 1984; Hall, *Liberalism*, ch. 7; L. Weiss, *Creating Capitalism*, Basil Blackwell, Oxford, 1988.

inventiveness, diligence and adaptability of modern trading states.[93] Imitating such virtues would require lowering the extraordinarily high levels of GNP given to consumption by means of increased taxation, less perhaps for direct industrial policy and more for the creation of suitable social infrastructures. If such policies are resisted because they are held to go against the American grain, this can only be ascribed to the particular character of Anglo-Saxon liberalism. As it happens, however, there are good reasons to believe that increased taxes, if mandated for educational or infrastructural renewal, might well be granted. Certainly individual states in America have been able to convince their citizenry of the need for greater taxation for industrial regeneration.[94] There is room for responsible national leadership to make a difference.

It is equally noticeable that the American economy has suffered from geopolitical over-extension, as seen most clearly in Vietnam. Involvement in Vietnam did not seem to have any immediate economic rationale, in terms of markets, investment or raw materials, and this has led Krasner to stress that this policy was the result of anti-communism – an *acte gratuit* whose extraordinary craziness will become more apparent in a moment.[95] There is certainly some truth to the claim that the 'best and the brightest', brought to Washington by Kennedy, suffered markedly from the arrogance of power, and should be held responsible for their actions. Nevertheless, Domhoff is surely right to argue that these advisers were but lesser men carrying out the implications of the grand strategy that America created between 1941 and 1950.[96] The responsibility of the advisers of the 1960s was, as had been the case with those who followed Bismarck, not to think their times for themselves. Still, it behoves us to try to understand the sources of post-war American grand strategy, not least so that the previous claim, that the United States has non-territorial possibilities closed to Britain, may be justified.

Discussion of the origins of American postwar strategy has been exceedingly lively for several years, and it is not possible here to give

[93]   R. Dore, *Flexible Rigidities*, Athlone Press, London, 1986; R. Dore, *Taking Japan Seriously*, Athlone Press, London, 1987; D. Okimoto, *Between MITI and the Market*, Stanford University Press, Stanford, 1988; Weiss, *Creating Capitalism*; Piore and Sabel, *The Second Industrial Divide*; F. C. Deyo, ed., *The Political Economy of the New Asian Industrialism*, Cornell University Press, Ithaca, 1987.
[94]   E. Vogel, *Comeback*, Touchstone, New York, 1985, ch. 10.
[95]   S. Krasner, *Defending the National Interest*, Princeton University Press, Princeton, 1978.
[96]   W. Domhoff, *The Power Elite and the State*, Aldine de Gruyter, New York, 1990, chs 5 and 6.

anything like a summary of recent research.[97] But, it now does seem apparent that no account will be satisfactory unless it recognizes the autonomous impact of four factors. First, the revisionist historians and their followers are surely quite correct to stress that the American state, owing to its liberal character and its historical lack of geopolitical involvement, was especially permeable – largely through the Council for Foreign Relations – to the wishes and demands of its domestic capitalists.[98] It was at this period, for example, that involvement in Vietnam became likely as South-east Asia became defined as part of 'the national interest'. But the revisionist account is incomplete. In particular, secondly, we must note that many state leaders had, from the turn of the century, geopolitical visions of their own, a remarkable number of which were formed in the surprisingly Kiplingesque surroundings of Groton.[99] This elite enjoyed the power it discovered during the war, and embraced empire willingly. Of course, there was a considerable overlap between the first and second sets of actors; this was scarcely surprising since the latter saw multilateralism as a means to ensure peace. None the less, if the statements of the political elite, public and private, are to be believed they were far more worried by questions of security than by the needs of the American economy, whether seen from their own point of view or as interpreted for them by capitalists and their experts. Consideration of the traditional balance of power led to the Truman administration's decisions to allow the multilateral norms they preferred to be diluted and to accept continental involvement in NATO.

A third set of actors were not American at all. The collapse of Britain and the rigorous if defensively inclined security demands of Stalin meant that many Europeans, most notably Bevin, actively sought an American presence.[100] This was an 'empire by invitation', and some part of its

[97] J. L. Gaddis, 'The Emerging Post-revisionist Synthesis', *Diplomatic History*, vol. 7, 1983 and *The Long Peace*, Oxford University Press, New York, 1987.
[98] G. Kolko, *The Politics of War*, Random House, New York, 1969; J. Frieden, 'Sectoral Conflict and US Foreign Economic Policy, 1914–40', *International Organisation*, vol. 41, 1988; Domhoff, *The Power Elite and the State*, ch. 5.
[99] H. K. Beale, *Theodore Roosevelt and the Rise of America to World Power*, Collier Books, New York, 1967; J. L. Gaddis, *The United States and the Origins of the Cold War, 1941–47*, Columbia University Press, New York, 1972; J. L. Gaddis, *Strategies of Containment*, Oxford University Press, New York, 1982; W. Widenor, *Henry Cabot Lodge and the Search for an American Foreign Policy*, University of California Press, Berkeley, 1980.
[100] V. Mastny, *Russia's Road to the Cold War*, Columbia University Press, New York, 1979.

dynamic came from allied actions.[101] Finally, the character of the grand strategy was markedly influenced by the nature of American institutions and experience. The American people – and, in particular, voters with ethnic ancestries in Ireland and Germany – had long been suspicious of foreign entanglements, and it did not prove easy to gain support for a global policy.[102]

In 1946 the Truman administration was faced with an ebullient Republican Congress, which was at once anti-communist and keen to balance the budget. It proved possible to turn fiercely anti-communist Republicans such as Vandenberg, who himself faced re-election in a constituency of mid-Western Polish-American voters, in an internationalist direction, and to split them from that fiscally cautious mainstream headed by Taft, which remained suspicious of foreign involvement. There is as yet no agreement amongst historians as to the exact input of public opinion on policy formation at this time, but there can be no doubt but that there was some. It would in principle have been possible to strike a simple 'spheres of influence' deal with the Soviet Union, as Kennan argued; that this did not happen was because the American people, and many of their leaders, saw foreign affairs in rather moralistic terms – involvement could be by crusade alone.[103] This all-or-nothing approach finally became cemented by the Korean War, which seemed to justify the charges of the 'loss of China' made by McCarthy. The fear of electoral retribution, probably much exaggerated in point of fact, made politicians rather reluctant to see the world in other than bipolar terms. This led to over-extension – not in Europe, it should be noted, but in the Third World where bipolar vision prevents proper appreciation of local forces and where there are few strategic interests of any significance.[104]

[101]   G. Lundestad, 'Empire by Invitation?', *Journal of Peace Research*, vol. 23, 1986.
[102]   F. G. Gilbert, *To the Farewell Address: Ideas of Early American Foreign Policy*, Princeton University Press, Princeton, 1961; Gaddis, *Origins of the Cold War*.
[103]   F. Klingberg, 'Cyclical Trends in American Foreign Policy Moods and Their Policy Implications', in C. W. Kegley and P. McGowan, eds, *Challenges to America: United States Foreign Policy in the 1980s*, Sage, Beverly Hills, 1979; S. Hoffmann, *Gulliver's Troubles, or the Setting of American Foreign Policy*, McGraw-Hill, New York, 1968.
[104]   S. Van Evera, 'American Strategic Interests: Why Europe Matters, Why the Third World Doesn't', testimony prepared for hearings before the Panel on Defense Burdensharing, Committee on Armed Services, US House of Representatives, 2 March 1988.

The United States has an alternative grand strategy that it can adopt. One important element of such a strategy is learning, against the tenor of American political experience, that states in the Third World need to be strengthened for developmental purposes; this does not represent an unadulterated attack on liberal principles, especially since the spread of nationalism is likely, as Kennan realized in the 1940s, to dilute the cohesion of the communist movement.[105] The second important element of an alternative American grand strategy is for the United States to realize the extent of its extraordinary power. It really does not matter if a state withdraws from the world market; this is likely to be temporary since the costs of such withdrawal, given the fact that it is capitalist and not socialist society that has abundant capital and significant markets, exact such an incredibly high price.

One of the most interesting questions in world politics today is whether modifications to post-war grand strategy can be made that will recognize regional dynamics and 'take class out of geopolitics'. It seems likely that capitalists can be convinced, given the obvious increase in market power even with the loss of Vietnam; they are unlikely to stand in the way of such a policy. Similarly, a determined political elite is likely to be able to achieve such a policy despite fear of electoral punishment. It is important to have international understanding so that no shocks will create such strong domestic pressure, as was the case at the end of President Carter's term of office, when the Soviet Union invaded Afghanistan. However, domestic pressures can all too easily be exaggerated. Kennedy was able to 'lose' Laos and Carter Zimbabwe without such punishment, largely because the future of these states was not defined in advance as something that would adversely affect American prestige. The same could have happened in Vietnam, perhaps as late as 1965; that it did not necessitates blaming the political elite of the time rather than the American people. There is room, in other words, for creative leadership.

Conclusion

The argument that has been made deserves summary. Doubt has been cast on the claim of hegemonic stability that the decline of Britain and the United States results from their bearing the burden of services for

---

[105] S. Hoffman, *Duties Beyond Borders*, Syracuse University Press, Syracuse, 1981; Gaddis, *Strategies of Containment*; Hall, *Liberalism*, ch. 7; Van Evera, 'American Strategic Interests'. For fuller justification of these points, see chs 4 and 6 in this volume.

capitalist society. In general, the decline of hegemons – of which the United States is in fact the only genuine representative – is best understood in traditional and neutral terms, as the result of geopolitical overextension and the inability to overcome social blockages. In particular, both Britain and the United States adhere to a full-blooded marketist ideology (seen most clearly in the freedom given to financial sectors and in the absence of industrial policies of varied types) that makes it hard for them to adapt within capitalist society. This more particular factor has been given separate analytic consideration because in the abstract there is no reason to believe that a hegemonic leader has to embrace every idea and institution beloved by Anglo-Saxon liberalism.

Two implications of the argument are worth highlighting. First, the theoretical presuppositions at work are largely realist: decline is seen as the result of a hegemon's own mistakes. This argument is perfectly compatible with the other elements of hegemonic stability theory; indeed the most distinguished theorist of that school oscillates between the sorts of arguments I have made and the false self-liquidating theory of hegemonic rule.[106] Secondly, a distinctive policy implication follows from the argument. As the external burdens of hegemony are not the fundamental reasons for the relative decline of the United States, policy drives emphasizing burden-sharing are effectively a distraction of time and energy. Renewal is in the hands of the United States alone.

Will the United States decline further as did Britain?. A central tenet of this chapter has been that the United States is in a much more advantageous position than was Britain. The uniqueness of its position as defender of capitalist society makes it likely that for some considerable and unspecifiable time the United States will be able to shore up its position by extracting seigniorage of various kinds from its allies. However, some social processes reminiscent of Britain seem to be at work in the United States; this suggests that decline may yet go much further, although, because it is larger, the United States is most unlikely to cease to be the main player in the modern world political economy. Despite the fact, for example, that American industrialists feature as heroes of a popular culture generally suspicious of Wall Street, the increasing importance of financial capital to the American economy is not in question; importantly, the sophistication of the equity market, not least when financed by junk bonds, places a disastrous premium on short-term returns only too familiar from a reading of British economic history. A shared Anglo-Saxon economic liberalism also seems present in the lack of

[106]   Gilpin, *War and Change*; Gilpin, *Political Economy of International Relations*.

industrial policy and of attempts to manufacture comparative advantage, although something like this may be happening at the state level in America today.

If all this is similar, there is one place at which the United States seems almost worse off than Britain. American politics are not at present coping creatively with the problems discussed in this chapter; it is proving especially difficult to contain or reverse decline by the means indicated, that is by raising taxes to enhance competitiveness and by adopting the alternative geopolitical strategy. These policies have forceful logics to recommend them in the abstract; at present they do not seem politically feasible. Why is this?

Some authors suggest that changes in economic organization are responsible: as banks and industry become internationalized, they increasingly favour free trade at the expense of domestic renewal.[107] There may be some truth in this, as there is in the argument that the greater internationalization of business diminishes domestic manufacturing employment in a way that affects the American electoral system.[108] But the argument is by no means convincing: it suggests a degree of coordination between business interests and foreign geopolitical and geoeconomic policy for which there is, at least as yet, little evidence.

Other authors have suggested that electoral pressures, particularly in a political system in which power is divided between the executive and legislative branches, make it hard to remain flexible, especially in foreign affairs. There may be some truth in this point as well, but it should not be accepted too easily. Democracy has opportunity/costs in all areas: there *is* a danger that moralistic swings of mood will replace calculation but the possibility remains that democratic review may enhance the policy process.

If I were to risk a judgement on the costs and benefits of democracy to the conduct of American foreign affairs, it would be to argue this: that the most serious mistakes of what has been generally an amazingly successful post-war foreign policy are attributable to autonomous elite actions, some of which, notably those concerning the Reagan administration's actions towards Iran, would have benefited greatly from more open democratic scrutiny. Democracy is a resource quite as much as a stumbling block, at least for an intelligent and determined elite.

This suggests a final factor whose impact is improperly understood but is of undoubted importance. During the Second World War something

---

[107]   Frieden, 'Sectoral Conflict'.
[108]   B. Harrison and B. Bluestone, *The Great U-Turn*, Basic Books, New York, 1988.

like a political class was created in the United States. If this class was at times constrained by the popular passions it had itself in part aroused and by the institutional surroundings in which it had to work, its fundamental unity meant that it could, when it acted skilfully, have its way most of the time. A determined political elite could still succeed in most of the tasks it set itself. But the unity of that class has been ruptured – by different responses to the student movement and to Vietnam and as the result of divided loyalties over Israel. With responsible leadership much could be done in the United States. At present, however, the fragmentation of the political elite suggests that American decline may not yet have bottomed out.

8

THE WEARY TITAN? ARMS
AND EMPIRE, 1870–1913

At the 1902 Colonial Conference, Joseph Chamberlain declared Great Britain to be 'a weary titan' staggering 'beneath the too vast orb of its fate'. There was, of course, an element of special pleading here: Chamberlain was seeking contributions from the Dominions to the burden of defence as part of his larger vision of imperial unity. A brilliant recent contribution by two leading economic historians has sought to separate what Chamberlain wished to conjoin. Davis and Huttenback agree that the burden of defence was very great but they also insist that the empire was never a strikingly good investment; this argument has been further developed by Patrick O'Brien.[1] Paul Kennedy recently challenged one element of this radical liberal case. While recognizing that the absolute costs of British defence were great, he insisted that costs need to be seen in the light of the great wealth of the economy. This point of methodology led to a substantive claim: the proportion of national

[1] L. E. Davis and R. E. Huttenback, *Mammon and the Pursuit of Empire: The Political Economy of British Imperialism*, Cambridge University Press, Cambridge, 1986; P. O'Brien, 'The Costs and Benefits of British Imperialism', *Past and Present*, no. 120, 1988. This chapter rests on a particular data base, and I gratefully acknowledge the Milton Fund of Harvard University and McGill University, both of which provided funds to enable me to employ John Hobson – for whose help I am indebted – as a research assistant. Our joint research resulted in an earlier article: J. A. Hall and J. M. Hobson, 'Re-appraising the Costs of British Imperialism in the Late Nineteenth and Early Twentieth Centuries', Department of Sociology, McGill University, Working Paper 91–9, 1991.

income devoted to defence may well, according to Kennedy, have been less in Britain than on the continent: the 'burden' of defence may not have been considerable.[2] In an interesting reply, O'Brien accepted the methodological point but continued to maintain that Britain's military burden *was* excessive.[3]

This chapter introduces new evidence so as to move as close as possible to a resolution of this disagreement in the debate about Britain's military burden. Such evidence is sorely needed. Bluntly, the figures offered by both Kennedy and O'Brien cannot give a reliable view of the weight of Britain's military burden. The crucial figures provided by both authors suffer from a similar conceptual failing, namely that they rest upon conversion into a single currency. Such currency conversion is likely to be particularly unreliable when based on market exchange rates because these do not give an accurate idea of differences in purchasing power.[4] Whilst Kennedy is to be applauded for refusing to accept the unindexed figures of Davis and Huttenback, on which O'Brien based his original case, little faith can be placed in A. J. P. Taylor's figures of 'Percentage of National Income Devoted to Armaments, 1914', which he offers as an alternative.[5] These figures were derived from Quincy Wright, who in turn relied upon the national income data produced by Kuznets in 1933.[6] One obvious problem with the latter's figures is that they are now rather old: sixty years of economic history should allow rather firmer conclusions! However, these figures are crucially weak because Kuznets had to use market exchange rates to convert different national incomes into then current US dollars. The gross national product figures used by O'Brien when seeking, in his reply to Kennedy, to go beyond absolute military

[2] P. Kennedy, 'Debate', *Past and Present*, no. 125, 1989.
[3] P. O'Brien, 'Reply', *Past and Present*, no. 125, 1989.
[4] P. O'Brien and C. Keyder, *Economic Growth in Britain and France, 1780–1914: Two Paths to the Twentieth Century*, Allen & Unwin, London, 1978, ch. 2; W. Beckerman, *International Comparisons of Real Incomes*, OECD, Paris, 1966, pp. 8, 34–5.
[5] Kennedy, 'Debate', pp. 190–1, citing A. J. P. Taylor, *The Struggle for Mastery in Europe, 1848–1918*, Oxford University Press, Oxford, 1954, table 6, p. xxix. Note that there are additional reasons for distrusting the Davis and Huttenback data, not least that their per capita estimates are inflated as the result of being based only on the population of England, Scotland and Wales. For details on this point, see Hall and Hobson, 'Re-appraising the Costs of British Imperialism', pp. 4–5.
[6] Q. Wright, *A Study of War*, 2nd Edn., Chicago University Press, Chicago, 1965, pp. 670–1; S. Kuznets, 'National Income', *Encyclopedia of the Social Sciences*, vol. 11, Macmillan, New York, 1933, table 1, p. 206.

spending so as to gauge Britain's 'real military burden' suffer from the same problem.[7] For the figures in question, those of Bairoch, also standardized national incomes (in this case into constant 1960 U.S. dollars) by use of market exchange rates, albeit with some 'ad hoc adjustments'.[8] Bairoch noted that his adjustment for differences in national price structures was 'not only very crude' but 'also in certain respects arbitrary'.[9] Better figures are required.

One way forward might be to utilize various recent data series which have standardized national income into constant US dollars by means of OECD purchasing power parities.[10] While such figures are an improvement on those used by Kennedy and O'Brien, the sheer fact that statisticians are compelled to make assumptions about the similarity of commodities produced in different countries at various points in time makes them problematic.[11] Rather than use any such set of generalist figures, and thereby encounter questionable assumptions about convertibility, I choose to work entirely with national currencies.[12] This makes complete sense. Absolute costs mean little given that some nation states are far wealthier than others: the real measure of the burden of the military *is* that of the proportion of national income devoted to military affairs.[13] So there is no reason whatsoever to bother with conversions into a single currency. My calculations accordingly make use of the best

[7]   P. A. Bairoch, 'Europe's Gross National Product: 1800–1975', *Journal of European Economic History*, vol. 5, 1976.
[8]   N. F. R. Crafts, 'New Estimates of G.N.P. in Europe', *Explorations in Economic History*, vol. 20, p. 388.
[9]   Bairoch, 'Europe's Gross National Product', pp. 275, 318.
[10]   Crafts, 'New Estimates', pp. 387–401; I. B. Kravis, 'Real G. D. P. Per Capita for More than One Hundred Countries', *Economic Journal*, vol. 88, 1978; I. B. Kravis, *World Product and Income*, Johns Hopkins University Press, Baltimore, 1982; A. Maddison, *Phases of Capitalist Development*, Oxford University Press, Oxford, 1962; A. Maddison, *The World Economy in the Twentieth Century*, OECD, Paris, 1989.
[11]   O'Brien and Keyder, *Economic Growth*, p. 34.
[12]   Military expenditure figures expressed in pounds sterling are, however, provided in Hall and Hobson, 'Re-appraising the Costs of British Imperialism', p. 3.
[13]   Agreement between Kennedy and O'Brien is shared by two other analysts, both of whom have produced evidence – in each case less extensive than that in this chapter – about the military burdens of the great powers in this period: see M. Mann, *Sources of Social Power*, vol. 2: *The Rise of Classes and Nation-States, 1760–1914*, Cambridge University Press, Cambridge, 1993, ch. 11 and A. Offer, 'The British Empire, 1870–1914: a Waste of Money?', *Economic History Review*, vol. 46, 1993. I thank these authors, together with Mary MacKinnon and E. A. Wrigley, for advice and encouragement.

available data on both military expenditure and national income specific to each country.[14] Two points must be made about these calculations. Firstly, all national income data have been standardized to one measure, net national product at factor cost; this procedure has necessitated some conversions, which are detailed in the appendix. Secondly, the figures for military spending *include* various extraordinary military expenditures that were financed by loans but *exclude* interest paid on debt.[15]

The results of my research are presented in the table. No support is lent by these figures to the view, advanced by Davis and Huttenback and powerfully re-stated by O'Brien, that Britain suffered in comparative terms from an excessive military burden. On the contrary, Britain's average is at the lower end of the international league table, although it is nowhere near as low as that of the United States. The weight of military spending was not so great as to cripple Britain.

Some reflections about the degree of robustness of these findings are in order. Consideration must certainly be given first to O'Brien's radically sceptical comment to the effect that there are no unambiguous conceptual notions nor valid statistical estimates of national income.[16] It is quite true that there are various statistical problems in the production of such data; awareness of this is the largest consideration in explaining the caution of the initial claim – 'to move as close as possible to a resolution' of the debate about the size of Britain's military burden. However, it is interesting to note that O'Brien himself relied on this type of formula both in an article on taxation in Britain and France between 1715 and 1810 and in a monograph on economic growth in the same two countries between 1780 and 1914.[17] The very great contribution made by these works frees

---

[14]   As is obvious from the table, it is not possible to produce a complete data series for every country. There are no reliable national income statistics before the mid-1880s for Japan and Russia, whilst 1872 was the first full fiscal year of the German Reich. In the latter case the costs of the Franco-Prussian war are therefore excluded: this means that the average military burden between 1872 and 1913 may be underestimated by as much as 0.2 per cent.

[15]   Calculating interest on debt is an extremely complicated exercise requiring such data as the length of such loans and their percentage rates (which differ within the internal accounts of each budget), as well as data showing what proportion of national debt was derived from military expenditure. This is simply too difficult for most of these countries. But, it is not my intention to foreclose discussion of this difficult area: on the contrary, much of the remainder of this chapter concentrates precisely on this problem.

[16]   O'Brien, 'Reply', p. 198.

[17]   P. O'Brien and P. Mathias, 'Taxation in Britain and France, 1715–1810: a Comparison of the Social and Economic Incidence of Taxes collected for the Central Governments', *Journal of European Economic History*, vol. 5, 1976;

TABLE Comparative real military burdens of the Great Powers, 1870–1913

Year	Britain	Italy	Germany	Russia	USA	Japan	France	Austria
1870	2.4	2.6	–	–	1.3	–	3.2	5.1
1871	2.2	2.1	–	–	0.9	–	2.9	5.0
1872	2.3	2.1	2.3	–	0.9	–	3.0	4.4
1873	2.0	1.9	2.4	–	1.0	–	3.1	4.8
1874	2.2	2.1	2.6	–	1.0	–	3.0	4.5
1875	2.2	2.4	3.0	–	0.9	–	3.1	4.3
1876	2.3	2.4	2.9	–	0.8	–	3.4	4.5
1877	2.3	2.5	3.1	–	0.6	–	3.6	4.2
1878	2.7	2.7	3.3	–	0.6	–	3.9	7.0
1879	2.9	2.5	3.1	–	0.7	–	3.8	4.7
1880	2.6	2.6	3.0	–	0.6	–	3.7	3.8
1881	2.3	2.9	3.0	–	0.7	–	3.8	3.7
1882	2.4	3.0	2.9	–	0.6	–	3.8	4.5
1883	2.6	3.6	2.7	–	0.6	–	4.0	3.6
1884	2.5	3.5	2.7	–	0.5	–	4.3	3.6
1885	2.7	3.6	2.8	4.1	0.6	2.4	4.6	3.4
1886	3.5	3.5	2.9	4.6	0.5	2.9	4.3	3.2
1887	2.7	4.0	3.3	3.7	0.5	3.2	3.8	4.2
1888	2.4	4.9	3.5	3.6	0.5	3.3	3.6	4.1
1889	2.1	5.9	3.3	4.3	0.6	3.1	3.7	3.6
1890	2.4	4.2	3.8	4.4	0.6	2.0	3.7	3.2
1891	2.4	3.9	3.5	4.9	0.7	2.7	4.3	3.1
1892	2.5	3.9	3.3	4.4	0.6	2.5	4.2	3.1
1893	2.5	3.6	3.4	4.4	0.7	2.6	4.2	3.1
1894	2.4	3.8	3.5	4.3	0.7	10.8	4.4	2.9
1895	2.4	3.4	3.3	4.8	0.7	9.0	4.3	2.8
1896	2.6	4.5	3.1	4.8	0.7	5.6	4.4	2.8
1897	2.6	3.9	3.1	4.5	0.6	6.9	4.3	3.0
1898	2.5	3.4	3.1	4.8	1.0	5.4	3.8	2.9
1899	2.6	3.3	3.1	3.9	1.9	6.3	3.9	2.7
1900	4.0	3.1	3.1	4.0	1.3	6.5	4.2	2.7
1901	7.0	3.2	3.6	3.9	1.4	5.2	4.3	2.7
1902	7.1	3.3	3.5	3.7	0.8	4.4	4.3	2.7
1903	5.9	2.9	3.2	4.1	0.9	6.5	4.0	2.8
1904	4.2	3.0	3.1	9.2	1.3	27.9	3.9	2.8
1905	3.7	2.9	3.1	13.8	1.1	30.6	3.9	2.5
1906	3.3	2.7	3.2	8.7	1.2	14.5	4.2	2.3
1907	3.0	2.7	3.5	5.4	0.9	7.6	3.8	2.2
1908	3.1	2.8	3.4	4.7	1.1	7.4	4 0	2.4
1909	3.1	2.9	3.5	4.3	1.1	6.4	4.1	3.0
1910	3.2	3.0	3.3	4.0	1.1	6.7	4.0	2.6
1911	3.3	3.3	3.1	4.3	1.2	6.2	4.5	2.4
1912	3.2	4.0	3.1	4.5	0.9	5.5	4.2	2.6
1913	3.2	5.1	3.9	5.1	1.0	5.1	4.8	3.2
Averages	3.1	3.3	3.2	5.1	0.9	8.2	4.0	3.1

Sources: See Appendix

me from despair about my own enterprise! But matters need not be left at this level of generality. Some particular points about the character of the figures deserve to be stressed.

The most important is that the figures used present the worst-case scenario for the general argument. While details in this matter can best be left to the appendix, an example of this conservatism is in order. P. C. Witt's figures were not used, even though these would have strengthened the argument.[18] An obvious virtue of his figures is the inclusion of payment for military pensions; this brings his figures into line with those of most other countries, especially Britain, whose 'non-effective services' accounted for approximately 18 per cent of total army spending until about 1900.[19] What is more striking is the inclusion of expenditure that had clear military purpose even though it is listed under civilian headings – a characteristic practice of the Wilhelmine state, keen not to draw the attention of neighbours to its militarism. Such expenditure includes specifically strategic railways, that is the laying of seven or eight parallel tracks to allow for rapid mobilization, and the widening of the north-east canals. If these expenditures were to be added to further costs for colonial troops and the military expeditions to East and West Africa, the military burden of Imperial Germany would have been perhaps 0.4 per cent higher between 1872 and 1913. Similarly, the French figures used do not include extraordinary expenditures. Inclusion of such payments might well increase the average of France's military burden to 4.5%. Here too the figures offer a worst-case scenario.

Witt also included – whereas I have not, in the previous paragraph and more generally – payment on interest on debt. More light must be cast on a difficult area. There was a marked difference between states in regard to borrowing for military expenditure. In Britain parliamentary control combined with Gladstonian orthodoxy to rule out any such borrowing in times of peace.[20] In contrast, most continental powers increasingly

O' Brien and Keyder, *Economic Growth in Britain and France*. In both these pieces of work, figures are given for commodity output rather than national income – which does not alter the similarity in the logic of the approach.

[18]   P. C. Witt, *Die Finanzpolitik des Deutschen Reiches von 1903 bis 1913*, Matthiesen Verlag, Lübeck and Hamburg, 1970, table 14, pp. 380–1.

[19]   See for example British Parliamentary Papers XLIX 1900, and various back issues. It should, however, be noted that British non-effective (as well as effective) rates of pay were the highest in the world: on this, see also n. 20.

[20]   This financial practice had long been judged a source of British military strength. In Selborne's words: '. . . its Credit (and its Navy) seem to me to be the two main pillars on which the strength of this country rests and each is essential to the other' (cited by P. Kennedy, *The Rise of the Anglo-German Antagonism, 1860–1914*, Allen & Unwin, London, 1980, p. 325). Cf. J.

financed their peacetime military expenditure by loans. Kennedy noted that the continental countries paid for this practice indirectly, in a way that does not show up in the table, through higher interest rates – which in theory would have disadvantaged their industries in comparison with those of Britain.[21] Differently put, the costs of military affairs were significantly greater than my figures allow.[22]

This is only one way of looking at loans, and an alternative approach, which might seem to cause a serious problem for the argument, must be evaluated. It is best to approach this matter circuitously by asking why Britain's military burden was so low.

One reason for the dislike of borrowing, founded in classical political economy, is that taxation *per se* is deemed to be generally unproductive.[23] But geopolitical necessity is the mother of fiscal invention, and it

Brewer, *The Sinews of Power*, Hutchinson, London, 1988; O' Brien, 'Costs and Benefits', p. 198; P. O' Brien, 'The Political Economy of British Taxation, 1660–1815', *Economic History Review*, vol. 41, 1988; K. Rasler and W. Thompson, 'Global Wars, Public Debts, and the Long Cycle', *World Politics*, vol. 35, 1990.
[21]   Kennedy, 'Debate', p. 190.
[22]   If the higher interest rates in Germany and Russia had the advantage of attracting surplus capital, the downside of the situation was an increase in instability. 'Financial convulsions', for example, followed the second Moroccan crisis, according to Kennedy, *The Rise of the Anglo-German Antagonism*, p. 303. On the Russian situation, see M. Falkus, *The Industrialisation of Russia, 1700–1914*, Macmillan, London, 1972, pp. 61, 72; A. Kahan, 'Government Policies and the Industrialisation of Russia', *Journal of Economic History*, vol. 27, 1967, pp. 71–3.
[23]   D. Ricardo, *The Principles of Political Economy and Taxation*, Pelican, London, 1971, pp. 168–72 and John Stuart Mill, *Principles of Political Economy*, George Routledge and Sons, 1895, book 5. Cf. H. V. Emy, 'The Impact of Financial Policy on English Party Politics before 1914', *Historical Journal*, vol. 15, 1972. The British political tradition effectively increased military spending, in comparison with the continental powers, by ruling out conscription – as O'Brien noted in 'Costs and Benefits', pp. 189–90. Continental military pay rates were inadequate for conscripts to live on, and they were forced to supplement their incomes from external sources. The resulting difference between German and British military recruitment costs after 1900 may have risen to as much as 0.7 per cent of net national product according to calculations in Hall and Hobson, 'Re-appraising the Costs of British Imperialism', pp. 21–2. This is a substantial figure, increasing Germany's 'real' military burden very sharply. Furthermore, it is important to stress that the costs of conscription to the advanced economies of Germany and France, that is the loss of labour power resulting in an effective diminution of net national product, do not appear in state budgetary records, and so are missing from the table. It is only fair to note, however, that the British style of recruitment owed as much to logistics as to liberalism. Britain needed volunteers rather than conscripts because long-term service was necessitated by the sheer length of voyages to and from the empire.

is likely that a genuine threat would have undermined the reluctance to pay taxes. Accordingly, the much more important reason accounting for relatively low military expenditure concerns the way Britain changed its grand strategy so as to maximize its assets. In naval affairs, crucially, redeployment took the place of construction: after 1905 domestic fleet size was maintained by recalling ships patrolling imperial waters, a move made possible by diplomatic moves neutralizing threats from France, the United States and Japan. What was happening deserves emphasis. The empire provided considerable relief to British taxpayers: had there been no empire, they might well have been the most heavily burdened in the world, for then construction rather than redeployment would have been necessary. And of course the greatest imperial aid was provided on the battlefields of Flanders.[24]

What has just been said can be expressed in economistic terms: the fiscal investment in the empire paid the dividend first of a diminished military burden and then of actual survival. But how much were those costs in the first place? It is worth stressing that my figures for Britain encompass *all* military expenditure, whether for Europe or the empire: the costs of maintaining the empire were insufficient to push Britain towards the top of the international league table. But what about the cost of acquiring the empire? If Britain refused to borrow during peacetime, it had often done so in wartime. Is O'Brien right to claim that the annual interest payments on debt, which were considerable, should be seen as part of Britain's military burden? More particularly, is it fair to make this claim on the ground that the money had been borrowed largely to finance colonial wars?[25]

Whilst it is not the case that all loans were taken out for military purposes, most did have military origins.[26] Tracing the development of the debt makes this clear. The debt began in earnest after 1694, standing in that year at £1.2 million. War soon led it to increase. After the Nine Years' War (1689–1699), the War of the Spanish Succession (1702–1713), and the War of the Quadruple Alliance (1718–1720), the debt had risen to £49.9 million. The Spanish War (1726–1729), the War of Jenkins's Ear (1739–1748), the Seven Years War (1756–1763) and the American War of Independence (1775–1783) increased the debt to a

[24]   Offer, 'The British Empire', pp. 231–6.

[25]   O'Brien, 'Costs and Benefits', pp. 193–4. See also his 'Political Economy of British Taxation'

[26]   From the end of the Crimean War until 1898, £41.4 million of a total £58.6 million taken out in loans for colonial purposes was in fact used for debt redemption and consolidation. On this point, see British Parliamentary Papers, 1898, LII Cd 8966, 'National Debt', pp. 16–19.

substantial £228.6 million. But, the really huge jump in the debt was occasioned by involvement in the Revolutionary and Napoleonic wars, which saw the debt rise from £234 million in 1793 to a colossal £816 million in 1815. Thereafter the debt was gradually reduced. By 1898, it stood at £588 million; it jumped to £640 million through the Boer War but returned to £587 million by 1914.[27]

There can be no doubt that Britain had to pay for past military involvement. The analytically interesting question raised by O'Brien is whether *all* that payment should be considered part of the imperial commitment. The answer must be a resounding no, for it is completely clear, *pace* O'Brien, that most of the military involvement that had led to loans had little to do with colonial or imperial affairs. A crude 'thought-experiment' makes this clear. Most of the debt was acquired in the eleven years after 1793. Quincy Wright labelled these wars as 'balance of power' in nature.[28] Holsti gives a more sophisticated picture, arguing that Empire was but one issue among combatants.[29] If 70 per cent of these wars were non-colonial, then the debt occasioned by colonial involvement would stand at only £407.4 million in 1815, that is almost exactly half of the actual total for that year.[30] If the annual interest repayments made after 1815 are halved, the interest figure ascribed by Davis and Huttenback as due to colonial involvement must be revised downwards by at least 50 per cent.[31] Inclusion of that much smaller figure would still not push Britain to the top of the international league table. The average military burden for Britain between 1870 and 1913 would remain below 4 per cent if this figure for debt repayment were included; it would probably have been in a range between 3.5 and 3.7 per cent.

This figure needs to be placed in context. Were it to be used, Britain's military burden would remain less than that of Russia and France, particularly if proper attention was given to France's extraordinary expenditures. More importantly, were the noted adjustments to be made for Germany – most obviously to allow for *all* military expenditures, the

27   British Parliamentary Papers, 1857–1858, XXXIII, 'National Debt', pp. 62–9, 70–83 and 'Public Debt, Its Origins and Progress', pp. 93–105; British Parliamentary Papers, 1898, LII, Cd 8966, pp. 6–9; British Parliamentary Papers *Statistical Abstract (UK)* (1914–16), vol. 62, Cd 8128, p. 10.
28   Wright, *A Study of War*, tables 36 and 37, pp. 645–6.
29   K. J. Holsti, *Peace and War: Armed Conflicts and International Order, 1648–1989*, Cambridge University Press, Cambridge, 1991, pp. 86–7.
30   £816 million (1815 debt figure) less £234 million (1793 debt figure) times 70 percent. Note that this derivation assumes, unrealistically, that all debt prior to 1793 was colonial in origin.
31   Davis and Huttenback, *Mammon and Empire*, table 6.4, p. 178.

expense of war in 1870 and 1871 and payments on debts incurred for military reasons – its military burden would remain greater than Britain's.[32] While the discussion as a whole shows that the numbers in the table are not – perhaps cannot be – absolutely precise, no fundamental reason for doubting the broad thrust of the initial conclusions has emerged.

When O'Brien published an amended version of his first paper he entitled it 'The Imperial Component in the Decline of the British Economy before 1914'.[33] Comments occasioned by this title allow highlighting of what *has* and what *has not* been claimed in this chapter.

The direct costs of empire were not significant enough to have caused relative decline in this period.[34] Britain did not suffer from 'fiscal over-stretch': on the contrary, its fiscal extraction rate, in comparison with that of most continental states, was low – and, after 1900, increasingly less regressive, not least as the result of the 'People's Budget' driven through by Lloyd George.[35] Nor was Britain over-extended in any more general way – rather there was a moderate and sensible balance between resources and commitment.[36] In this connection, it is worth insisting that Germany rather than Britain was over-extended, less because of the military burden *per se* than because of a diplomatic failure that led to its having to face war on two fronts.[37]

All of this does not entail, as a direct consequence, any uncritical and total endorsement of empire. Whilst it is true that imperial troops helped on the Flanders battlefields, naval forces would not have had to be

---

[32] This statement takes into account the diminution by 0.2 per cent of the average of Germany's military burden between 1872 and 1913 discussed in the second part of the appendix; it would hold even if the expenses of 1871 and 1872 were omitted. Inclusion of the more imponderable factors discussed – the hidden costs of recruitment and the burden of high interest rates – would strengthen the argument still further.

[33] This paper appeared in M. Mann, ed., *The Rise and Decline of the Nation State*, Basil Blackwell, Oxford, 1990.

[34] It is important to remember, however, that the direct military costs of the empire *increased* in the inter-war years, largely owing to the rise of various nationalisms. For further argument and references on this point, see the previous chapter.

[35] For details, see J. M. Hobson, 'The Tax-seeking State: Protectionism, Taxation and State Structures in Germany, Russia, Britain and America, 1870–1914', PhD dissertation, London University, 1991.

[36] A. L. Friedberg, *The Weary Titan: Britain and the Experience of Relative Decline, 1895–1905*, Princeton University Press, Princeton, 1988, ch. 7 interestingly goes even further in arguing that Britain would have been wise to spend *more* rather than *less* on defence.

[37] J. Snyder, *Myths of Empire*, Cornell University Press, Ithaca, 1991, ch. 3.

redeployed to home waters had they been there in the first place: naval superiority was guaranteed by the level of spending that had taken place. Furthermore, a weight of evidence suggests that the empire created problems for the British economy, especially in the longer run. The colonies provided an outlet for Britain's oldest industries.[38] The empire tended to shield inefficiency, the opportunity cost of which was the failure to create industries with higher growth rates. As a result, Britain paid less attention to the important capital goods sector.[39] And it may well be that possession of empire hurt the economy in a less tangible way. It is hard to concentrate on two things at the same time. Accordingly, the failure of the British elite to respond to economic slow-down may best be ascribed to the fact that their attention was so concentrated on geopolitical prestige.

All in all, there remains much to be said for O'Brien's claim that an early 'delinking of the economy from commerce with the empire may have promoted faster productivity growth and the structural changes required by the British economy to meet the challenges of the twentieth century'.[40] But even if (perhaps especially if) the empire had given massive economic returns, was its possession altogether wise in geopolitical terms? In 1805 William Playfair, friend and follower of Smith, warned against grabbing too much of the world on the grounds that this would lead to resentment. Is there not a modicum of sense in his view that 'if there were no such possessions, or if they were equally divided, there would be very little cause for war amongst nations'?[41]

[38] A. Cairncross, *Home and Foreign Investment, 1870–1913: Studies in Capital Accumulation*, Harvester, Brighton, 1975, pp. 103–208, 222–246.

[39] F. Crouzet, 'Trade and Empire: the British Experience from the Establishment of Free Trade until the First World War', in B. M. Ratcliffe, ed., *Britain and Her World, 1750–1914*, Manchester University Press, Manchester, 1975, pp. 224–5, 227; W. A. Lewis, 'International Economics': International Competition in Manufactures', *American Economic Review*, vol. 47, 1957, p. 583; C. P. Kindleberger, *Economic Response: Comparative Studies in Trade, Finance and Growth*, Harvard University Press, Cambridge, 1978; M. De Cecco, *Money and Empire: the International Gold Standard 1890–1914*, Basil Blackwell, Oxford, 1974; D. H. Aldcroft and H. W. Richardson, *The British Economy 1870–1939*, Macmillan, London, 1969, pp. 72–4; E. J. Hobsbawm, *Industry and Empire*, Penguin, London, 1969, pp. 116–26.

[40] O'Brien, 'Costs and Benefits', p. 170. I note but cannot here resolve the interesting technical challenge to some parts of this view mounted by Offer, 'The British Empire', pp. 216–22.

[41] W. Playfair, *An inquiry into the permanent causes of the decline and fall of powerful and wealthy nations, illustrated by four engraved charts. Designed to show how the prosperity of the British empire may be prolonged*, Greenland and Norris, London, 1805, p. 292.

Appendix

A   Military Expenditures

BRITAIN

B. R. Mitchell and P. Deane, *Abstract of British Historical Statistics*, Cambridge University Press, Cambridge, 1962, Public Finance Tables, pp. 397–8.

ITALY

1870–1910: Stato Maggiore Dell'Esercito, *L'Esercito Italiano dall' Unita Alla Grande Guerra 1861–1918*, Rome, 1980, pp. 508–9. 1911–1913: P. Ercolani, *Lo Sviluppo Economico in Italia: Storia dell' Economia Italiana negli ultimi cento anni*, Franco Angeli, Milan, 1978, p. 446. Note that the 1884 figure was taken from N. Choucri and R. North, 'Nations in Conflict: Data on National Growth and International Violence for 6 European Major Powers, 1870–1914', Inter-University Consortium for Political and Social Research, Print-Out Data Base, no. 7425, Ann Arbor, 1985.

Whilst the figures used here for 1870–1913 include extraordinary with ordinary military expenditures, they omit military pensions, which should be included.

GERMANY

S. Andic and J. Veverka, 'The Growth of Government Expenditure in Germany since the Unification', *Finanz Archiv*, vol. 23, 1964.

Andic and Veverka's figures do not encompass all military expenditures. P. C. Witt, *Die Finanzpolitik des Deutschen Reiches von 1903 bis 1913*, Matthiesen Verlag, Lübeck and Hamburg, 1970, table 14, pp. 380–1, provides, as discussed in the text, a more complete set of figures, which, had they been used, would have increased the average of Imperial Germany's military burden between 1872 and 1913 by 0.4 per cent.

RUSSIA

P. A. Khromov, *Ekonomicheskoe razvitie Rosii v XIX–XX Vekakh 1800–1917*, Institute of Economics of the Academy of Sciences, Moscow, 1950, pp. 514–29.[1] Note that some military expenditure took place locally. Such expenditures were minimal up to 1907 but consumed approximately 0.2 per cent of net national product between 1910 and 1913.[2] These figures have been excluded, as have all local expenditures elsewhere.

AMERICA

Historical Statistics of the United States: Colonial Times to 1970, Department of Commerce, Bureau of the Census, Washington, 1975, Series Y 457–465, p. 1114.

JAPAN

K. Emi and Y. Shionoya, *Government Expenditure*, vol. 7 of K. Ohkawa, M. Shinohara and M. Umemura, eds. *Estimates of Long-term Economic Statistics of Japan since 1868*, Toyokeizai Shinposha, Tokyo, 1966, table 10, pp. 186–7, 212–13. See also K. Ohkawa and H. Rosovsky, *Japanese Economic Growth: Trend Acceleration in the Twentieth Century*, Oxford University Press, Oxford, 1973.

FRANCE

Annuaire Statistique de la France, vol. 33, 'Résum Rétrospectif', Paris, 1913, pp. 140–1. See also vol. 34, 'Résum Rétrospectif', Paris, 1914.

French figures do not include extraordinary military spending. The average military burden for France between 1870 and 1913 might well rise to 4.5 per cent had such expenditure been included.

AUSTRIA

As will be explained in part B of this appendix, Hungary has been omitted from these estimates. The military expenditures for Austria-

---

[1] P. Gregory provides figures for three-yearly intervals between 1885 and 1913 in *Russian National Income, 1885–1913*, Cambridge University Press, Cambridge, 1982, table F1 in Appendix F, p. 257.

[2] Gregory, *Russian National Income*, table 3.1, pp. 56–7 and especially table F1 in Appendix F, p. 257.

Hungary are not straightforward. Austria had its own separate army (the *Landwehr*), as did Hungary (the *Honved*). However, there was also a common army and a common navy in the Dual Monarchy. Thus it is important to separate out the Austrian part of the common services.

Fortunately, there was an agreement that Austria would contribute approximately 70 per cent and Hungary 30 per cent of total joint expenditures.[3] I have therefore estimated 70 per cent of the common services and aggregated this figure with the *Landwehr* expenditures. However, the ratio of expenditures between the two halves changed in 1908; thereafter Austria contributed 63.6 per cent and Hungary 36.4 per cent. So the estimates change after 1908 accordingly. My source for this is R. von Kesslitz, 'Die Lasten der Militärischen Rüstungen Österreich-Ungarns im Neuesten Zeit (1868–1912)', Kriegsarchiv, Vienna MS. Allg. Nr. 54 II. 45. 163, pp. 181–4, 387–8, date unknown but probably 1912.[4] Note that the 1913 figure was only approximate, and that it was calculated on the basis of 63.4 per cent of the figure given in A. Paulinyi, 'Die Sogenannte Gemeinsame Wirtschaftspolitik Österreich-Ungarns', in A. Wandruszka and P. Urbanitsch, eds, *Die Habsburgermonarchie 1848–1918*, vol. 1: *Die Wirtschaftliche Entwicklung*, Verlag der Österreichischen Akademie der Wissenschaft, Vienna, 1973, p. 574.

B National Income

BRITAIN

There are several main national income data series. The one selected here is that of C. Feinstein, 'Income and Investment in the United Kingdom, 1856–1914', *Economic Journal*, vol. 71, 1961. It is important to note that these figures are the lowest available. Although they are similar to the rival series up to 1900, they diverge thereafter. If four alternative sets of data for each of the years 1900–1913 are averaged out, and the difference between them and the Feinstein data is then calculated, a

---

[3] J. Wysocki, 'Die Österreichische Finanzpolitik', in A. Wandruszka and P. Urbanitsch, eds, *Die Habsburgermonarchie, 1848–1918*, vol. 1: *Die Wirtschaftliche Entwicklung*, Verlag der Österreichische Akademie der Wissenschaft, Vienna, 1973, pp. 68–105.

[4] This source was kindly pointed out by David Stevenson. Cf. W. Wagner, 'Die K (U) Armee-Gliederung und Aufgabenstellung, 1866 bis 1918', in A. Wandruszka and P. Urbanitsch, eds, *Die Habsburgermonarchie, 1848–1918*, vol. 5: *Die Bewaffenete Machte*, Verlag der Österreichischen Akademie der Wissenschaft, Vienna, 1987, table 4, pp. 590–1.

figure approximately 4 per cent lower is reached.[5] Furthermore, the Feinstein data are a considerable 7 per cent lower than the highest of these four data series.[6] It is worth emphasizing that the Feinstein data series presents a worst-case scenario for my argument. As an appromixate guide, the military burden would be 0.2 per cent lower if the Deane (1968) figures were used, and 0.1 per cent lower if we were to use an average of the four remaining alternative data series. Note that a difference of 0.2 per cent of national income translates into a military expenditure figure of ± £4.5 million. This is a significant sum given that total military expenditure in 1913 was £72.5 million.

ITALY

G. Fuà, *Notes on Italian Economic Growth, 1861–1914* (Giuffrè, Milan, 1965), pp. 61–2. These figures are presented in 1938 prices. They were deflated to current prices using the price index in Ercolani, *Lo Sviluppo Economico in Italia: Storia dell' Economia Italiana negli ultimi cento anni*, pp. 437–8 (see above). These are a revised estimate of the ISTAT figures. Note that Fuà has revised them marginally upwards. The Fuà figures will therefore give a slightly lower estimate of the military burden.

GERMANY

W. G. Hoffmann, *Das Wachstum der Deutschen Wirtschaft seit der Mitte des 19 Jahrhunderts*, Springer Verlag, New York, 1965, pp. 506–9.

The Hoffmann data series has been widely used. Recently, it has been coming under scrutiny from various economic historians. In particular, R. Fremdling has argued that the Hoffmann data (net national income in current prices) give a downward bias in the period 1850–1913 of as much

---

[5] P. Deane, 'New Estimates of the Gross National Product for the United Kingdom, 1830–1914', *The Review of Income and Wealth*, Series 14, 1968; P. Deane and W. A. Cole, *British Economic Growth, 1688–1958*, Cambridge University Press, Cambridge, 1967; J. B. Jeffreys and D. Walters, 'National Income and Expenditure of the United Kingdom, 1870–1914', *The Review of Income and Wealth*, Series 5, 1955; A. R. Prest, 'National Income of the United Kingdom, 1870–1946', *Economic Journal*, vol. 58, 1949.

[6] Deane, 'New Estimates'. These figures were depreciated to net national product using the capital consumption figures in Feinstein, 'Income and Investment', p. 374.

as 5 per cent.[7] From the point of view of this chapter, this is significant. For 1913, for example, the military burden would have to be reduced from 3.9 to 3.7 per cent.

If Fremdling is correct, the average German military burden between 1872 and 1913 would be about 0.2 per cent higher than the figures presented in the table. This is because of a countervailing factor. The military expenditure figures should be revised upwards, as noted in the text, on the basis presented in Witt, *Die Finanzpolitik des Deutschen Reiches von 1903 bis 1913*, table 14, pp. 380–1. The upward revision of the military burden would be approximately 0.4 per cent. Adding this figure to Germany's military burden, and then subtracting 0.2 per cent to allow for the criticism of the Hoffmann data creates the 0.2 per cent figure already quoted. In sum, the military burden presented in the table represents a worse-case scenario–especially when we recall that various considerations raised in the text (the expense of war in 1870 and 1871, the payment on debt incurred for military reasons and the more imponderable burdens of high interest rates and conscription) would add still more to the figure for Germany's military burden.

RUSSIA

P. Gregory, *Russian National Income, 1885–1913*, Cambridge University Press, Cambridge, 1982, table 3.2, pp. 58–9. These figures had to be adjusted to net national product at factor cost, since Gregory supplies estimates of net national product at market prices. To derive national income from net national product at market prices, indirect taxes and government enterprise surplus have been subtracted. These figures were taken from Khromov, *Ekonomicheskoe razvitie Rosii v XIX–XX Vekakh 1800–1917*. Finally, 'subsidies' to the private sector have been added. Because these figures are unavailable for the whole period, a figure of 50 million roubles for the years 1885–1900 and 100m roubles for the years 1901–13 have been assumed. These figures accord appromixately with those produced by Gregory in his *Russian National Income*, chart F1 in Appendix F, p. 252, column 7. Gregory has calculated net national product at factor cost for the year 1913 at 18,701 million roubles compared with our estimate of 18,746 million

---

[7]   R. Fremdling, 'German National Accounts for the Nineteenth and Early Twentieth Centuries: A Critical Assessment', *Vierteljahrschrift für Social und Wirtschaftgesichte*, vol. 75, 1988 and 'Productivity Comparison between Great Britain and Germany, 1885–1913', *Scandinavian Economic History Review*, vol. 39, 1991.

roubles; this amounts to a 0.2 per cent difference. As my figures for net national product are high, they produce a Russian military burden which represents a worst-case scenario for the general argument.

AMERICA

The figures were taken from *Historical Statistics of the United States: Colonial Times to 1970*, series F71–F97, p. 231. These figures are based on the data of S. Kuznets.[8] Note that, with the exception of those for 1873–6, they have been produced only for five-year averages. It has been necessary to make one amendment to these data. Kuznets views military expenditures as an *intermediate* rather than a *final* product. He has therefore omitted this form of government expenditure from his net national product figures.[9] However, given that all other net national product data used in this essay include military expenditures, they have beed added to the Kuznets estimates. This addition was *not* made for 1912 and 1913: the figures given for those years are probably too high–so *underestimating* the military burden–as they are based on an average for 1912–16.

JAPAN

As with the Russian data, the most reliable set of Japanese data derive net national product at market prices. These are taken from K. Ohkawa and M. Shinohara, *Patterns of Japanese Economic Development: a Quantitative Appraisal*, Yale University Press, London, 1979, table A7, pp. 266–7. Total indirect taxes and government enterprise surplus were then subtracted, then estimates for subsidies added. These figures were taken from Emi and Shionoya, *Government Expenditure*, table 7A, p. 172, table 7B, pp. 174–5.

FRANCE

These figures were taken from M. Lèvy-Leboyer and F. Bourguignon, *The French Economy in the Nineteenth Century: an Essay in*

[8] S. Kuznets, 'Long Term Change in the National Income of the United States since 1870', in *Income and Wealth of the United States: Trends and Structures*, series 2, Bowes and Bowes, Cambridge, 1952 and *National Product since 1869*, NBER, New York, 1946, table 2.1, p. 86.

[9] S. Kuznets, 'Discussion of the New Department of Commerce Data Series, 'National Income: A New Version'', *Review of Economics and Statistics*, vol. 30, 1948.

Econometric Analysis, Cambridge University Press, Cambridge, 1990, table A-1, pp. 315–17

AUSTRIA

The figures for Austria-Hungary are highly problematical. For Hungary there are no figures for any years before 1913. Moreover, most of the figures that have been produced are based on the Marxist definition of net material product–a definition which omits government and private sector services not directly related to the production process (as well as omitting net product from abroad).[10] As a result, these national income figures are much too low and would, if used, lead to a considerable exaggeration of the military burden. However, more reasonable sets of data have been constructed by F. Fellner, E. Waizner and D. F. Good.[11] Note that these figures cover Austria-Hungary. However, these data are for the years 1911–13, and are weighted towards 1911. Furthermore, they are not produced prior to these years.

The Hungarian figures have therefore been omitted. Use has simply been made of Austrian national income data. In this context, the most complete set of figures is produced by A. Kausel, 'Österreichs Volkseinkommen 1830 bis 1913', in Wandruszka and Urbanitsch, *Die Habsburgermonarchie 1848–1918*, vol. 1: *Die Wirtschaftliche Entwicklung*, pp. 692–3 (see above). These figures are problematic for several reasons. They are not net national product but gross domestic product figures. They have *not* been depreciated and aggregated with income from abroad for the following reason. The military expenditure figures include the spending made by Bosnia-Herzegovina, which

[10] G. Ránki and I. T. Berend, 'National Income and Capital Accumulation in Hungary, 1867–1914', in their *Underdevelopment and Economic Growth: Studies in Hungarian Social and Economic History*, Akademiai Kiado, Budapest, 1970; G. Ránki and I. T. Berend, *Hungary: a Century of Economic Development*, David and Charles, Newton Abbot, 1974, especially p. 74; L. Katus, 'Economic Growth in Hungary during the Age of Dualism', in E. Pamlényi, ed., *Social Economic Researchers on the History of East Central Europe*, Akademiai Kiado, Budapest, 1970. For a criticism of these figures, see J. Komlos, *The Habsburg Monarchy as a Customs Union: Economic Development in Austria-Hungary in the Nineteenth Century*, Princeton University Press, Princeton, 1983, pp. 208–13.

[11] F. Fellner, 'Das Volkseinkommen Österreichs und Ungarns', *Statistisches Monatschrift*, vol. 42, 1916; E. Waizner, 'Das Volkseinkommen Alt-Österreichs und seine Verteilung auf die Nachfolgestaaten', *Metronom*, vol. 7, 1928; D. F. Good, *The Economic Rise of the Habsburg Empire, 1750–1914*, University of California Press, Berkeley, 1984, pp. 266–75.

probably represented about 5 per cent of the total. By using the gross domestic product figures, we can effectively absorb the Bosnia-Herzegovina military spending figure; the differences approximixately cancel out.

CONCLUSION

THE STATE OF
POST-MODERNISM

Contemporary social theory makes a striking claim: that the age of high modernity is over, leaving us members of a post-modern world. There is much about this claim – vagueness, idealism and relativism – that makes it highly questionable, as I hope to show on another occasion.[1] But this book can usefully conclude by briefly considering one entirely concrete argument put forward by post-modernists, and by others, to the effect that the nation state, seen as central to modernity, is now losing its powers. If this is so, this book becomes of historical rather than general interest. As it happens, several of the considerations raised cast doubt on the notion that the nation state has withered away or is about to do so.[2] But let us begin by spelling out why it seems that nation states have lost out in the contemporary world.

Cultural theorists argue that the production of meaning, the preserve of nation states once schooling systems were introduced, has now become

---

[1] A particularly clear account of post-modernism is N. Mouzelis, 'The Modern and the Postmodern in Social Thought', Inaugural Lecture, London School of Economics, 1992.

[2] Fundamental scepticism towards this view is offered by M. Mann, 'Nation-states in Europe and Other Continents: Diversifying, Developing, Not Dying', *Daedalus*, vol. 122, 1993. I am very much at one with Mann's argument, differing, however, in giving a more statist reading of the European Community and in offering a different reading of the future of social democracy.

truly transnational.[3] Such thinkers clearly have in mind the continuing impact of American culture, but they add a view of a more cosmopolitan transnational life-style tinged with vague anti-American flavour. Another indicator of nation states' declining powers of control is sometimes taken to be the huge contemporary increase in the numbers of those who hold more than one passport.

Theorists of the economy concentrate on the importance of globalization.[4] The creation of genuinely transnational production – that is a qualitative leap beyond a mere increase in international trade – is such as to 'hollow out' many of the traditional powers of the state. Large transnational companies can know far more about modern technologies than do modern nation states within which they operate; in consequence, the latter are often seen bribing and begging the former to locate their operations on a particular piece of territory. More obviously, states can no longer think of their currencies as national preserves. All in all, the increased tempo of interaction within capitalism may be such as to create (or rather to make more powerful) a new world class structure: an officer of a major transnational company, armed with an MBA from Harvard and the right to fly first class, is not in the same boat as most of us; rather, such a person has no need of any national boat whatever. An important consequence of such developments has been the creation of new forms of sovereignty, with the European Community characteristically being seen as a new transnational form suitable for modern circumstances.

But there is a third area of change, that of geopolitics, which is more hinted at than analysed by post-modernists, even though it makes their case most effectively. Much more is involved than the ending of the Cold War. Rather, it is possible to locate novel developmental tendencies, mostly interrelated and mutually supportive, which suggest that major war is now less likely. These deserve separate consideration.

1   Overwhelmingly, the most important novelty is the presence of nuclear weapons, together with new technologies of surveillance that diminish the uncertainties of armed adversaries.[5] Human beings often become rational, capable of accurately assessing their self-interest,

3   F. Jameson, 'Marxism and Postmodernism', *New Left Review*, no. 176, 1989.
4   A representative set of papers on this topic is the special issue of *Government and Opposition*, vol. 28, 1993.
5   Two particularly helpful accounts on which I have relied are R. Jervis, *The Meaning of the Nuclear Revolution: Statecraft and the Prospect of Armageddon*, Cornell University Press, Ithaca, 1989 and McGeorge Bundy, *Danger and Survival: Choices about the Bomb in the First Fifty Years*, Random House, New York, 1988.

only when the stakes are high. The possibility of destruction seems to have made the political elites of both superpowers averse to risk.

2   In recent years, the recognition given to nationalism as a principle of world politics has increased. There is a very positive side to this development, which much recent commentary has ignored. Militarily, expansion no longer brings security as nuclear missiles ignore the size of any empire or buffer-zone belonging to a leading state. Further, if possession of territory increased power and wealth in the agrarian era, it no longer has that role, for two reasons. Negatively, nationalist movements have the capacity to make the retention of imperial possessions prohibitively expensive. Positively, economic success seems ever more dependent on the creation of human capital capable of allowing one's economy to move up the product cycle; one way of helping such movement is participation in advanced markets rather than trading with secure colonial markets – whose capacity to absorb one's products, given their poverty, was in anycase often exaggerated. Europe was made to realize this largely within the two decades after 1945; the behaviour of Gorbachov suggests that the principle is now commonly understood.[6]

3   Marx famously remarked that re-enacted historical events have an air of farce about them; this can indeed be so. But sometimes historical events can catch up with theories that have preceded them, and there are good reasons for believing that this is true of the hope that interdependence would limit geopolitical conflict. The demand for free trade now begins to have domestic political roots, given that employment often depends upon companies whose very being depends upon world trade; both votes and campaign funds are now available to those who resist protectionism.[7] Some indication of what is involved can be gained by noting that perhaps a third of world trade is now intra-firm in character – something that makes nonsense of any simple view of national accounts.[8] More important than this, however, is the fact that economic success depends upon participation in the market. The history of the world economy in recent years has seen that nations

[6]   C. Kaysen, 'Is War Obsolete?', *International Security*, vol. 14, 1990.
[7]   I. M. Destler and J. Odell, *Anti-protection: Changing Forces in United States Politics*, Institute for International Economics, Washington, 1987; H. Milner, 'Resisting the Protectionist Temptation: Industry and the Making of Trade Policy in France and the United States during the 1970s', *International Organisation*, vol. 41, 1987.
[8]   R. Reich, *The Work of Nations*, Basic Books, New York, 1991.

which protect their industries for any length of time after their initial nurturing condemn their societies to increasing poverty. Argentina is the prime example of the false trail of protectionism, but the Latin American practice of import-substitution-industrialization makes the general point equally well, especially, as noted in chapter 4, when compared to the export-led growth of the East Asian newly industrializing countries.[9] The underlying structural fact explaining this seems to be that the speed of technological change is now so fast that not to be involved in it invites inefficiency.

4 Societies that are heavily involved in world trade and that seek to move up the product cycle are likely to generate pressures for liberalization. Economic success in these circumstances depends ever more upon the willing participation of educated labour, of people whose jobs depend upon freedom of movement and information. If this goose is to lay a golden egg, it is imperative that rigidly authoritarian and ideocratic regimes loosen their hold. And if that hold is not loosened demands will be made, especially by students, for liberalization from below. The pressure generated by this segment is of more significance than that generated by European working classes at the end of the nineteenth century.[10] Every time such pressure is successful, the long-term chances of geopolitical conflict are reduced; for there is something to the liberal notion that authoritarian regimes are more likely than democracies to wage aggressive war.[11]

What are we to make of these interrelated claims? It is worth re-emphasising the argument of chapter 1 immediately: nation states were

[9] I draw here principally on: C. Waisman, *Reversal of Development in Argentina*, Princeton University Press, Princeton, 1987; F. C. Deyo, ed., *The Political Economy of the New Asian Industrialism*, Cornell University Press, Ithaca, 1987; and N. Mouzelis, *Politics in the Semi-periphery*, Macmillan, London, 1986. Cf. ch. 4 in this volume.

[10] J. A. Hall, 'Classes and Elites, Wars and Social Evolution', *Sociology*, vol. 22, 1988.

[11] This is a careful formulation owing much to J. Snyder, *Myths of Empire*, Cornell University Press, Ithaca, 1991. If democracy can help geopolitical calculation, so too can the presence of unitary authoritarian regimes. The most dangerous situation is that in which authoritarianism co-exists with popular mobilization. The breakup of the Soviet Union may lead to an increase of regimes of this latter type, making geopolitical blunders more rather than less likely in the near future. The general contention that the state still matters is reinforced by this consideration.

never completely autonomous, for they always had to exist within the larger societies of capitalism and the state system. Realization of this may allow for more balanced judgement in the long run, for an appreciation of developments and of diversities as opposed to the declaration of a total change in human affairs. Certainly many, but not all, social conditions have changed; but states have always adapted in the past, and sensitivity must be shown to their new strategies. To that end, let us consider in turn how advanced and less developed countries are faring in the contemporary world.

State power continues to structure the political economy of the advanced world in important ways. The United States still has a predominant position within capitalist society, as noted in chapter 7, and it is likely to be able to continue to structure international norms to suit its own interests – even though this will surely lead to increased tensions with Japan and Europe.[12] It is far too early to declare that the Cold War has changed all this by lessening the obligations felt by Japan and Europe to their military protector. The Gulf War showed extant American primacy, and the continuing ability to extract seigniorial rights; the possibility of further not-so-small wars and the inevitable revival of Russian power look set to cement this pattern.

Nor should too much be made of the transnationalism of the European Community. Most obviously, the degree of economic cooperation within Europe rests upon the peace provided by the United States, making it dependent, a secondary rather than a primary actor in world affairs. Moreover, European states show no sign of wishing to get rid of their protector; on the contrary, the increase in German power makes that protection welcome even to France, whose sudden interest in NATO is one of the more amusing twists of contemporary international affairs. Mention of France and Germany ought to remind us that the Community had its origins in the desire of French statesmen to control Germany;[13] statist considerations of this sort have most definitely not died out today. This applies even to monetary affairs: monetary union may yet be defeated by German loyalty to their Deutschmark.

If one were to summarise all of this it would be to say that there have been great changes, notably the creation of a single market and of a

---

[12]   Mann, 'Nation-states in Europe and Other Continents', p. 139 argues in favour of socialist control of the international market, not least because he seems to regard national social democracy as more or less doomed. I am more optimistic about the latter, and see no way to achieve the former. For further argument on this point, see ch. 2.

[13]   A. Milward, *The Reconstruction of Western Europe, 1945–51*, University of California Press, Berkeley, 1984.

European law to regulate it, and that they have a certain dynamism of their own. But these changes are essentially all in the economic field; elsewhere, the European Community remains an international organization, a place where heads of governments meet. The Bosnian debacle makes it apparent that the Community has no *single* voice in geopolitical affairs. Further, no real attempt is being made as yet to create a single European identity, which might anyway be disliked and resisted. This may change. The desire of peoples to the south and the east to enter Europe, not least when driven out by nationalist conflicts, may lead to the creation of a shared fortress for the wealthy. More likely, it will lead to an increase of nation state power, that is to the passing of ever harsher *national* citizenship laws designed to exclude the unwanted.

It would be possible to continue to talk about statist interests when discussing East Asia. But let us turn instead to making an analytic point of more general relevance. Whilst it is indeed true that the speed of capitalist interaction has increased, it is none the less wholly facile to equate this with an inevitable decline of state power. More is involved here than the leading state continuing to use its geopolitical muscle in order to gain economic advantage. The point to be made is that states are adapting. It is true that states can no longer compete militarily with ease; nor can they do so economically by means of protection, currency control or direct economic planning, at which they seem to be rather inept. But states can and do create competitiveness in novel ways.

On the one hand, successful states manage the market pragmatically. The secret of East Asian economic success, as noted in chapter 4, seems to lie in protecting infant industries, which are then escorted onto the market. Similarly, the German state provided seed money to encourage the development of several computer firms, subsequently allowing the market to decide which of them was the best – a striking contrast to Britain's misguided attempt to develop its computer industry by investing all state funds in a single company. Italian small businesses were significantly helped by the Christian Democratic state by means of a generous loan policy.[14] The Japanese state helps its corporations by funding basic research, by helping to market manufactured products and, above all, by providing information.[15]

On the other hand, many states realize the need to increase competitiveness by providing better social infrastructures. Let us recall that Adam

---

[14] L. Weiss, *Creating Capitalism: Small Business and the State since 1945*, Basil Blackwell, Oxford, 1988.
[15] R. J. Samuels, *The Business of the Japanese State*, Cornell University Press, Ithaca, 1987.

Smith, unalarmed by the discovery that new nations could threaten the wealth of established economic leaders, expected such leaders to abandon old industries to new countries and to adopt wholly new trades and techniques.[16] Put another way, the future of the advanced world must lie in a high-wage, high-productivity economy – certainly not in the cutting of wages. This places an enormous premium on education designed to allow a skilled work-force to respond speedily and flexibly to market opportunities.[17] Austria, Japan, Switzerland, Holland and Denmark are all examples of societies that have developed social skills allowing rapid adaptation to changes in the world market.[18] It is noticeable that the political economies of these countries varies, but that social democracy – the extension of citizenship in combination with openness to the market – remains, as we noted in chapter 2, a viable option within contemporary capitalism.

But the concentration on the advanced world encouraged by postmodernism is an outrageous piece of ethnocentrism that hides from our attention a banal and brutal fact. Most countries in the less developed world have not even reached the stage of having states, let alone the stage of being able to go beyond them. Chapter 5 noted that the situation within the less developed world is extremely varied. Some countries have national histories such that state building and market integration are likely to follow, thereby making economic development within capitalism possible.

However, many more countries are not based on national experiences, have puny states and are nowhere near controlling their territories, let alone integrating their markets: such countries have little chance of breaking chains of dependency. Formal sovereignty in such cases has resulted from the post-war reverence for the norms of sovereignty and non-intervention; this should not hide the fact that we are dealing with 'quasi-states'.[19] More is at issue than the fact that there may be no more newly industrializing countries.[20] Rather, many such states are not doing well at establishing basic order, making life within them 'poor, nasty,

[16]   I. Hont, 'The 'Rich Country – Poor Country' Debate in Classical Scottish Political Economy', in I. Hont and M. Ignatieff, eds, *Wealth and Virtue*, Cambridge University Press, Cambridge, 1983.
[17]   Cf. M. Piore and C. Sabel, *The Second Industrial Divide*, Basic Books, New York, 1984.
[18]   P. Katzenstein, *Small States in World Markets*, Cornell University Press, Ithaca, 1985; R. Dore, *Flexible Rigidities*, Athlone Press, London, 1986.
[19]   R. H. Jackson, *Quasi-states: Sovereignty, International Relations, and the Third World*, Cambridge University Press, Cambridge, 1990.
[20]   R. Broad and J. Cavanagh, 'No More NICs', *Foreign Policy*, no. 72, 1988.

brutish, and short'. More rather than less state power is needed at this stage in the history of the world. This is not of course, as many chapters in this book point out, to say that mere despotism is equivalent to genuine state strength. But states need to be established before citizenship rights can be secured within them.

This leads to a final reflection. It is important to return to the claim that major geopolitical conflict is now less likely. Optimism entertained in this regard is really about 'us' rather than 'them'. But a large and sobering dose of pessimism should not and cannot be avoided when contemplating the fate of the vast majority of humanity. Economic development is not proceeding smoothly for many. If this is offensive to liberal values, at first sight it might seem not to matter in terms of traditional *realpolitik*. Are these countries not weak and helpless? Is it not the case that most of them scarcely matter economically, as is so clearly shown by trade and investment figures? Such a position seems to me as blind as it is cruel. I have always feared that nuclear weapons may fall into the hands of leaders of mobilized and ideocratic societies who feel, justly or unjustly, aggrieved at the advanced world; the behaviour of Saddam Hussein, already the possessor of terrifying chemical weapons and reputedly close to the nuclear threshold, has turned private nightmare into public horror. The moral to be drawn from this is simple: aiding development is a geopolitical if not an economic necessity. The difficulty with this is that we face a dilemma, noted at chapter 6, between that respect for sovereignty which created international order after 1945 and the desire to extend liberalism, by allowing intervention on behalf of universal human rights. If ways can occasionally be found to escape this dilemma, it is salutary to emphasize that more often we act without the benefit of clearly identified goals. [21]

[21] S. Hoffman, *Duties Beyond Borders*, State University of New York Press, Syracuse, 1981.

INDEX

social controls in 37
and the United States 92, 173,
174, 175–6
Jefferson, Thomas 102
Johnson, Lyndon 39

Kadar, Janos 55
Kant, I. 129, 164
Perpetual Peace 158
Kennan, George 158, 182, 183
Kennedy, John F. 180, 183
Kennedy, Paul 177, 187–8, 189, 193
*The Rise and Fall of the Great
Powers* 149
Kenyatta, Jomo 129
Keohane, R. 152
Keynes, John Maynard 29–30, 33
Kindleberger, C. 152
Kissinger, Henry 158
Kohl, Helmut 58
Korea 79, 81, 82, 86
democratization 117
see also South Korea
Korean War 182
Kornai, Janos 56
Krasner, S. 180
Kuznets, S. 188

Labour Party, British 43, 168
landownership
and the consolidation of
democracy 108
in imperial China 5–6
medieval 17
land reform, in East Asia 116–17
late development
and growth 155–6
and nationalism 125
and state power 76–98
Latin America
Argentina 81, 107, 115–16, 209
authoritarianism in 92
Brazil 95, 98, 107, 115–16
capital exports 174
chances for consolidating
democracy 115–16
civil society in 113
democracy in 80, 90–2
liberalism and democracy 107,
108, 118

and nationalism 126
in the present world order 95, 98
state power and economic
development 79, 80, 90–2
legal codification, and the Christian
church 16–17
legitimacy, level of and bounded
autonomy 82
Lenin, V.I. 43, 125
Lévi-Strauss, Claude x, 78
liberalism
in Britain 160–1, 171
and capitalism 29–30
and decline 150, 184–5
and democratization 104–6, 107,
117, 118–19, 122
and the diffusion of conflict 42–7,
142–3
and economic development 213
embedded 172
and nationalism 148
war and foreign policy 157–9
liberalization
and the collapse of socialism 55,
56–7, 57–8, 70–4, 75
and the consolidation of
democracy 115–16
liberty, and commerce 22
Linz, J. 146
Liska, George 152
List, Friedrich 154
Lloyd George, David 196
logic of the asocial society,
nationalism as 129–31, 141
logic of industry, and
nationalism 127, 141, 143
London School of Economics 129
Louis XIV, King of France 25
Louis XVI, King of France 73
Lynch, John 133

McCarthy, Joseph 182
Machiavelli, N. 27
Macmillan, Harold 170
McNeill, W. H. 24
Malinowski, B. 129
Mann, Michael xi–xii, 4, 8, 24, 47,
48
on decline 151